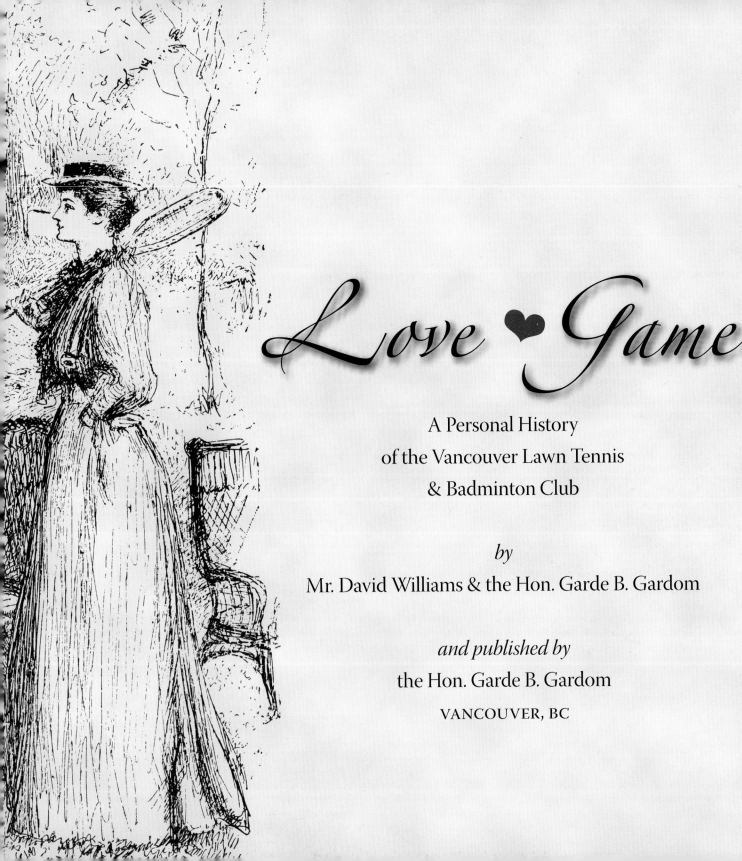

Love ♥ Game

A Personal History
of the Vancouver Lawn Tennis
& Badminton Club

by

Mr. David Williams & the Hon. Garde B. Gardom

and published by

the Hon. Garde B. Gardom

VANCOUVER, BC

Love Game is published by the Hon. Garde B. Gardom and all net proceeds from its sale will be divided 50/50 between the Vancouver Lawn Tennis & Badminton Club's Legacy Fund to assist its promising Juniors, and the Salvation Army to enhance its good works.

Library and Archives Canada Cataloguing in Publication

Williams, David Ricardo, 1923-
   **Love game : a personal history of the Vancouver Lawn
   Tennis & Badminton Club** / David Ricardo Williams & Garde B. Gardom.

Includes bibliographical references and index.
ISBN 978-0-9809351-0-3

   1. Vancouver Lawn Tennis and Badminton Club--History. 2. Vancouver
   (B.C.)—History. I. Gardom, Garde B. (Garde Basil), 1924-
   II. Title.

GV997.V35W54 2008
796.342'06071133   C2008-905718-X

Published by
Hon. Garde B. Gardom
2122 SW Marine Drive
Vancouver, BC
Canada V5P 6B5

ISBN 978-0-9809351-0-3

Editorial services provided by Philip Sherwood, www.lifewriters.ca, Tel. 1.800.864.9152
Book design by Wm. Glasgow & Neil Klassen, Abbotsford, BC
Printed in Canada by Friesen Printers, Altona, Manitoba

Contents

Publishing team (L-R, back): Neil Klassen, Philip Sherwood, Ian Adam, Bill Glasgow, Barbara Wallace, Ted Horsey and (front) Dick Hibbard, Arthur Jeffery, and Garde Gardom.

iv

Preface

In 1990, the directors of the Vancouver Lawn Tennis and Badminton Club commissioned David Williams Q.C., of Duncan, B.C., to write a history of the Club for its Centenary celebration in 1997. Although a lawyer by profession, he also was the author of a number of books, including a biography of B.C.'s first judge, the famous Sir Matthew Bailey Begbie. David was never a member of the Vancouver Lawn Tennis and Badminton Club, however he played here many times and by coincidence, he graduated along with me from the University of British Columbia's second law class in 1949. Well do I recall his infectious chuckle, cultivated discourse, and passion for lawn tennis. After conducting extensive research, interviewing, and receiving assistance from many Club members, David submitted his initial manuscript in late 1993, which was reviewed by Gordon Cooper, Ian Angus, and several directors. Our Centenary came and went before his manuscript was finalized and unfortunately in January 1999, he died in his beloved Duncan.

In 2004 I volunteered, with the board's blessing — and without charge save out-of-pocket expenses — to complete David's work and ensure that the history was published. I had a good working knowledge of the Club, its members, and administration, having been an active member for over sixty years. My wife Helen is also a member, as are my daughter, Kim, and her daughter, Cara. Three other daughters — Karen, Brione, and Brita — were members for years. During this time I worked on a number of Committees, served as a director, was president from 1964 until 1966, acted as the Club's solicitor, revised its bylaws, and eventually was installed as an Honorary Life Member.

Producing his book called for a lot of research regarding how and where Tennis, Badminton, Squash and Table Tennis came into being, plus an extensive and comprehensive time line. It also required a great deal of editing, researching the Club's archives, conducting many additional interviews, adding material of interest, selecting photographs and other memorabilia, writing sections on its endeavours from 1993 to 2007 — plus working with professional book editors, designers, and printers.

David described his manuscript as: "An account of the life of the VLTBC and the major events and the trends affecting it." I have added to his tennis, badminton, squash, and social activities references, plus I've covered swimming, fitness, and table tennis, as well as referring to the City of Vancouver and other communities and the happenings of the times which impinged on our members' activities.

This work is in a sense a biography of the Club — not a social history, nor an almanac of events, nor of the people David and I have mentioned except where they're relevant to particular issues or events, but they are by no means the only ones who have contributed to the Club's welfare and progress. As David said, "There have been thousand of members over the years, many of them prominent citizens, many of them ordinary citizens, some with unusual characteristics, in fact a few that were downright eccentric. Each one, however, shared a common and invigorating interest — the racquet sports."

During its first three decades, the VLTBC was a tennis club, together with croquet and lawn bowling for a short time at the beginning of the twentieth century. Badminton arrived in 1928 with the construction of our badminton hall and in 1961 squash became available, completing the trilogy.

David's manuscript reveals that he described the first 50 years of our Club's life in greater detail than its second 50 years. This was deliberate. The first half-century were its formative years and though the Club has experienced many worrying times since, the account of those early years chronicled many extremely difficult situations when it might easily have failed to survive.

The admirable devotion and willingness of members in every era to take on responsibilities to keep the VLTBC afloat is apparent after even only a cursory examination of its history. No doubt the parlous state of the Club in those earlier years caused the directors many a sleepless night! A surprising fact which emerged was that the company which everyone loved to hate — the Canadian Pacific Railway — often proved to be the Club's saviour and also was its somewhat behind-the-scenes banker.

The research for this project evoked many familiar and well-remembered images, both of those living and those gone before. For David, two stood out most clearly. Harry Monk, the long-time, pipe-smoking secretary-manager who would strike terror into the heart of any junior who failed to observe court decorum. And Jack Bromwich, the Australian Davis Cupper, who, when playing his opponent in the first round of the 1939 Western Canadian singles — a most unfortunate fellow whose tennis and attire were abysmal. His underwear hung well below his shorts, he failed to earn a single point, and occasionally the poor soul would turn to the spectators witnessing his slaughter and shout, "I'm not afraid, I'm not afraid!"

What stands out most clearly to me first of all is the camaraderie and character of the Club, as well as its capacity to weather all sorts of often-repeating storms. As baseball's Yogi Berra used to say, "It's déjà vu all over again." Or, if you prefer the more complete French expression, *"Plus ça change, plus c'est la même chose."* Secondly, I sense that the Club has become more impersonal, with fewer members knowing each other and, apart from the collegiality of play, they are less frequently involved in our myriad of activities and responsibilities.

Although some may wish otherwise, the Club, its members and staff obviously were, and continue to be buffeted and shaped by the general events of the day.

As is often the case, it takes a generation for anyone to become much interested in an account of the prior goings-on of their time. This is especially true in the case of relatively youthful enterprises such as the City of Vancouver and our Club. However, it is useful to collate the events of the past, as history is the ongoing dialogue between our past and present. Whether we like it or not, it shapes us. Hence we must learn from the past and profit from the past, but never become shackled by it. With all of this in mind, *Love Game* categorizes chronological periods from 1877 until 2007. At the beginning of each chapter, passing reference has been made to what was going on in the world, in Canada, in our province, and in our city — all of which in one way or another impacted our members.

The material in this book is drawn from divers sources. These include the Minutes of the Club — which, like many such formal tomes, result from animated discussion yet turgidly record the issues and the decisions taken. They are substantially intact, but contain some gaps — notably 1889–1905, 1907–10, and 1951–53. If any readers have these missing Club Minutes, or know where they can be located, please let me know and also contact our Archives Committee. Also, any donations of useful archival material would be welcomed, perhaps to be included in any next biography of the Club — to be written when and by whom, the Good Lord only knows.

I am indeed grateful to everyone who agreed to be interviewed as well as those who provided David and me with written recollections and anecdotes, which were important sources of information. Their names, along with a brief bibliography, are in the Appendix. Newspaper articles were also used, as well as the vast collection of archival material lovingly and painstakingly assembled by the Club's first and longest-serving archivist, Al Stevenson. One can't say enough good about Al — without question the best tennis archivist Canada ever had. And gratis too. In 1981, General Manager Graham Laxton recommended that Al compile a history of the Club — however that never came to pass.

Other Club members have been very helpful in offering suggestions and information and I cannot begin to mention them all, but they know who they are. In particular, the remarkable and ever-helpful Ted Horsey, Joan McMaster, Rosemary Cunningham of the Archives Committee, Al Stevenson's good friend Arthur Jeffery, and Dick Hibbard and Ian Adam have been exceptionally supportive. The Club's tennis pros, as well as Graham Laxton and Janis Ostling, always seemed able at short notice to ferret out some needed information and documents.

And of course many thanks to my spirited production team: Philip Sherwood for his editing, Neil Klassen and Bill Glasgow for designing the book, Jorge Rocha of Friesen's Corporation for its printing plus Murray Todd of Todd Graphics and Bob Annable of Capilano Golf & Country Club for recommending them. Also my gratitude to David's widow, Mrs. Laura Williams, for her enthusiasm and cooperation, and lastly to my secretary, Barbara Wallace, who laboured above and beyond call.

Happy Reading.

David Ricardo Williams,
Q.C., BA, LLB

David Williams was born in Kamloops in 1923. Soon after the family moved to Vancouver where David attended Lord Byng High School. In 1949 he graduated from the University of British Columbia. He was one of the founders of the B.C. Forests Museum and served on UBC's Board of Governors and its Senate. He practised law in Duncan and, in 1980, was appointed Adjunct Professor of Law at the University of Victoria.

He also became one of our Province's foremost biographers. His 1977 book, *The Man for a New Century: Sir Matthew Baillie Begbie* was awarded the UBC Medal for Canadian Biography. It was reprinted as *Matthew Baillie Begbie* in 1980. In 1982 Williams completed *Simon Peter Gunanoot: Trapline Outlaw*, and a biography of Chief Justice Lyman Poore Duff, *Duff: A Life in the Law.* His biography of the famed Mayor of Vancouver, *The Remarkable Gerald Grattan McGeer*, was published in 1986. Williams wrote his only novel, *Ace of Pentacles* (Sono Nis), in 1990, and followed this with *Yesterday, Today and Tomorrow: A History of Vancouver's Terminal City Club* (1992).

His non-fiction study, *With Malice Aforethought* (1993), won the Crime writers of Canada award for best book of actual crime. Williams wrote *Just Lawyers: Seven Portraits* for the Osgoode Society for Canadian Legal History (1995) plus *Call in Pinkerton's: American Detectives at Work for Canada* (1998).

HONOURS:
UBC's medal for Canadian biography
The Hubert Evans Non-fiction Prize
Crime Writers of Canada Award
Honorary Life Member of the Writers Union of
    Canada.

Mr. Williams and his wife Laura (Bapty) Williams had five sons and one daughter. He enjoyed tennis at the Victoria Lawn and he often played at the Vancouver Lawn Tennis and Badminton Club and at the South Cowichan Lawn Tennis Club.

Mr. Williams died on January 29, 1999.

The Honourable Garde Basil Gardom,
O.B.C., Q.C., BA, LLB., LLD (Hon)

Garde Gardom was born in Banff, Alberta in 1924. He attended Dewdney, Prince of Wales and Banff Elementary Schools, Point Grey Junior High and Magee High School in Vancouver. In 1949 he graduated from the University of British Columbia.

He practiced law in Vancouver and then entered provincial politics, and was elected as an MLA six times. Along with Dr. Pat McGeer, he served the constituents of Vancouver-Point Grey from 1966 until 1986.

Mr. Gardom was appointed Attorney General and Government House Leader in 1975 ultimately to become B.C.'s longest-serving House Leader. During his years in Premier Bill Bennett's Cabinet, he initiated COUNTERATTACK against drinking and driving, and amongst other legislation the Ombudsman Act, Aid for Victims of Crime, the right to sue the Crown, and the Family Relations Act. As B.C.'s first Minister of Intergovernmental Relations, he was our Province's lead Minister in the constitutional negotiations resulting in the Patriation of the Canadian Constitution from the U.K. Together with his duties on many Legislative Boards and Committees, he also assumed responsibility for B.C.'s Official Visits Program for EXPO '86.

After retiring from politics Mr Gardom served as Agent General for British Columbia for the United Kingdom and Western Europe from 1987 to 1992.

On April 21, 1995, the Honourable Garde B. Gardom was sworn in as B.C.'s 26th Lieutenant Governor and served until September 25, 2001.

HONOURS:
Order of British Columbia
Honorary LLD – U.B.C. and the University of Victoria
Freeman of the City of London
Knight of Justice, The Order of St. John
Rotary's Paul Harris Fellow
Member of the B.C. Sports Hall of Fame
Lifetime Achievement Award, U.B.C.
Honorary Colonel, The British Columbia Regiment (DCO)

Mr. Gardom and his wife Helen (Mackenzie) Gardom live in Vancouver where they enjoy their four daughters and eleven grandchildren, their Standard Poodles, Angus and Henry, the outdoors, fishing, gardening, basketball, rugby, football, and all racquet sports—especially at the Vancouver Lawn Tennis and Badminton Club.

This book is dedicated to

Everyone who enjoys and engages in Racquet Sports,

The conviviality and health they engender,

And The Vancouver Lawn Tennis & Badminton Club—

Long may they, and it, flourish.

Real or Court Tennis was played at Hampton Court and enjoyed by royalty and the very wealthy in England during the reign of Henry VIII.

CHAPTER 1

The Evolution of Tennis

Its Arrival in British Columbia, our Club's Origins, Members, and Finances

The Birth of Tennis

The origin of the game goes back a long way — to the Egyptians, the Persians, the Arabs, the Holy Roman Emperor Charlemagne, and in AD 1100 to the French with their *jeu de paume* (game of the palm), or *tenez* — "take it / play." The French never took long to gamble and in the fourteenth century their Royal Council's Louis d'Orléans often lost up to two thousand gold francs, of which his ever-starving peasants were little aware. During the papal schisms and the ongoing wars with England, one of France's calls to arms in 1393 banned tennis to promote the use of archery and the crossbow. It did. However, *tenez* was soon again permitted.

To the purist, "tennis" means the game that was played by royalty and the aristocracy during the medieval era and the Renaissance. The court was enclosed — about the same width as the one we use today, and one and one-half times its length. The racquet resembled an elongated squash racquet and the ball was hard — not as hard as a cricket ball, but not as soft as today's tennis balls. Surprisingly, *Court Real* or Royal Tennis, is still played today. Its shrine is at England's Hampton Court, the magnificent palace of Henry VIII where in 1530 his majesty built a raftered court which is still used. Adherents of Royal Tennis continue to follow its original rules, including its complicated scoring — points being made for hitting the ball into designated nooks and crannies. It's a helter-skelter endeavour, possessing certain characteristics of jai lai and squash. While it is not played on the West Coast of North America, tournaments are regularly held in New England, New York, and the United Kingdom. As might be expected, aficionados of Royal Tennis tend to regard modern players as somewhat nouveau. So the tradition continues, but only to a select few of ample means with a keen interest.

In the early 1870s, England's Major Walter

"Tenez" or *"la Longue Paume des Champs Elissees,"* as it was played in France in the early nineteenth century.

> **In Singapore the sport was first played in 1878 and there referred to as "niminy piminy,"… a game fit only for weak women.**

2

Wingfield, pioneered his game *sphairistike* — Greek for "sphere" and "stick" — which soon became known as lawn tennis. Apart from the shape of the court, the size of the racquets, and the "bounce" of the balls, this is the game we love and play today. After a failed attempt by Wingfield to patent his idea, the Marylebone Cricket Club drew up a set of rules in 1875, which led to the rapid spread of tennis throughout the United Kingdom. The All England Lawn Tennis & Croquet Club — Wimbledon — was founded in 1877 and subsequently became tennis's holiest of holies. Tennis soon found favour in English military circles and quickly spread to the Empire's colonies and possessions around the world — the Brits were everywhere. In Singapore the sport was first played in 1878 and there referred to as "niminy piminy," i.e., sissy — for some felt it was a game fit only for "weak" women. How women and times change! In Canada, the game caught on and in 1876 the Toronto Lawn and Tennis Club was founded, followed by the Ottawa Tennis Club in 1881.

Lawn Tennis Arrives in B.C.

Lawn tennis was pioneered in B.C. by Sir Matthew Baillie Begbie, a bachelor and the formidable and renowned first Chief Justice of British Columbia. In addition to his legal prowess, he was a man of many accomplishments — the first president of the Union Club of B.C., a musician, an

1500s

1579 Francis Drake, English privateer and navigator, is the first European to enter the Strait of Juan de Fuca. **1588** The Spanish Armada defeated by the English Fleet; ascendancy of British Fleet begins. **1602** East India Company formed in Amsterdam.

avid reader, and also a most gracious host. He was visiting England when Major Wingfield introduced his sport and no doubt saw it played. In 1877, soon after his return, Sir Matthew laid out three lawn courts on the spacious grounds of his large home in Victoria and became the first person to play tennis in our province, and among the first to do so in Canada.

1886 – Lawn Tennis Starts in Duncan

Nine years later, in 1886, the South Cowichan Lawn Tennis Club (SCLTC) was founded on a portion of the Corfield dairy farm at Cowichan Bay near Duncan. Although it wasn't Canada's first club, the SCLTC enjoys the distinction of being the oldest club in the country where lawn tennis has been played continuously on its six courts.

Initially Duncan had two clubs — the Duncan, and the SCLTC, where British-born Noel Staples became the leading light. Staples owned a sporting goods store in Duncan and was an all-round sportsman as well as an excellent tennis coach. He stressed agility and mixes of shots, and also pioneered two-handed backhands and topspin drives — virtually unheard of then. His most successful student was his daughter Kay who, along with Jean Eckhardt (later Bardsley), became the top-ranked juniors in the Pacific Northwest and Canada.

Mr. Corfield willed part of his farm to the SCLTC as long as the club functioned. If the club failed, the land was to revert to the residue of his estate. Fortunately, as the result of lots of hard work and dedicated members, the SCLTC is still going strong and no doubt will continue to do so. It enjoys a great heritage. Interestingly, at one time Mr. Corfield hired a farmhand, the renowned poet Robert Service, who wrote his first poem there before he set out for the Yukon and fame.

The Founding of the City of Vancouver and the Great Fire of 1886

Every British Columbian can thank those people of foresight who decided to honour the memory of the Royal Navy's Captain George Vancouver from Kings Lynn in Norfolk by naming our city — and our Club — after him. Vancouver, as a midshipman (along with William Bligh, later to become Master of the *Bounty* and weathered its ill-famed mutiny) first sailed into our waters off Nootka Sound in 1777 with the world-renowned navigator and explorer Captain James Cook. Then in 1792, the now Captain Vancouver, commanding *HMS Discovery* along with *HMS Resolution*, returned here to seek the Northwest Passage and met our first citizens, the Salish, Musqueam, Capilano, and Kitsilano First Nations. Captain Vancouver painstakingly and meticulously charted five thousand miles of our coastline — charts that today are still accurate and useable. A remarkable man!

Our present-day city of Vancouver started as two settlements: Hastings Mill — a tiny "dry" (no liquor) company town — and Granville. As was the case in most of B.C., our towns and communities took English names — e.g., Hastings, commemorating the famous battle of AD 1066. Hastings Mill and Granville amalgamated in April 1886 to become the City of Vancouver and within one month elected our first mayor — M.A. McLean — who won with 242 votes,

3

1600s · 1700s

1606 Rembrandt van Rijn born. **1665** Newton formulates the Law of Gravity. **1666** Great Fire of London. **1667** Champs Elysees designed. **1607** Hudson's Bay Company founded. **1703** Peter the Great moves Russian capital from Moscow to St. Petersburg.

Downtown Vancouver in 1887, looking east along Water Street to Cambie and Abbott streets.

edging out his opponent Richard Alexander's 225 votes. A closely fought contest! McLean presided at City Hall, formerly the Customs House of the Crown Colony of B.C.

By the beginning of June, the population of Vancouver had soared to over two thousand and the city boasted a daily newspaper, two weeklies, and an office of the Bank of Montreal. But 13 days into the month, tragedy struck. Some clearing fires — started to burn stumps and felled branches — were beset by a mighty westerly wind. Almost instantly they became an inferno and in less than two hours consumed almost all of the newly founded community. But the settlers, far from daunted, immediately started to rebuild, buoyed by the knowledge that two years earlier, the Canadian Pacific Railway (CPR) had chosen us as the Pacific Terminus of its transcontinental railroad — for which the CPR received a grant of 6,458 acres.

1888 — Tennis Starts in Vancouver at the City Tennis Club

In 1888, H.O. Bell-Irving had a lawn court at the corner of Gore and Alexander Streets. About the same time, Vancouver's first tennis club,

✦
5
✦

An oil painting by John Innes depicts the first meeting of Vancouver's first City Council on May 10, 1886.

THE BADGE OF VANCOUVER
1886 - 1903

The Founders of Vancouver

1886

Our City Is Their Monument

.OUR FIRST "CITY HALL"

The Crown Colony of British Columbia built this cottage and called it the "Customs House". After Confederation it became the "Court House". In 1886 it was, for a few days, an improvised "City Hall".

An appreciation by the Citizens of Vancouver on the 70th Anniversary of the Incorporation of Vancouver, as a city, April 6th, 1886.

CITY ARCHIVES, CITY HALL, VANCOUVER, CANADA

Cover of *The Founders of Vancouver,* a booklet honouring some of Vancouver's earliest eminent citizens.

6

the City Tennis Club, got under way. According to the North Pacific International Lawn Tennis Association, that year the winner of the first B.C. championships was J.T. Williams. Possibly that tournament was held on Mr. Bell-Irving's court, but more likely at the City Tennis Club, which according to Al Stevenson's *History of Tennis in British Columbia,* was on Georgia Street between Thurlow and Bute. However an 1894 photograph is captioned, "A view of the plank tennis courts of Vancouver Lawn Tennis Club." But since it didn't start until 1897, that property must be the City Tennis Club. This was borne out by Mr. A.P. Horne who, in a 1953 interview recalled, "When I first came to Vancouver in 1889, I joined a little club with two wooden courts opposite the old Hotel Vancouver." (Wooden court play was somewhat similar to playing on lawn as the ball skidded on both surfaces, although more predictably on wood than on the grass.) However others say that the City Tennis Club's courts were on CPR land between Georgia and Dunsmuir streets, opposite the present-day Hudson's Bay department store. So at one time the City Tennis Club must have enjoyed two locations. There is no question that establishing two clubs with tennis courts only two years after the devastating fire of 1886 was no small accomplishment. Committed were our pioneers! The Brockton Athletic Club also put in some lawn courts at Brockton Point in 1893 in conjunction with its cricket pitch and rugby field — a lovely site.

1700s

1710 St. Paul's Cathedral in London completed. **1725** Casanova born. St. Mark's Square in Venice painted by Canaletto. **1759** Wolfe defeats Montcalm at Plains of Abraham. **1776** U.S. War of Independence. **1787** UK convicts arrive in Botany Bay, Australia.

1897 – Genesis of the Vancouver Lawn Tennis Club

As both the population and prosperity of the rebuilt City rapidly increased, some enterprising tennis players began to think about forming a lawn court club on property that it would own rather than lease. So, on October 2, 1897, with D.G. MacDonald in the chair and A.P. Horne as honorary secretary, a meeting was held at the old Hotel Vancouver at the corner of Georgia and Granville streets that proved to be our Club's genesis. Fortunately the Minutes of that meeting, recorded by Mr. Horne, have survived. Horne was a well-respected city businessman who became the father figure of the VLTBC and the object of affection of many of its members. He lived to the ripe old age of 98.

Most interesting those Minutes were — 17 prominent men attended. Most were identified by surname only, so that when we read the name "Angus," we have to speculate as to whether this was R.B. Angus or his brother Forrest. The former was the general manager of the Bank of Montreal plus a director of the CPR. Forrest was the president of the British Columbia Sugar Refinery Company, to be succeeded by B.T. Rogers — one of our members — who married a daughter of James Angus, a third brother. So, which Angus attended that October meeting? Forrest lived in B.C. and R.B. in Montreal, so we presume it was Forrest. However, the City Tennis Club courts were on CPR land, the meeting was held at the CPR's Hotel Vancouver, and the soon-to-be-founded club was established on land in the West End partly owned by R.B. Angus as nominee for the CPR. So take your choice, but it's our guess that it was R.B. Angus who attended.

1898 – Incorporation of the Vancouver Lawn Tennis Society

The Minutes of that 1897 October meeting referred to an earlier, undated occasion when a group explored the possibility of starting a lawn tennis club and concluded that it was feasible. Hence the first order of business on October 2 was a resolution to form the "Vancouver Lawn Tennis Club" and elect officers and directors. Although he was not present at the meeting, R.M. Marpole was elected as its first president. He served until 1904, thus forging another link with the CPR, for he was the general superintendent of its Pacific division. Marpole Avenue to the south of us is named after him.

The directors — then called a "Committee" — were authorized to acquire suitable grounds and draw up a constitution and rules. Membership fees were set — an entrance fee of $5 for "gentlemen" plus annual dues of $10. For the "ladies" it was $2.50 and $5 respectively. They also ruled that should any members "leave Vancouver before the first of May their subscriptions would be refunded." Those were the days, my friends!

Taken in the light of the Land Registry documents, which are referred to later, all of this seemed to indicate that the club expected to be in operation by May of 1898, though presumably not on grass because it couldn't be planted in the winter, so turf was acquired from a CPR park. Thus, we can safely assume that tennis — played on cinder as well as some lawn — along with croquet started in 1898 at the Vancouver Lawn

7

1700s

1789 Captain Bligh and the Mutiny on the Bounty. Members of France's Estates General meet in a tennis court near Versailles and swear an oath (The Tennis Court Oath) demanding a constitution for France. The Parisian mob storms the Bastille.

The Vancouver Lawn Tennis Club on Denman Street, 1904.

1700s

1791 Spain's Jose Maria Narvaez anchors off Point Grey. **1792** Captain Vancouver meets the Musqueam, charts our West Coast and asserts Sovereignty for George III - to become New Caledonia which encompasses all of today's Oregon, Washington, and

Tennis Club (VLTC) on the grounds it acquired between Denman and Bidwell streets.

Representatives of the City Tennis Club also attended that October meeting at the Hotel Vancouver, and since it hadn't achieved its aim of establishing grass, its representatives offered to merge with the newly founded VLTC, bringing its assets, which were unstated, and its liabilities, "which didn't exceed thirty dollars." The merger was agreed to, and upon paying their subscriptions, the City Tennis Club members became members of the newly formed VLTC.

No additional Minutes of the new club can be found until those of 1905, however the acquisition of the Denman Street property has been traced in the Vancouver Land Titles Office. Details concerning the development of the grounds, the courts, and their use between 1898 and 1905 have not been located, so we can only imagine what took place following that historic meeting at the Hotel Vancouver. No doubt the Committee was hard at work behind the scenes — deciding what part of the city was most suitable for the Club, then finding a property, and finally raising funds to pay for it and build the courts. Early on they decided to incorporate a society to purchase or lease the Denman Street property and in turn to lease or sub-lease it to their VLTC. The reasoning was that the society would become the nominee of the Club and its members and as such better shelter its principal asset from any economic storms. If the Club went broke, the land would be beyond the reach of creditors. As will be seen, much the same reasoning was used on later occasions. And so the Vancouver Lawn Association Society came into being.

9

B.C. **1803** The Louisiana Purchase. **1805** Following Lord Nelson's victory over the combined French and Spanish fleets at the Battle of Trafalgar, British naval supremacy is confirmed. **1808** Simon Fraser reaches the mouth of the Fraser; Charles Darwin

Acquiring VLTC's Courts

On April 1, 1898, the first of several land trans-actions took place. William Farrell and Yorkshire Guarantee and Security Corporation leased four lots to Messrs. Richard Marpole and D.G. MacDonell in trust for the VLTC. The leases ran until November 1902 at an annual rent of $120 plus taxes, and included an option to purchase for $1,000 per lot. Mr. Farrell, the founder of B.C. Telephone Company — already a prominent businessman and later to become one of Vancouver's wealthiest citizens — signed the lease as agent in British Columbia for the Yorkshire, which was headquartered in Huddersfield, England and had purchased the property as an investment.

The Club used its four lots until 1902, when it acquired more in order to expand. On June 9, 1902, Marpole and MacDonell assigned their option to purchase to the Vancouver Lawn Association Society, which exercised it and then purchased three more lots for a thousand dollars a piece. Robert Kerr Houlgate — who had replaced Farrell as agent for Yorkshire and acted as its general investment manager in B.C. — executed the conveyances. The Society then bought another lot for $700, registered in the names of the Right Honourable Lord Strathcona and Mount Royal and Richard B. Angus, both of who were nominees for the CPR. One more was purchased from Yorkshire for an additional $1,200. In each of these dealings, it is dif-ficult to ignore the involvement of many high-powered individuals and corporations — in particular the CPR.

The "net" result of all this (please pardon the pun), was that the Society owned nine city lots, amounting

10

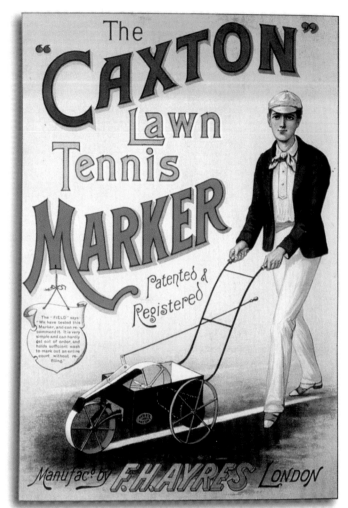

An 1881 poster advertises the Caxton Lawn Tennis Marker and promotes its ability to "mark out an entire court without refilling."

to half a block on Barclay Street bounded by Denman Street to the west and Bidwell Street to the east. This is where the VLTC eventually laid out nine grass courts, four cinder courts, and two croquet lawns, plus building a pavilion with changing rooms for the

1800s

("Origin of Species") born. **1812** Napoleon retreats from Moscow. **1815** Napoleon defeated at Waterloo, exiled to St. Helena. **1827** Ludwig van Beethoven dies. **1831** Faraday discovers electro-magnetism. **1846** U.S. President Polk hives off Washington

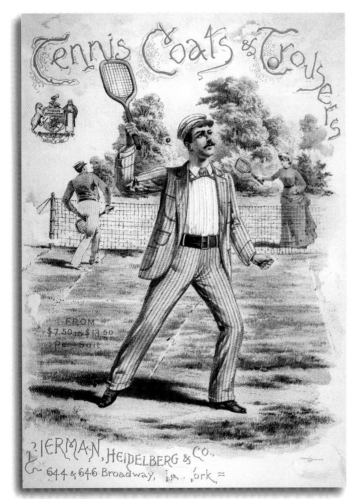

An advertisement from the 1890s for men's fashionable tennis attire.

Croquet, Lawn Tennis, Lawn Bowling

In those days croquet, lawn tennis, and lawn bowling — which was then called "bowls" — went together. When The All England Lawn Tennis & Croquet Club was formed in 1877, all three sports were played there. Its first game of lawn tennis took place on a croquet lawn. In England, clearly the three games commanded equal respect, but in Vancouver they were different. The harmony at the Denman Street grounds of the VLTC lasted about 10 years, during which croquet pitches doubled as greens for lawn bowling. Both croquet and bowls were very much a part of Club life of the time, however this was soon to change, for the tennis players increasingly coveted more space.

Goodbye Croquet — Goodbye Bowls

By 1911, pressure from the tennis fraternity resulted in a resolution being passed to discontinue croquet and bowling. However, the croquet and bowling devotees enlisted support and a few months later the resolution was rescinded and a committee was appointed to "look after the croquet and bowling interests." This merely postponed their demise for a while, as when the three tennis courts were closed for returfing, the tennis faction reclaimed the croquet lawns — thereby terminating both bowling and croquet at the Denman Street grounds. When the Club later moved to our present location at 16th Avenue, croquet and bowling greens were once again established, but hardly a month after our opening the directors reported, "The bowling greens have been turned into tennis for the time being and nets and posts have been purchased."

◆
11
◆

lady and gentlemen members. The financial arrangement between the Club and the Society wasn't complicated. The Club paid rent to cover the municipal taxes and reimbursed the Society for its expenses for construction of the facilities, repairs, and maintenance. It was excellent progress.

1800s

Major Walter Clopton Wingfield at age 40, holding Sphairistike racket.

Major Walter C. Wingfield, the inventor of *sphairistike*, which became know as "lawn tennis." He is shown here in tennis garb typical of the 1870s.

12

The "time being" however, became forever and so croquet and lawn bowling disappeared, much to the dismay of their supporters. Today, croquet continues to be leisurely battled at two locations — Brock House, and the West Point Grey Lawn and Bowling Club at 6th Avenue and Trimble Street.

Lawn bowling did attempt a weak comeback at the Club in the late 1950s and early '60s. At this time, our long-time neighbour on 15th Avenue, the Terminal City Lawn Bowling Club, was experiencing severe financial problems. A less-than-strenuous dialogue ensued with them as to how the two "lawns" could be combined. Alas, since the VLTBC was burdened with its own financial challenges, it was not to be, and so the City of Vancouver assumed control of the Terminal City Club and reconstituted it as the Granville Park Lawn Bowling Club. In retrospect it seems that if we could have worked out an agreement, it would have provided us with a complementary sport and increased our membership, old and young, for a large percentage of bowlers today are under 45 years old and the best ones much younger than that.

Lawyers, Businessmen, and The Establishment

The VLTC was establishing itself in the West End at the same time as the area was becoming a popular residential neighbourhood for up-and-coming businessmen and successful professionals, typical of whom was J.W. deB. Farris (later Senator Farris), a rising young lawyer who became a Club member and remained one for most of his long life. The eminent lawyer Sir Charles Hibbert Tupper also lived there.

for the Cariboo Gold Rush. The dollar becomes Canada's official monetary unit. **1859** the "Pig War" in the San Juans. **1862** New Westminster's Royal Columbian Hospital opens—patients pay $5 a week. **1864** Governor Douglas retires. **1865** Abraham

Tupper was one of the founders of the Vancouver law firm which still bears his name and has been our solicitors since 1993.

In the decade before World War I, Club Committee members — directors — were from the Who's Who of early Vancouver business and society. Eric W. Hamber, who achieved great wealth and position, eventually became Lieutenant Governor of British Columbia. Equally impressive were: R.L. Maitland and D.S. Montgomery (brother of "Monty," General Bernard Montgomery, commander of the British Eighth Army in North Africa during World War II and victor at El Alamein), A.E. Jukes, R. Bell-Irving, Watkin Boultbee, Gordon Runkle, and Major Leckie — all names still familiar to many Vancouverites. Lawyers seemed to proliferate. George Housser joined the Club in 1912, as did Reginald Symes. E. Cave-Browne-Cave was also a well-known figure. He was once introduced to a Colonel Holme, who rejoined that his name was "Holme-Sweet-Holme." Cave-Brown-Cave became president

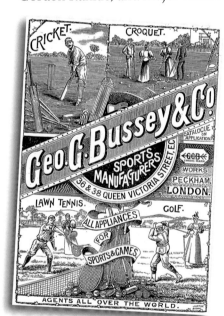

Geo. Bussey & Co. 1880 advertisement for all manner of gentlemen's sporting goods, including lawn tennis equipment.

in 1908 and held office for 12 years — still a Club record.

Bankers

We encouraged clerks of banks and other institutions, e.g., the Yorkshire, having agencies in other cities in the province, to become members by granting them special consideration such as foregoing entrance fees, refunding a portion of their dues if they were transferred from Vancouver, and to sweeten the pot, letting them and our lawyers schedule their own tournaments. One can only speculate as to why lowly bank clerks, whose monthly wage was not more than $30 or $40, would be invited to hobnob with the Club's then more affluent members. One explanation could be that in that era bank clerks, though poorly paid, were "gentlemen," often from good English families, who had been sent to the "colonies" to make their way — equipped with tennis racquets, crested blazers, and white flannel trousers, which were then *de rigueur*.

Those special privileges, however, only applied to clerks who worked for the Bank of Montreal or the Canadian Bank of Commerce. The manager of the Imperial Bank of Canada — which merged many years later with the Canadian Bank of Commerce to form the Canadian Imperial Bank of Commerce — wrote unavailingly to the Club in 1907 to ask for similar dispensations. No luck. Which offers us a clue as to why only employees of those two banks were given preferential treatment — the Club had close ties with R.B. Angus, and via him with the Bank of Montreal, which at that time was the bank of Vancouver's establishment.

✦
13
✦

1800s

Lincoln assassinated. **1866** Our Crown Colonies unite to become British Columbia. **1867** Confederation — Canada comes into being. The typewriter is invented. Prussia's Bismark unites Germany. **1868** B.C.'s Capital moves from the Royal City (New

1800s

Westminster) to Victoria. **1870** Charles Dickens dies. **1871** We join Canada, or Canada joins us! John McCreight is B.C.'s first premier. **1872** Emily Carr born in Victoria. Vancouver's first school. Samuel Morse (inventor of the Morse Code) dies. **1873** North West Mounted

The pleasure of a tea break was an essential part of an afternoon of tennis. Watercolour by E.F. Brewtnall, 1891.

The Canadian Bank of Commerce didn't enjoy quite the same status, although the Club later had dealings with it, or more accurately with the trustees of the pension fund of its employees (at that time banks could not lend by way of mortgages on land, but pension funds could) and borrowed from those trustees the money necessary to purchase our 16th Avenue premises, which was secured by a mortgage on the Denman Street property. However, not long after we moved to 16th Avenue, the concessions which allowed those lesser mortals to join without paying entrance fees were rescinded. One wonders if the foreclosure of the Club's property on Denman Street by the Commerce trustees pension fund fuelled that decision.

Merit Players, Players, and Tea Members

In general, we operated like any private club, receiving applications from those wishing to join either as Playing Members or Tea Members — as Social Members were then called. However there was another category — Merit Players — for whom the ordinary rules of qualification didn't apply. This was reserved for those whose game was superior and whose membership would improve our standard of play and enhance the Club's image. Instead of having to endure a waiting list, they were closely scrutinized by our Tennis Committee and played a set or two with some designated members, who would evaluate their character and competence and report back.

E.J.H. Cardinall joined the Club in 1911 as one of our first Merit Players. He went on to become an outstanding player, a secretary of the Club, and a member of the British Columbia Sports Hall of Fame and Museum (BCSHFM). Known to all as "Cardy," he sported a bristly moustache, a brusque manner, and brooked no nonsense. Cardy was soon put to work evaluating other players. A 1911 motion records that it was "moved by C.R. Elderton and seconded by A.E. Jukes that Messrs. Cardinall and Gilliatt be asked to give Messrs. Meredith, J.I.F. Somerville and J. Bevan and G. Bray a game — and report on their play with view to admitting them as Merit Players." Cardy and Gilliatt were both excellent players

✦
15
✦

1800s

Police formed. Marconi (inventor of the telegraph) born. **1875** Vote denied to Chinese and Aboriginal people. Deas Island Fish Cannery opens. **1876** Alexander Graham Bell invents the telephone and Thomas Edison the phonograph. **1877** Vancouver's

These lovely ladies are dressed in fashionable tennis attire of 1897.

tion as a badminton player, a lawyer, Club president, and as a Justice of the Supreme Court of B.C. W.G. Murrin, who later became president of the British Columbia Electric Railway Company as well as president of the Club, was put to the same test and passed. Only one woman Merit Player has been identified — Mrs. Verley, the wife of one of our first pros.

During that time another outstanding player emerged, Ashley S. Milne, whose tennis career coincided with that of Cardinall and who was cut from the same cloth. Both had an imposing presence, both had combustible fuses readily set off by the other, and both were domineering — although Ashley tended to exercise his influence more from the sidelines. He was a Brit, born in India, and possessed a prickly personality. Passionately devoted to the game, he and his wife raised their three children — Jean, Susie, and Colin — to become excellent players.

More Women and Junior Issues

In 1907 the Club examined the restrictions on the number of members and decided that there should be more women. Huzzah! Questions concerning the privileges of juniors also occupied much time — ones that continue to arise. When could juniors play? If they were talented, could they play with senior members during senior hours and could they use the locker rooms?

but, regrettably, there is no record of the results of this particular test. One may assume though that Meredith passed. This was undoubtedly Elmore Meredith, a lawyer, whose firm years later acted for the Club and whose son Ken achieved great distinc-

Hastings Street built. B.C.'s first Governor, Sir James Douglas dies. **1880** Helen Keller born. **1883** Canada adopts Standard Time and establishes time zones. **1884** Vancouver Post Office opens on Granville Street. **1885** Cornelius Van Horne drives last spike

"The Champion" — the elegant Edwardian "Gibson Girl" in sports attire with a tennis racquet. From a 1907 print by Harrison Fisher.

In 1907, in a spirit of liberality, the Club decreed that junior members could play at the same time as anyone else. This spirit of equality did not extend to the guests of junior members — also, the Club forbade schoolboys, let alone schoolgirls, from being admitted as guests.

Early Tournaments, Great Players, and No Spikes

The Club soon joined the North Pacific International Lawn Tennis Association (NPILTA) — forerunner of the present Pacific Northwest Tennis Association — which was founded in 1902 due to the efforts of a superb player from Victoria, R.B. "Bobby" Powell. Before World War I, the VLTC and the Victoria Lawn Tennis Club were the only British Columbia members of that Association. The NPILTA favoured the use of spikes by players on the grass, but we resisted this heresy and banned them, following the rules of the Lawn Tennis Association of England. Lawn tennis, after all, is not baseball.

All sorts of tournaments were held at the Denman Street grounds, but the first reference to specific competitors didn't appear until 1908, when it was recorded that Miss Hotchkiss beat Miss Beckett to win the ladies' championship. The customs of the era dictated that women were only identified by their surnames, and men used the initials of their Christian names. Miss Beckett was a Vancouverite, and Miss Hotchkiss, aged 22, was from California, who went on to have a remarkable career as Hazel Wightman, and donor of the Wightman Cup for international competition. The year after her appearance in Vancouver, she won the U.S. women's singles, and for two years, playing with Helen Wills (Moody), she took the women's doubles at Forest Hills and once at Wimbledon. She played competitively until 1943 when, at the age of 57, she won the U.S. indoor doubles. Mrs. Wightman's worldwide devotion to tennis was recognized by Great Britain

◆
17
◆

at Craigellachie. Louis Riel hanged. Chinese immigration restricted—$50 head tax. First issue Vancouver's first newspaper. **1886** Vancouver's first newspaper—The Weekly Herald and North Pacific News and Vancouver's terrible fire. Council applies to

The 1913 Canadian Davis Cup Team is still considered by many to have been the best ever to represent Canada in that tournament. Back row, left to right: H. G. Mayes, B. P. (Bernie) Schwengers, and J. F. Foulkes. Seated: R.B. (Bobby) Powell, the captain.

✦
18
✦

B.C. Sports Hall of Fame & Museum

Canada for a lease of Stanley Park. Statue of Liberty erected in New York Harbour. **1887** Hertz predicts radio waves. Vancouver's first train arrives—the CPR. Our first electric street lights. Rudolph Diesel patents his engine. **1892** Terminal City Club. WCTU

when she was made an Honorary Member of the British Empire (MBE). She died in 1974.

In 1910, the Starr–Reynolds–Starr competition, with its three pages of carefully crafted rules, was established and a cup donated by its namesakes, L.M. and C.D. Starr and Captain J.J. Reynolds from Victoria.

In open tournament, players from Victoria dominated until the outbreak of World War I. Three names stand out: J.F. Foulkes, R.B. Powell, and B.P. Schwengers — then B.C.'s best all-round athlete, excelling in soccer, rugby, and professional baseball. All three were familiar figures at tournaments at Denman and in 1912 Schwengers (uncle of Club member and Olympian basketball athlete Dr. Pat McGeer) captured the Canadian Men's Open, an event witnessed by a thousand spectators! Powell played at Wimbledon in 1899, where he won the Consolation Plate in men's singles and, with an American partner, reached the finals of the men's doubles only to lose in five sets. In 1913 he captained Canada's winning Davis Cup team of Foulkes, Schwengers, and Colonel H.G. Mayes — all four from B.C. and still considered to be the best team Canada has ever produced. Mayes, who had coached the famous Suzanne Lenglen, was much admired by his contemporaries. He became the Chief Bayonet Instructor for the Canadian Army and later was killed in action in France in 1915.

Early Dollars and Cents

During its years at Denman, the Club, though not prosperous, was solvent. It managed to end each year with a small surplus (in the first year it was $184 — with 365 members), but not nearly enough to accumulate a capital fund to provide a reasonable equity in any new development, which would have to be financed almost exclusively from borrowings. Then, as now, the directors grappled with financing. How to treat entrance fees? Should they be taken into revenue on operations, or should they be capitalized as a rainy-day endowment fund? It was so easy to fall prey to the temptation, as some of our succeeding directors did, to treat entrance fees as current income in order to keep our dues low. For example, in 1913 the directors decided that appropriation of the entrance fees into current income would continue "temporarily until sale of the Denman Street grounds." "Temporarily" soon became more the rule than the exception. For the Club to embark on an ambitious expansion program by moving to 16th Avenue and Fir with such a modest financial base, small membership, and even smaller surpluses appeared foolhardy — yet such was the optimism of the times that anything seemed possible.

✦
19
✦

1800s

Children's Home. **1893** Henry Ford builds his first car. **1894** St. Paul's 20-bed hospital. Grouse Mountain named. **1895** Roentgen discovers x-rays. **1897** Vancouver's first symphony orchestra. 2,000 fishers from Japan fish the Fraser. **1895** Christ Church

The Vancouver Lawn Tennis Club Executive Committee, 1914. Back row: C.F.H. Walker, Charles Dawson, Michael Greaves, F.A. Jones, T.W. Wyndham, A.S. Milne. Middle row: A.B. Given, A.H. Edwards, Julius Griffith, E. Cave-Browne-Cave, E.N. Maltby, T.J. Derby, J.G. Stark. Front row: Duncan Carmichael, Mrs. Wyndham, Miss K. Taylor, Mrs. Lisle Fraser, Jim Hutchinson. The Committee is shown on the steps of the elegant McLure clubhouse, which would be demolished in 1957 to make room for our new parking lot.

CHAPTER 2

1914–1917 • Settling In

Our Proposed Move to 16th Avenue and Fir Street

Planning the Club's move to the more spacious 16th Avenue property began during the real estate boom in Vancouver just prior to World War I, when land prices were skyrocketing. The value of the Denman Street property — the Club's principal asset, though technically owned by the Vancouver Lawn Association Society — continued to rise and the directors were sure that it could be sold at a handsome price, enabling them to purchase and develop new and larger facilities. They proceeded with their plans with unshackled optimism. But the real estate bubble burst and instead of being able to sell at a high price, the Club was forced to borrow and diminish its equity. However, looking back it is difficult to fault the directors — many landowners in Vancouver suffered similar losses as the real estate market plummeted.

The proposed move to 16th Avenue was largely a result of the blandishments of the CPR. As already acknowledged, CPR director R.B. Angus was probably instrumental in the formation of the VLTC and securing the grounds on Denman Street. As well, before World War I the CPR owned large tracts of present-day Vancouver and was developing Shaughnessy as a prime residential area. Anxious to attract the well-heeled citizens of Vancouver — many of who played lawn tennis — to this new subdivision, the CPR encouraged the Club to abandon its Denman Street property and relocate to ritzier South Granville. Not that the West End had become shabby — far from it — but tony Shaughnessy was on the "heights," was well-removed from the commerciality of the city, had large residential lots, and possessed an air of exclusivity. Also, the Denman Street property needed a new clubhouse — estimated to cost $3,750 — which did not go over well with its members.

So the Club started the negotiations with the CPR that culminated in the move to the

The Vancouver Lawn Tennis Club

MEMBERSHIP TICKET

1923

Name *W. C. Ross*

TICKETS MUST BE PRESENTED AT THE GATE
DURING TOURNAMENTS

—SECRETARY-TREASURER

present location. Three men figured prominently in those dealings: Club President E. Cave-Browne-Cave; F.G. Crickmay, who was a perennial vice-president; and Newton J. Ker. Crickmay was a surveyor who had worked for the CPR for a number of years before establishing his own business. Ker was the CPR's land agent in charge of the Shaughnessy subdivision and represented the company in its dealings with the Club. In later years he too became a president. It was probably his idea that the move to 16th and Fir would be to the Club's advantage as well as serve the commercial interests of the CPR in its promotion of their Shaughnessy Heights lots.

Financing the Purchase of 16th and Fir

At a Club meeting in October 1911 — with Cave-Brown-Cave and Crickmay present, but not Ker — the Club launched its proposal to sell its Denman Street property and buy 20 town lots from the CPR, comprising just over three acres. They secured a short-term option for $40,000 from the CPR. An additional $25,000 would be needed to lay out the courts — both lawn and cinder, as well as the bowling and croquet greens — and erect a presentable clubhouse. So all told the Club faced an outlay of $65,000. The purchaser would be the Vancouver Lawn Association Society, the legal owner of the Denman Street grounds, on the security of which the Society had already borrowed $10,000 for their capital improvements. Since the value of the Denman Street property was estimated at $115,000, there appeared to be ample funds to support the required borrowings for the new site. But it soon became apparent that this wasn't the case.

The Club directors were impressed by the 16th and Fir location, with its gentle slope to the north providing an outstanding view as well as easy-to-construct bleachers for spectators, which were built in 1919. Our more senior members will recall sitting in those stands with a high fence shielding them from passers-by on 16th Avenue. Next, with another example of good forward planning, the directors contemplated indoor tennis courts as well as badminton courts, but lack of money ruled that out. The Club

All white, all flannel—typical pre-World War I tennis garb for men, modeled here by England's Reggie and Laurie Doherty.

exercised its option with the CPR and the Vancouver Lawn Association Society borrowed a further $15,000, escalating the mortgage on the Denman Street property to $25,000. It also borrowed $6,000 from a member, F.L. Beecher. Hence the Club was successful in borrowing enough money to purchase the property and complete the courts, but still lacked the necessary $10,000 to build a clubhouse. The directors were hopeful that this could be financed as well, and decided to use the financial cushion of the Denman Street grounds to provide those funds, and so they put Denman on the market. The risk in all of this was that if the Denman Street property didn't sell, the Club would have its new property but no money for a clubhouse.

1914 — Our New Grounds and the Elegant McLure Clubhouse Open

In March 1914, once we were assured that the funds to complete the clubhouse could be borrowed, we

Cornerstone Holy Rosary Cathedral laid. **1899** Vancouver's first horseless carriage. Vancouver Board of Trade's first banquet - $12.50 per plate including a quart of Mumm's Champagne. South Africa Boer War begins. "Soldiers of the Queen, my boys."

approved the plans, which had been designed by the renowned Victoria architect Samuel McLure and his partner, Cecil Croker Fox. On June 22, the VLTC held an "at home" at its new grounds and grand new clubhouse. *The Vancouver Sun* reported:

> The formal opening of the handsome new clubhouse recently completed for the Shaughnessy Heights Lawn Tennis Club took place Saturday last attracting a smart and numerous company who during the afternoon were spectators at the match between their club and a contingent of players from Victoria. The members took full advantage of the privilege of inviting guests to enjoy the opening and the games that followed.

The Club held its first tournament a month later — the Starr-Reynolds Cup — in which as said, teams from Victoria, Seattle, and Portland vied with the VLTC. Overall, the Americans prevailed. However A.S. Milne and Bev Rhodes in doubles extended the Americans to five sets in all their matches and Captain J.F. Foulkes of Victoria, still a redoubtable player, also acquitted himself well. Unfortunately, B.C.'s two best players, Bobby Powell and Bernie Schwengers, were elsewhere playing Davis Cup matches for Canada. Had they been present, undoubtedly they would have produced a win.

16th Avenue and Fir and the Environs

Our new grounds were very much in the hinterlands, a largely primeval, heavily forested, and streamed wilderness with swarms of mosquitoes and all sorts of wild animals and everything that accompanied them. 16th Avenue was then the boundary between Vancouver and the municipality of Point Grey, which didn't become part of Vancouver until 1928. Our property extended south to 16th Avenue, north to 15th Avenue, west to Pine Street, and east to Fir Street. Some good homes were located further west toward Arbutus Boulevard. Beyond that was a dairy farm and a swamp — Skunk Hollow — through which a boardwalk led to Dunbar. To the south lay the mainly undeveloped Shaughnessy Heights.

The Club could be reached by a B.C. Electric streetcar — originally the Shaughnessy Heights Line — to 25th Avenue. However, by virtue of a disagreement with the new municipality of Point Grey, for a while it only ran to 16th Avenue. Its price was right — eight fares for a quarter! Some years earlier, in 1909, the Interurban, with its big electric engines, had flatcar-ed materials to the CPR's Shaughnessy Heights subdivision — which is higher, so that when it snows, it gets much more than central Vancouver. One of the tracklayers, who earned $2.50 for a 10-hour day, was 22-year-old William Henry Pratt, who later was destined to become the famous horror movie actor Boris Karloff.

The Interurban, known as The Sockeye Ltd., ran from False Creek along Arbutus Boulevard to Eburne — later called Marpole. So from the beginning, the Club was easily accessible. The Interurban's passenger service was excellent, usually two heavy cars with wicker seats, and it really whizzed. Would that it was around now! George Kidd, general manager of the B.C. Electric, also had many dealings with the CPR, so there was more useful "linkage," as networking then was called. The B.C. Electric printed *The Buzzer*, a

24

1800s

Baden Powell starts the Boy Scouts. Johann Strauss (Vienna's "Waltz King") dies. **1900** First North Vancouver Ferry. Vancouver's population increases to 25,000. **1901** Queen Victoria dies. Brooklyn Bridge opens. **1902** Woodwards' store opens, followed

weekly periodical with timetables and information about city events. Later they operated an open observation car that toured the city during the summer with its well known, cheery, and memorable raconteur, Ted Lyons.

Initially we installed 13 courts — nine grass, which came from the gardens of Colonel Victor Spencer at 2nd Avenue and Trimble Street, plus four clay, or cinder — as well as the short-lived bowling and croquet lawns, where the badminton hall now sits. From the stately Tudor-style clubhouse on the southeast portion of our property, members enjoyed views of our new courts plus the magnificent mountains on the North Shore. On a clear, warm summer evening we could watch the sun until it slowly set over Bowen Island. It was a lovely, charming lifestyle, made even more attractive by cups of freshly brewed tea that cost only 5¢!

Excerpts from the Club Minutes of this early era provide some fascinating vignettes. Mrs. Guttridge, wife of the groundskeeper — who earned $75 a month — sold the tennis balls, provided they were paid for at the time of purchase. Credit was not extended. An assistant groundskeeper was hired at 25¢ an hour. Later on the groundskeeper got $95 a month, with his wife catering Sunday teas for $1.50 an hour and dinners for $3 an hour. The ladies wanted a shower bath installed, but since it would cost $167, it was deemed too expensive. Hot showers for the men were only available on Wednesdays and Saturdays, and the furnace was turned off on Sundays. Annual dues (subscriptions) were $20 for men and $15 for ladies. Secretary Cardinall was paid $450 a year. When he

THE BUZZER

Published Weekly by the British Columbia Electric Company Limited

Vol. 46   Vancouver, B.C., Friday, April 21, 1961   No. 16

Capilano Explored

Trip recalled by pioneer

Early adventure takes young men of 1890 to land of the Lions.

North Vancouver's Capilano Valley with its beautiful artificial lake behind Cleveland Dam draws thousands of visitors every year.

And it holds a special place in the memory of one of Vancouver's pioneer citizens, A.P. Horne, of South Vancouver.

Now over 90, Mr. Horne vividly recalls a day in the spring of 1890 when he and two other young men, Henry Mackay and Robert Fripp, decided to follow the Capilano to its source.

—Continued on page 2

25

1900s

next year by the Hudson's Bay. **1903** Wright brothers' flight. Perms for ladies. Our first sky-scraper—Dominion Trust Building—at Hastings and Cambie. Suspension bridge over the Capilano River. Royal Vancouver Yacht Club. Sir Richard McBride becomes

retired in 1930, he was granted an honorary life membership as well as hosts of well-deserved accolades.

1914 — The Outbreak of World War I and Financial Hardship

No sooner did we make the move to 16th and Fir than the Great War (World War I) started. A number of members joined the Home Guard, membership and revenues plummeted, and open tournaments were suspended, although Club matches continued — notably the Patriotic Tournament, which was held in 1918 to raise money for the war effort. The winner of the men's singles was A.S. Milne, who had recently returned from active duty. He also won the doubles, playing with T.D. Stevens, as well as the mixed, playing with his wife.

The Club, though never very flush with cash, put what money it could into Victory Bonds. It also assured members who had enlisted that at war's end they would be readmitted without further entrance fees. The first war fatality of the VLTC community was Sgt. James Guttridge, our groundskeeper, who had enlisted in the 29th Battalion. Members contributed to a testimonial for his widow, and in 1919 the Club commissioned a war memorial plaque which now hangs in the foyer.

By 1917, the Club was experiencing financial hardship. Declining membership and reduced revenues made it impossible to pay the CPR loan of $16,000 as well as the $3,000 outstanding on F.L. Beecher's original loan of $6,000. The Club also owed $15,000 on its first mortgage on our property. As a result, we were forced to return our property to the CPR, which graciously waived any claim for debt, assumed responsibility for the mortgage, and agreed to give the Club a five-year lease of the site for $600 per year plus taxes for the first year, and a negotiated rent for the remaining four years. This extraordinarily generous arrangement ensured that we could continue to operate. In 1918 and 1919 the financial situation continued to be precarious, with the operating surplus recorded as being barely over $50. By 1920 things were improving and the Club accepted with equanimity the CPR's rent increase to $1,000 a year. The obligation to Mr. Beecher was also settled. He too was generous and agreed to accept $1,500 as payment in full for his $3,000, provided it was paid forthwith. A grateful Club found the money.

1916 — The Denman Street Grounds are Foreclosed

The Denman Street property came to a melancholy end. The enormous downturn in Vancouver's real estate market as well as the outbreak of war in 1914 combined to prevent a sale and the recovery of the Club's investment. In 1916 its property was foreclosed by the mortgagee (the trustees of the pension fund of the Canadian Bank of Commerce), despite the anguished pleas of our directors that had it not been for the absence of 90 members on active service in France and the resultant loss of income, the mortgage payments could have been maintained. In 1925, the pension fund trustees sold the property to the City of Vancouver for $40,000. Eventually the City built the King George High School on the land immediately east of St. Paul's Hospital.

1900s

Premier and later B.C.'s first Agent General in the U.K. **1904** Russo-Japanese War. Marlene Dietrich born. Rotary International founded. First Fraser River bridge. Bill Miner robs train near Mission. Novocain. Tea bags. License plates for B.C. cars.

The CPR Once More Our Landlord

With the Club once again becoming a tenant, no significant improvements or alterations could be made without the approval of the landlord, the CPR. Even to install a "shower bath in the ladies' and men's locker rooms" required consultation. And when a member complained that he was unable to have a hot shower "at eight p.m.," the secretary was instructed to notify him "that the question was under consideration by the CPR." So the Club continued to operate close to the brink — notwithstanding that the CPR responded to that crisis by paying for half the cost of a new hot water tank!

Our new role as tenant made the Vancouver Lawn Association Society redundant. In 1924 it was wound up and $74.24 — all the money that remained — was turned over to the Club. In 1925 the friendly CPR once more agreed to extend its lease for an additional five years at $1,000 per annum plus City taxes. That same year the City decided to pave 15th Avenue and charged the adjoining property owners with a substantial amount of the costs. This resulted in a sharp increase in our property taxes — which we could ill afford — so the CPR agreed to pay half of that increase. Such assistance undoubtedly stemmed from the continued presence of the CPR's Newton Ker, first as honorary vice-president and later, as president of the Club.

Did he make it? This comic tennis photograph depicts male and female tennis clothing of the early twentieth century.

27

1900s

1905 Empress Hotel construction starts. First Auto Club Race—11 cars—five finish, all Oldsmobiles. English Bay bathhouse. Vancouver High School—later King Edward—opens. **1906** Vancouver General Hospital and Spencer's store open. SOS adopted

Competitors and spectators assembled on the steps of the McLure clubhouse during a 1920 tennis tournament.

CHAPTER 3

The Evolution of Badminton

Its Arrival in British Columbia, Building our Hall, Members, Tennis, and the Press

The Birth of Badminton

Modern badminton evolved from the ancient game of "battledore and shuttlecock," which was played by two people with small wooden racquets strung with parchment or gut, and shuttlecocks made of light material — usually cork — with feathers attached. The origins of the game go back two thousand years. Ancient Greek drawings depict it and for centuries it was played in Japan, India, Siam (Thailand), and China. It spread to Europe around AD 1500, where it became popular among children. The shuttlecocks — or "birdies" — were made of goose feathers, as are the best ones today. As Real Tennis was evolving into the modern game, so battledore and shuttlecock was becoming modern badminton. The game was popular in the British community at Pune in India in the 1870s, and it was there that its rules were developed, which remain much the same today. About that time the Duke of Beaufort introduced the game to England at "Badminton," his country estate in Gloucestershire. The name stuck.

Badminton Comes to B.C.

In North America, badminton was first played in 1878 at a club in New York. By 1896, Vancouver had a badminton club and the City of Vancouver archivist Major J. S. Matthews claimed that it was first played in the Imperial Opera House at Pender and Beatty streets and later at the Beatty Street Armouries of the B.C. Regiment (Duke of Connaught's Own), which by 1910 had several courts. Annual dues were $5, shuttles cost $1.50 a dozen, and players boiled their own water for tea. Toward the end of the 1920s, the Hill Club at 25th Avenue and Oak Street, with its three first-rate courts, became Vancouver's premier club. It was here that Eileen George and her husband Jack Underhill established their reputations as top-ranked players. They later became members of the Club. Jack won the Canadian singles five successive times, 1928–1932, and Eileen took the women's crown in 1927.

Duncan — B.C.'s First Badminton Capital

Vancouver Island's tiny town of Duncan was B.C.'s first badminton capital and home to an extraordinary array of talent, mainly of British background. In the mid-1920s, their Ian McTaggert Cowan and Jerry Gorges entered the Dominion championships in Ottawa and between them took all titles. Marjorie Leeming, who lived in Victoria but often played in Duncan, was outstanding at badminton in addition to her considerable tennis prowess. Anna Kier, later Anna Kier Patrick, was born in Duncan and had become a superb player by 1930, when she moved to Vancouver. As a member of the Club, she compiled a record unmatched by any other woman in B.C., winning the Canadian singles three times — the first in 1932 — as well as numerous National titles in the women's and mixed. Noel Radford, another Duncanite, often played with and against her and in 1932 they won the Canadian mixed. He also took the B.C. men's singles, defeating Dick Birch who, though not born in Duncan, grew up there.

Birch's enviable talent was obvious early in his career. He moved to Vancouver and in 1933 became one of Canada's outstanding players — a reputation that still endures. In Vancouver he joined the Hill Club and later our Club and for a time belonged to both. In one of his City championship victories he defeated Jack Brawn, whose real prowess was tennis. But being a racquets natural, Jack was no slouch

MR. and MRS. J. E. UNDERHILL

Jack and Eileen Underhill were perennial badminton champions in the 1920s and beyond.

at badminton either. Birch won the Canadian singles twice while a Club member, plus a third time in 1948 after he moved to Toronto. He won the Canadian

1900s

as international distress signal. **1907** Vancouver's Canadian Club, Jericho Club and Vancouver Stock Exchange founded. Canada's first gas station opens at Cambie and Smithe. **1908** UBC founded. B.C.'s first airplane flight—from Richmond's Minoru Park.

mixed nine times (sometimes playing with Anna Kier Patrick) and the men's doubles once. He recalled the first time he played with Anna Kier Patrick in the Canadian mixed in 1934. In the semi-finals, they walloped the eastern Canadian defending champions 15-0, 15-1— much to their own amazement and even more so to those of the eastern Canadian establishment. Westerners had burst on the scene and drubbed them. Huzzah!

Other excellent players from Duncan were lefty Art Peel (who later, as manager of the Marine Building branch of the Bank of Montreal, became the Club's "friendly" banker), who together with H.R. Partington, published an excellent account of the history of badminton in B.C. Norm Mustart and Eric Leney were other notables, with Eric reaching the finals of the B.C. championships in 1931— held at the Club — where he had the misfortune to meet Jack Underhill, who at that time was the top-ranked player in the country. And so, little, laid-back, very

The Vancouver Lawn Tennis Club Constitution (Revised to April, 1927).

English, tea-and-crumpety Duncan with its remarkable tennis history was also the spawning ground for our province's top badminton players in the 1930s.

Finances and Proposals to Build our Badminton Hall

The Club's financial position in the mid-1920s, though not critical, was certainly worrisome and for the first time the directors gave serious thought to cutting expenses by converting our lawn courts to asphalt or clay. This did not sit at all well with the history conscious powers-that-be at the CPR, who diplomatically advised the Club of their displeasure, so that the idea was dropped.

The directors then looked for ways to increase revenue. For when the rains came, our grass courts for a good part of the year lay idle. A badminton hall appeared to be the answer. Badminton in the winter, tennis in the summer. Each sport would have separate fees, but members of each could enjoy year-round use of the clubhouse. The directors also felt that, notwithstanding the Club's cozy relationship with the CPR, there was no assurance of our continued tenancy at an affordable rent once our lease expired in 1930. Hence, it seemed like a good idea to work toward repurchasing the property from the CPR, erecting a badminton hall, and operating year-round.

So in 1927, upon Mr. Ker's intervention, the CPR agreed to return 16th and Fir to us for $40,000 with a discount of 10% for cash — not much more than it had spent 10 years earlier when it took our property back. The fairness of this arrangement was verified by independent appraisal. The CPR then gave the Club

31

1900s

New Westminster Salmonbellies win lacrosse's Mann Cup. Vancouver's first Horse Show. Ex-Lax invented. **1909** Longshoremen strike—35¢ an hour for day work, 45¢ for night. **1910** First talking motion picture. Madame Curie receives her second Nobel

Vancouver Tennis Club to Build Badminton Courts

Members To Form Company

Premises to Be Purchased From Canadian Pacific Railway

Members of Vancouver Lawn Tennis Club, at a special general meeting held in the Board of Trade Building, Tuesday night, unanimously approved of the scheme whereby the club shall erect a building suitable for the housing of five or six badminton courts. As permission to erect the proposed building within 10 feet of Fifteenth ave. has been granted, there will be six courts in the building.

This scheme provides that a limited liability company shall be formed to purchase the club premises from the C. P. R. and that all assets of the club be transferred to the company. The club at present holds an option on the grounds, good until the end of the year.

Assets Transferred

Under the scheme all assets of the clubs, which at present are held in trust by Messrs. A. P. Horne and E. J. H. Cardinall, shall be transferred to Messrs. A. P. Horne, P. L. Lyford and E. J. H. Cardinall, as trustees, who shall transfer the assets of the club to the new company upon instruction from the executive committee of the club.

The assets of the club will be appraised before being transferred to the company and the trustees shall receive an issue of shares at a par value equivalent to such appraised value. The trustees hold the shares in trust for the present ordinary members of the club, to be issued to the members upon payment of their dues and assessments for 1928.

Committee to Meet

A special committee, to be appointed, will meet at the Quadra Club, Thursday night, to consider ways and means of floating the company. The company will have a capitalization of $60,000, more or less.

It is also proposed to make alterations in the present clubhouse, so as to permit the use of the same throughout the year. The tea room will be enlarged and a fireplace added, etc.

Under the new arrangements the tennis and badminton affairs of the club will be conducted independently of each other, the business and financial arrangements being in the hands of the directors or a board of management appointed by the directors and chosen among the shareholders, with an equal number from the tennis and badminton sections of the club.

NEW COMPANIES REGISTER WITH B.C. CHARTERS

Vancouver Incorporations Monopolize List

VICTORIA, Nov. 9.—Fourteen new companies were granted certificates of incorporation during the week ending today. The list was notable for the fact that all 14 were Vancouver concerns. Although the mainland city invariably dominates the roster it seldom monopolizes it entirely. The list follows:

The Portland Canal Brokerage Co., Ltd., $10,000, Vancouver (private).

Pitt Lake Farms, Ltd., $180,000, Vancouver (private).

Astor Lunch, Ltd., $25,000, Vancouver (private).

The Big Bend Platinum & Gold Mining Co., Ltd. (non-personal liability), $100,000, Vancouver (public).

Quaker Bakery, Ltd., $10,000, Vancouver (private).

Oppenheimer Bros., Fraser & Wood, Ltd., $10,000, Vancouver (private).

Independent Investment Co., Ltd., $50,000, Vancouver (private).

The Woman's Bakery, Ltd., $50,000, Vancouver (private).

Provincial Motors, Ltd., $25,000, Vancouver (private).

Moore Logging Company, Ltd., $25,000, Vancouver (private).

Canadian Spring Company, Ltd., $10,000, Vancouver (private).

The Livingston Syndicate, Ltd. (non-personal liability), $100,000, Vancouver (private).

Tahatsa Mining Company, Ltd. (non-personal liability), $250,000, Vancouver Lawn Tennis & Badminton Club, Ltd., $75,000, Vancouver (public).

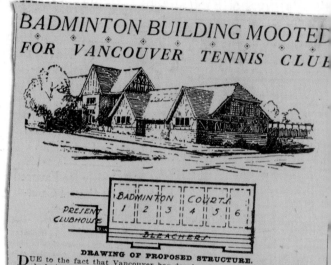

BADMINTON BUILDING MOOTED FOR VANCOUVER TENNIS CLUB

DRAWING OF PROPOSED STRUCTURE.

DUE to the fact that Vancouver has developed so rapidly as a Canadian badminton centre, holding at various times, several national titles, the fact has been increasingly borne home that facilities for the playing of this popular winter game must be improved—more especially, too, since the Canadian championships are to be played here in the spring of 1929. Over the signatures of President A. P. Horne and Secretary E. J. H. Cardinall of the Vancouver Lawn Tennis Club, notices of a general meeting of the members of that organization to consider a scheme to erect a building for badminton and indoor tennis on club property at the northeast corner of Fifteenth avenue west and Fir street, were in the mails today. The gathering has been called for Tuesday, October 25, at 8 p.m., in the Board of Trade Building, Pender and Hamilton streets, to authorize the executive to purchase the present property bounded by Fifteenth and Sixteenth avenues, Fir and Cedar streets, from the C.P.R. at a price of $40,000, and to proceed with the erection of the building which would provide for five or six courts, the number depending on the decision of the appeal board of the Town Planning Commission to allow the building within ten or twenty feet from the street line. The club has been given an option at the above figure until the end of the year. The club has leased the property, comprising three acres, on the basis of rental and payment of water rates and taxes. Provision for a full-sized tennis court would make it possible for the holding of exhibition matches where Australian, New Zealand or Japanese Davis Cup stars were passing through Vancouver during unsettled weather. Seating accommodation would be provided for approximately 700 persons. The exit for the public would be on Fifteenth avenue. In the event that the members support the proposal it is the intention to conduct the tennis and badminton activities quite separately, the entire arrangements being under the control of a board of management.

Above: Notice of the incorporation of the Vancouver Lawn Tennis & Badminton Club, Ltd.

Left: A 1927 news clip reporting on the construction of the badminton hall and the formation of the new company.

A 1927 news clip shows a perspective rendering and plan for the Club's proposed badminton hall.

Tennis Star Coming

Montrealer Will Be Hope of the East in Canadian Championships Which Start at the Vancouver Courts Next Monday Morning

JACK WRIGHT

ONE of Canada's representatives in the Davis Cup play, who showed a lot of class in disposing of the Cuban invasion recently. He will represent Quebec in the big net event here next week and is expected to travel far in the singles against the American stars from the Pacific Coast cities. Wright gained a lot of popularity by his dashing play during the last Canadian tourney here.

Jack Wright was one of the best Canadian tennis players in the 1920s. He played in the Davis Cup in 1927.

an option until August 1928 to arrange financing to pay for the property and build a badminton hall. At that time some hoped to also raise funds to construct two squash courts, but that was not to be, and over 30 years elapsed before that came about.

Hand in glove with those developments was the decision in October 1927 — following a spirited meeting of 454 of our Club members at the Board of Trade building at Pender and Hamilton — to build a six-court badminton hall for an estimated $13,000–$15,000. The plan won the approval of everyone. The municipal zoning authority gave assent, the CPR was in accord, and the architect for the endeavour, H. Blackadder, graciously agreed to take half his fees in debentures.

The Club Incorporates

Several complicated corporate and legal transactions followed. On December 31, 1927, the physical assets and cash belonging to the Vancouver Lawn Tennis Club were transferred to A.P. Horne, P.L. Lyford, and E.J.H. Cardinall as trustees, pending the incorporation of the new entity, the Vancouver Lawn Tennis & Badminton Club Limited (VLTBC). Many changes and amendments took place before the share structure and Articles of Association of the new company were settled. By coincidence, H.G. Garrett, the B.C. Registrar of Companies who issued the certificate of incorporation, was a stalwart competitor from Victoria who frequently played and sometimes won tournaments at our Club. Our new company then entered into an agreement with the CPR through its nominee, the Royal Trust Company, to purchase the property on terms even more favourable than those

◆
33
◆

1910s

Prize for Chemistry. Iodine, neon lighting, electric washing machines and chemotherapy invented. "A Pretty Girl is Like a Melody." Man fined $10 for car speeding — 12 mph! George V crowned. Florence Nightingale dies. **1911** Irving Berlin's "I Want a Girl

A copy of the Debenture that the Vancouver Lawn Tennis & Badminton Club, Ltd. Issued in 1929.

Prospectus for the Badminton Hall.

first proposed. Our $40,000 agreement for purchase called for a down payment of $10,000, with the balance payable in annual instalments of $2,000 commencing in 1930, with interest at 7% and the first payment of principal deferred for two years. A generous arrangement.

Debentures Issued

To meet these financial obligations, the Club decided to sell debentures. In 1928, it authorized $40,000 30-year debentures, at 7% to mature in 1958. A trust deed between the Club and the Toronto General Trusts Corporation specified the security for the debenture holders would be the Club's equity in its land and improvements as well as some 60 bits and pieces of its assets — "lawn mowers, rollers, hoses, wheelbarrows, eleven sets of single sticks, a weed gun, a megaphone, a shower curtain, nets, a waste paper basket, and one screwdriver." Nothing was overlooked! Under the trust deed, the Club also had to annually pay into a sinking fund which, when accumulated with interest, they hoped would be sufficient to retire any outstanding debentures when they matured 30 years later, on September 1, 1958.

We Failed to Make Payments

These plans proved to be excessively optimistic and literally before the ink was dry, the Club again faced financial distress. It couldn't sell all of its debentures, it couldn't meet its interest payments, and it couldn't deal with its sinking fund requirements, so it was forced to borrow money from the Royal Bank, which loaned us funds secured by way of our unis-

sued debentures. We were also unable to repay our old bank loan and had to borrow from a member, W. Bailey, part of whose loan was represented by debentures. And with no cash available, our lawyers accepted debentures for their fees.

There were two main reasons for these difficulties — the onset of the Great Depression, plus the inability to raise money from many members who had opposed these expansion plans. In late 1928, president P.L. Lyford referred to this discord at the first annual general meeting (AGM) of our shareholders of the Club, held in our just-completed badminton hall. In speaking of the Club's accomplishments he said, "I deplore the indifference and lack of support on the part of a large proportion of the membership which I find very difficult to understand." No doubt he was referring to the members of the old tennis club. This hostility was probably sparked by the loss of two tennis courts, as well as the Club's "tennis sector" not being placated by the upgrade of the clubhouse for year-round use, the addition of a fireplace in the lounge, and an enlarged tearoom. This was not the only time in which a president uttered such a lament. Twenty-five years later, Colin Walker voiced similar sentiments on the occasion of another major building campaign — our new clubhouse and swimming pool. And re tennis, we heard it again in 2004.

1928 — Building and Opening Our Badminton Hall

Not surprisingly, the construction of the badminton hall experienced some teething pains, the most alarming of which was that the roof was constructed five feet below its specified height. Also, as work proceeded, an underground stream — where at one time salmon probably spawned — was discovered on the site, which caused drainage problems and warping of the floor. Sadly, no one netted a fat sockeye, but fortunately the construction was at a stage when rectification was not too difficult. Twenty-five years later that stream resurfaced, again causing drainage problems — but once more nary a salmon! With Sherwood Lett in the chair, the directors approved an additional $1,600, but not a penny more, to refigure the roof. This delayed the official opening of the badminton hall from October until November 17, 1928. A gala ball followed on November 23. From this point on, large Club meetings took place in the hall. Previously, large meetings and the annual balls had been held downtown at the Aztec Room of the Hotel Georgia and at the Hotel Vancouver.

✦
35
✦

Badminton's Early Stars

In one sense the badminton hall's christening occurred in January of 1929 when we hosted the Canadian badminton championships, a highly successful event that also turned a handsome profit. Jack Underhill, who had won the Canadian men's singles in 1928, successfully defended his title as a Club member. His future wife, Eileen (then George), accomplished a similar feat. Actually, she won a national title before her husband did. She won our Club championships from 1926 to 1931 while Jack took them in 1929, '31, '32, and '35. VLTBC's members were delighted when Jack and Eileen came to us from the Hill Badminton Club, as they were both exceptional players and graciously helped our upcoming players.

1910s

incorporated. Canada's first parachute jump in Richmond. Oakhalla Prison Farm opens—25 inmates. Duke and Duchess of Connaught open the Court House. Point Atkinson Lighthouse. **1913** First crossword puzzle published. Birks Building opens.

The fancy-dress Badminton Scrambles were held in our badminton hall during the 1930s and '40s. Secretary Harry Monk is seen in the photo above, front row and centre, in the Indian headdress.

Badminton Activities

From the outset, our badminton courts were immensely popular, attracting many players, especially juniors. This was in marked contrast to our tennis juniors, whose numbers were steadily dwindling. Family memberships then did not exist and tennis members didn't want, or couldn't afford, to pay for their children to play both tennis and badminton. Tennis was primarily a summer sport, however badminton was ideal during our cold, wet, and sometimes snowy winters, and then it generated much the same interest as skiing does today. But in the city for a while, badminton took a bit of a back seat and was mainly played in church halls, however soon it became heralded as not only a sport but also a social life. There were lots of laughs, lots of social functions, the competition was strong, and everyone got along well and mixed with each other, most certainly at our Club.

Scrambles

Mel Scott and Dick Birch well recalled badminton's social side. Mel joined the Club as a junior in 1936, wishing to become part of that "very lively and sociable bunch." Once a month, on a Saturday evening, there would be a "Scrambles." Each player would buy a ticket and draw lots for a partner. After the matches they would gather in the lounge, enjoy some gramophone music plus a snack and a beer or a mickey under the table — no licensed liquor then. President Sid Winsby said he'd never forget our "Costumed Scrambles" in 1942. It was wild.

1928 — Club Colours, Blazers, and Crest

The Minutes of 1928 reveal that our Club colours were to be cardinal (scarlet) and white, and members could wear a white blazer with cardinal trimmings and a cardinal monogram. However, the proper shade of cardinal proved impossible to obtain, and so the colours were changed to the present-day green and white. At a later date our crest was designed — consisting of a shield with crossed tennis and badminton racquets flanked by a tennis ball, a shuttlecock, and later a squash ball. It is appealing yet not complicated. In those early days, any member could wear our blazer. However the crest had to be awarded.

Problems with Members

During this period of corporate reorganization while the negotiations with the CPR were proceeding and efforts to forestall financial disaster were taking place, Club life went on. Among other things that the directors had to deal with were the peccadilloes of some members. One member, against all regulations, insisted on playing with a female partner — not his wife — and at a time of day when ladies were not permitted on the courts! What to do? A polite warning letter was written. On a more serious note, the fraudulent activity of one of our best players caused more than a little embarrassment. He borrowed money from a groundskeeper and

37

8 million. "St. Louis Blues." Lipstick, bobby pins and submachine guns invented. Naval guns placed in Stanley Park. Zeppelins bomb London. **1915** Lusitania torpedoed. Chlorine gas at Ypres. First C.N.R. (Canadian Northern) train. **1916** Tanks invented.

In 1933 Dick Birch became known as one of Canada's outstanding badminton players. His reputation still endures.

38

repaid it with a cheque for a larger amount — and asked the trusting groundskeeper for the difference in cash, which he got. However the cheque bounced. The Club quickly reimbursed our groundskeeper and reprimanded the member, but didn't expel him as he was one of our "talented" players. Exercising his fraudulent talent at another club, the member borrowed more money from another grounds-keeper and once more furnished a worthless cheque. That was one scam too many, so the Club promptly gave him the boot.

Number of Members

Since the Club's early years, it has been a constant challenge to attract enough members to assure financial stability without over-whelming the use of our facilities. When the Club was prospering the directors imposed strict limits upon membership, but in times of financial stress those restrictions were eased. We also added new facilities to attract new members such as the badminton hall and, much later, the swimming pool and the squash and fitness facili-ties. In 1933 we even advertised.

1910s

Vancouver's first grain elevator. First Trans-Canada telephone call. **1917** U.S. declares war. Vimy Ridge. "Mademoiselle from Armentieres," "Pack Up Your Troubles in Your Old Kit-bag." Russian Revolution—Lenin and Communism take control. Helen MacGill

However, over the years it became apparent that our existing members are best at recruiting new members.

With the advent of badminton in 1928, tennis membership was fixed at 375 and badminton at 300. Why they permitted 75 more tennis players than badminton players we don't know, especially since the badminton sector of the Club was more profitable and their facilities needed little maintenance, whereas the lawn courts required constant care.

Juniors

The board was constantly called upon to prescribe rules for the use of the tennis courts and clubhouse. A major topic was the playing privileges for juniors. When should they be permitted to play? On weekdays before 4:00 p.m. when seniors arrived, or should they be restricted to our lower courts neighbouring 15th Avenue, rather than our grass courts? And if a junior player was especially talented, should he or she — in the first few decades most juniors were male — be given special dispensation to play with seniors during senior hours? And if so, was that fair? Also, if there was disparity, could that be remedied by letting them play longer on Sunday mornings on the clay? And if rules forbade junior play on certain courts on certain days of the week, could they enter the clubhouse and sip a Stone's Ginger Beer, a Canada Dry, homemade lemonade, or a barley water cooled by a block of ice? Those were the issues of the day.

And it was not until 1928 that the juniors got a locker room. Prior to that, they changed at home or in the smelly equipment room under the clubhouse where our groundskeeper, Tom Williamson, stored his mowers, rollers, and most everything else. Tom was a grand guy. Young Merton Lechtzier — who lived next to the Club on 16th Avenue until he got married — recalls going to the Dutch door of Tom's equipment room to ask for old tennis balls. Although not then a member, Merton always got a few to rally with me on 16th Avenue, when there was little traffic.

Tennis for the Ladies

While the privileges of the junior members occupied a great deal of the directors' time in the 1920s and '30s, an even more pressing issue was that of court use for the ladies. Not long after our move to 16th Avenue, they were restricted to certain hours of play on weekdays and none on Sundays — the justification being that the men "worked" and couldn't play during the workday, unlike their homemaker wives. However that attitude soon changed and our women were granted unrestricted play on weekdays as well as on Sunday after 2:30 p.m. Some male members fought these changes and made an unsuccessful attempt at an AGM to require the ladies to stop play at 4:00 p.m. on at least two days a week. The women and their supporters retaliated by lobbying for an exception to the Sunday rule by allowing "girls in offices" — women in the workforce, most of whom were in insurance, banks, or shipping companies — to play all day on Sunday. That too was unsuccessful. But by 1924 all restrictions were swept away and women members were treated equally. Hosanna! To emphasize their newly found parity, their dues, which had always been lower then the men's, were raised to those of their male counterparts. While gender equality existed on

1910s

becomes Canada's first female Judge. Income Tax introduced as a "Temporary Measure." Einstein's Theory of Relativity. Henry Ford grants equal pay to female employees. Birdseye frozen foods. "Darktown Strutters' Ball." Daylight Savings Time first initiated

the courts, it took several decades to reach the Club executive, for it was not until 1952 when the first woman director, Doris Betchly, was elected.

Tennis Play and Players

In those early days, the end of play for tennis each evening was signalled by the lowering of the flag — the Union Jack — and by the sounding of a gong. Woe betide anyone who continued playing! Charming practices of a bygone age.

During this time, some members were more equal than others. As mentioned earlier, this favouritism had existed in the Club for many years. A talented male applicant, following a practice set with a designated Club member who assessed his skills and character, could avoid the waiting list and immediately become a Merit Player. In 1925 the directors designated a grass court on which, during certain hours, six leading Club players could play without having to yield to those waiting. This peer group was under the supervision of A.S. Milne, who was given the power to co-opt other players in order to give these elite members additional practice time. Other members of this talented ensemble were the brothers G.H. and W.J. Peers, J.A. McGill, M.M. Greaves, and T.L.C. McMaster. It's not clear how long this policy lasted, but one suspects not for too long.

As has been previously discussed, before World War I, B.C. Men's Open tennis was dominated by players from Victoria. In women's events the honours were more equally shared. In Club tournaments prior to 1914, E.J.H. Cardinall's name leads all the rest. A.S. Milne came to the fore in 1913, and in 1919 he cap-

tured the B.C. singles. With one or two exceptions, there is no record of the winners of the Club ladies events until 1920 when his wife won the singles.

After World War I, no male player dominated the Club championships until the advent of Jack Brawn in 1929 — whose record of victories is eclipsed only by that of Art Jeffery whose championship career commenced in 1942. B.A. "Bev" Rhodes took the men's singles in the Mainland championship in 1919 and '20, but is not listed as winning a Club tournament at any time. Perhaps he didn't play or was beaten by St. L. Keith Verley, Club champion in 1920 and '21. In women's Club singles during the 1920s, those who achieved notable successes — besides Mrs. Milne — were Mrs. Lorna Fraser Ross and Mrs. D. Gillespie Patrick. During this time no Club member, male or female, won a Canadian title. Marjorie Leeming of Victoria, who often played at the Club, was the only woman then to achieve national success, capturing the women's singles in the Canadian championships of 1925 and '26.

The quality of play was much better here than at other clubs in the Lower Mainland, so much so that in early 1921 the Club passed this resolution: "On the motion of Mr. Rhodes, seconded by Mr. Milne, it was unanimously agreed that at least four of the Club's leading players be eliminated from taking part in the Vancouver and District Tennis League matches, with view to making the matches more even." In July of that year the Club held the first City Open tournament and Milne and Cardinall, those two formidable gladiators both on and off the court, met in the finals of the men's singles. As expected, it was a barnburner. Cardinall

40

1910s

in Newfoundland. **1918** Baron von Richtofen shot down. November 11, 1918, WWI ends, 14 million killed, 21 million wounded. U.S. airmail. Mary Ellen Smith first female MLA. Daylight saving time. Kotex. **1919** Treaty of Versailles. Woodrow Wilson,

went ahead 11-9, 1-6, 7-5, but Milne, with his extraordinary perseverance, won the next two and the match. Milne then paired with Rhodes to defeat the Peers brothers.

Other Tennis Venues

In the first quarter of the twentieth century, Hastings Park had an indoor clay facility. It came to an end when the roof collapsed following a heavy snowfall. Kitsilano Park had some public grass courts and Vancouver's first Pro Tour, featuring France's Suzanne Lenglen, was played at the Denman Street Arena. This was also the home of B.C.'s hockey greats, the Vancouver Millionaires, winners of the Stanley Cup in 1915 against the Ottawa Senators and runners-up to the Toronto Arenas in 1918. Cyclone Taylor, father of Club member John Taylor, was a standout for Vancouver.

The flamboyant and remarkably agile Mlle Lenglen soon became, and will probably always remain, a tennis legend. Invincible from 1919 to 1926, she had a prima ballerina-like approach to the game, flying through the air and covering the court like a panther. What flair! What élan! To Mademoiselle, the court was very much a stage — her stage. She would grandly enter clad in a floor-length mink or ocelot, which she shed. After blowing kisses to all those assembled, she started to perform, adorned in the finest silk there was. Cotton togs for Mlle Suzanne? *Non, merci.*

Two unidentified men (at left) with Suzanne Lenglen and Col. H.G. Mayes, c. 1924. Mlle Lenglen was a French tennis legend, elegant in both her attire and tennis prowess.

✦
41
✦

Vancouver's Premium Tennis and Badminton Facility

The Club was then not only home to most of the region's top players, but it also boasted a larger membership and better facilities than the other clubs — Point Grey in Kerrisdale; Jericho, with its spectacular

Lloyd George, Georges Clemenceau divide much of Europe and the Mideast. First airmail—Vancouver to Seattle. Prince of Wales visits. Vancouver eggs $1 a dozen. **1920** First Canadian Transcontinental flight, Halifax to Vancouver—10 days. Prohibition

view on Point Grey Road; the Laurel Club next to the Vancouver General Hospital; and our neighbour to the west, the British Columbia Electric Railway Tennis Club at 15th and Pine. Because of this, we were inevitably called upon to host more than our share of city tournaments, which the directors considered a mite unfair and urged other clubs to assist.

Similar complaints were voiced about the Canadian Lawn Tennis championships. Why, our directors lamented, when the tournament was played in B.C., should it be held here more frequently than in Victoria? Well, attendance was a factor. Victoria had excellent grass courts but it lacked a commodious clubhouse, and more importantly, Victoria's population wasn't large enough to draw a profitable number of spectators. And so the Club came to see itself — and not without justification — as being somewhat of an "easy mark" for those wishing to use its facilities without having to pay for them.

The division of tournament profits, if any, between the Canadian Lawn Tennis Association (CLTA) and the host club was another source of contention prior to World War II. This did not so much concern the gate receipts as the expenses incurred. For example, should the Club be expected to absorb the costs of special preparation and of selling and collecting tickets, or should they be shared? If complimentary tickets were given to the Lieutenant Governor of British Columbia or to the Mayor of Vancouver, should free tickets also be offered to their entourage? If so, should the resultant loss of revenue be charged to the CLTA or be shared jointly? Today those questions may seem trifling, but then they certainly were not.

Our VLTBC Canadian Tennis Champions

When Jack Brawn was 13 years old, he watched the 1925 Canadian championships at the Club. Brawn, who was to enjoy an illustrious career both in tennis and the military, played in the under-17s. When reminiscing, he said that the finest men's doubles match he witnessed, outside of Wimbledon, was at that 1925 Canadian championships when Willard Crocker and Dr. Jack Wright, both of Montreal, beat Wally Scott from Tacoma and Leon deTurenne from Seattle. Scott was a pioneer of the American twist serve which gave the ball such a kick it more than often bounced into the adjoining courts.

Of the three open tournaments held during the 1920s, the Canadian Open headed the list for the Americans. However, it was only held occasionally at the Club, whereas the Mainland of British Columbia Tournament and the British Columbia championships were played here annually. Of the two the former, especially after its evolution into the Western Canadian championships in 1929, attracted the stronger entry, but visiting players would often play in each. In 1923, Marjorie Leeming won the women's singles and, with lawyer Marshall Gordon, also of Victoria, the mixed doubles. She repeated her singles victory in 1926.

When the Canadian championships were held at the Club, they were combined with the Western Canadian. In 1927 Jack Wright, who defeated deTurenne, was the last Canadian to win a men's Canadian singles at the Club for many years, though he did take the Western Canadian in 1931. At that

in U.S. Pantages Polar Bear Club swim in English Bay. **1921** Bill Tilden first American to win Wimbledon. Russian Revolution ends. Start of knee length skirts. Canada's motto "A Mare Usque Ad Mare," adopted. Capital Theatre opens. **1922** three radio

tournament Ellsworth Vines, later to become a world-ranking player but then an up-and-coming American junior, won the junior men's singles. He referred to Cardinall, who ran the tournament and took nonsense from no one, saying, "He was the only official who convinced me that he would scratch anyone who showed up late for a match." No one messed around with Cardy!

In 1930, Bradshaw Harrison from Duncan, who had won the B.C. championships in 1928 and was later fifth-ranked in the United States, took the Western Canadian. He was a fiery-tempered competitor and once hurled his racquet over our bleachers, over our fence and right onto 16th Avenue. Someone was sent to retrieve it, but alas, a passer-by had absconded it, no doubt believing that tennis racquets, as well as pennies, did indeed fall from heaven! The winner of both the junior girls' and the women's singles at that 1930 tournament was the rising and soon-to-be internationally famous Alice Marble.

Trophies

Permanent trophies posed difficulties. Club officials were skittish about letting them out of their sight because, no matter how well intentioned the winners were, they sometimes lost them. When Leon deTurenne won the Mainland singles event in 1922 — beating A.S. Milne in straight sets — he was allowed to take the trophy to Seattle upon his written undertaking that "I have received the Vancouver Lawn Tennis Cup and will take good care of it until it is returned in July 1923. So help me God!" He was as good as his word.

However Club member Mrs. N. Diamond caused some chagrin when she won a trophy and volunteered to pay for the inscription of her name if she was allowed to keep it for the coming year. She took it to O.B. Allan, the well-known jewellery store, and left it there in her name rather than that of the Club. Some months later she told our secretary manager that she'd sent it to Birks jewellers but that when she went to pick it up, Birks said that they had no record of it. She insisted that she had left it with Birks and that "they must have lost it." The Club then wrote Birks who,

E.J.H. Cardinall

✦
43
✦

1920s

stations in Vancouver. B.C. changes from driving on the left to the right side of the road. Flappers do the Charleston. Maidenform bras. Cellophane. Banting at the U of T discovers insulin. UBC's Great Trek. Vancouver's Yvonne de Carlo (star of TV's "The

to keep the peace, supplied a replacement. Not long after, Mrs. Diamond realized she'd made a mistake and contacted O.B. Allan, also a Club member, who was puzzled at her long delay in coming for the cup. The Club sheepishly apologized to Birks and paid for the replacement cup. Mrs. Diamond was a good player but possessed a none-too-spry memory! Since that time the Club's policy is to retain possession of the trophies.

Learning to Play the Lawn, Rankings, and Private Courts

Upcoming juniors on both sides of the border, especially from California, looked on our open tournaments as an opportunity to learn to play on grass, ruin our baselines, improve their rankings, and with luck, achieve distinction and possibly stardom. The regional tennis associations on the Pacific Coast also took those results into account when compiling their rankings. Rankings often result from vagaries of the draw — nothing new about this, for complaints about the draw are perennial.

Not often, however, do players go to the lengths of Jamaica-born St. L. Keith Verley, one of the best players in the Club and B.C. In 1920 he accused the Tournament Committee of rigging the draw in the men's doubles by placing two other players, who were on the committee, into the easy half. At a late-evening meeting of the directors, marvellously-mannered Keith was hauled on the carpet and apologized — a *contretemps* that inflicted little damage to his career. He won the B.C. men's singles in 1922 and '23 and some years later became the Club pro. He could always pinpoint his shots and played men's doubles

with his cronies until well into his 90s. Following a game in his later years, he and his friends were in the locker room, discussing how each would prefer to die. One said, "while hitting a match-winning volley," while another mused, "serving an ace at match point." However Verley, being a quiet but extremely keen ladies' man, said he'd "far prefer to be shot by a jealous husband." Hmm.

A lot of homes in old Shaughnessy had private lawn courts. The residences of John Hendry at 3802 Angus Drive, R.S. Lennier at 1737 Matthews Avenue, and the Bell-Irvings at 1837 Hosmer Avenue to name a few. Diminutive Helen Mackenzie put one in at her dad's home at 2206 S.W. Marine Drive, fertilizing, rolling, and marking the lines. They also had an English squash court. Later, as Helen Gardom, she steadily carried her other half to the Haggart Cup — and Bar by winning twice.

Exhibitions and Tourneys

Throughout this period, tournaments and play flourished at the Club. The longest documented set played at the Club in any year, in any tournament, was a 1925 match between J.D. Forsyth and W.H.E. Richards. When play was called on account of darkness, the score in the final set was 32–32. No tie-breakers then! During the decade following World War I, Australia and England played several outstanding exhibition matches here. The first, in 1919, featured Australians Norman Brookes and Gerald Patterson. They were to play each other in singles and then pair up against A.S. Milne and Bev Rhodes in doubles. Brookes defeated Patterson in the singles

Munsters") born. **1923** Time Magazine and Hertz U-Drive. "Tea for Two." "Yes, We Have No Bananas." Immigration Act virtually bans Chinese—only 44 arrive over the next 24 years. In Berlin a loaf of bread rose in price from 1/2 mark to 201 billion marks.

W.C. ROSS   A.P. HORNE   NICHOLSON   KINMOND   CARDINA

Left to right:
W.C. Ross, A.P. Horne,
F.D. Nicholson,
R.D. Kinmond,
E.J.H. Cardinall.

Enthusiastic Helen
Mackenzie con-
vinced her father
to put in a lawn
tennis court at their
Marine Drive home.

and Rhodes and Milne played creditably against the Aussies, but lost in four sets.

The Australian Davis Cup team put on an exhibition in 1921. Its star was young John Hawkes who seven years later, playing with Helen Wills Moody, won the mixed doubles at Wimbledon. Two years later, in 1923, the "fair dinkums" played another exhibition, this time against the Club's locals, and whipped them pretty good. G.H. Peers in singles played well but lost in three sets. John Hawkes, then the reigning Australian doubles champion, teamed with J.O. Anderson to handily defeat our A.S. Milne and W.H. Richards.

In 1928 the English Davis Cup team, which had played in the U.S. Open at Forest Hills, came to Vancouver for an exhibition. The top-ranked English player, Edward Higgs, had been beaten at Forest Hills by Jack Wright — one of Canada's outstanding players of the century. Wright had taken the great Bill Tilden to five sets in 1927 before Tilden prevailed. The next-

ranked Englishman, H.W. "Bunny" Austin, also came to Vancouver where he experienced stiff opposition playing Geoff Peers. Peers won the first set, overwhelming Austin with his superb serve and excellent overhead. However Austin quickly recovered and won the next two sets at love. He later remarked that Geoff Peers was the "best first set player" he had ever encountered. Faint praise.

In many ways the 1920s were the Club's formative years. During this decade, it not only became the tennis club of the city's establishment — counting amongst its members the *crème de la crème* of society — but was also home to the majority of B.C.'s best players. Our facilities were also considered to be the best, rivalled perhaps only by the Victoria Lawn Tennis Club. We were the venue of choice of the CLTA for the Canadian championships as well as all the major provincial tennis tournaments. Much of the credit for this success was due to Cardinall, our secretary man-

✦
45
✦

1920s

1924 Lenin dies, Stalin takes over. Vancouver Cenotaph unveiled. B.C. Electric runs two streetcars. "Rhapsody in Blue." F.B.I. founded. Hitler writes Mein Kampf. Bridge invented. **1925** U.B.C. campus opens in Point Grey. Grand Ole Opry broadcast. Motels

ager from 1921 until 1930, who knew everything about tennis. A non-tennis player, H.L. Haines, succeeded Cardinall — perhaps a good thing as for in the next decade, badminton became our pre-eminent activity.

The Press — The Fourth Estate

For years we granted playing privileges to members of the fourth estate, who generally earned very little. It was a good policy and the newspapermen and women welcomed it. British Columbia's first newspaper, *The Province*, began as a weekly in Victoria in 1894 and then moved to Vancouver where it became a daily, publishing its first edition on March 26, 1898. The Southam family bought *The Province* in 1923 and it remained the major newspaper in B.C. until its disastrous three- and one-half-year strike from 1946 until 1949. At that point *The Vancouver Sun*, which was first published in 1912, took over the top spot. Sam Cromie — father of the Club's Don and Peter — bought the *Sun* in 1917 and became its publisher. The Cromies owned it until 1963. The editorial policy of *The Province* was politically conservative while the *Sun*'s was liberal. *The Morning News Herald* started as a co-operative in 1933 but folded in 1957.

Both *The Vancouver Sun* and *The Province* carried numerous detailed and colourful articles about tennis and badminton tournaments. Club Secretary Cardinall's 1927 and 1929 scrapbook contains dozens of newspaper clippings about the draws, the rush to purchase advance tickets, the results — game by game, set by set, day by day — rafts of pictures, catchy cut lines and accounts such as Cardy "invading Toronto and from that centre of culture, shipping the Canadian Nationals west to our far-flung Pacific slopes." We also read about "the hard-hitting Misses Eileen and Helen Kloepfer winning the Junior Patriotic in the third set." Plus detailed accounts of "darkness halting a final set" — no lights then. *The Province* printed manicured sketches of our proposed badminton hall and carried stories about the Club's world-famous visitors and "the crack (not today's 'crack') racketeers from California."

These papers also extensively covered the Club's splendiferous parties and major social events — even to the point of naming all those who attended. Articles reported on Club members "enjoying McLure's huge open fireplace, its crackling logs, tea and supper and a rubber of bridge." The fashion and attire of tennis were also of interest to the press. When an edict came from Wimbledon that "limbs of the female persuasion must be clothed with silk, chiffon, cashmere or mere cotton," much was made of Cardinall's subsequent ruling that "hose at the VLTBC had become *de trop* and that ladies could play *sans* them."

Articles usually contained pictures of the competitors, the officials, and spectators — especially the ladies in their attire of the times. During the 1890s this included corseted, hooped dresses, picture hats, skirts, parasols, and fans in case they perspired. Women did not sweat in those days! Gentlemen were pictured with their long-sleeved shirts, bright sashes, side-whiskers, frock coats, boaters, and the young blades sporting gardenias in their lapels. Men, in their long white flannels, were often asked by their tailors, "Do you dress on the right or the left side?"

In those days most of the female frame remained covered, especially at the beach. A notable exception

1920s

start. Second Narrows first bridge opens. **1926** Grouse Mountain Chalet opens. Orpheum Theatre built. Impressionist painter Claude Monet dies. **1927** Lindberg flies New York to Paris. Canada's first Old Age Pension. H. Y. Louie incorporated and Hotel

attracted the attention of the press. "A lady caught swimming at English Bay was a sight to see. Right up to her knees bare naked!" And they also took pictures of the flappers of the Roaring Twenties, charlestoning with their floppy hats, floppy dresses, with no doubt a mickey concealed in their floppy purses for their other half.

For many years Pat Wallace ran an excellent "Women's Page" in *The Province* which reported on Club activities. This was in addition to the regular sports page where affable and dapper Club member Pat Slattery — the Club's answer to Hollywood's Adolph Menjou — regularly penned lively sports articles. Pat liked his tennis, but equally enjoyed writing both about it and badminton. His style was as breezy as his attire, and is evident in his observation that Dorothy Walton of Toronto was "the smoothest shuttler we'd seen since fiery Anna Kier Patrick was Queen Bee of Canada's players." Not since his time has the Club enjoyed such extensive and colourful sports coverage.

During the 1950s, Mildred Jeffery, who toiled in the public relations department of the B.C. Electric under President Dal Grauer and Harold Merilees, was our enthusiastic publicity guru and ensured the newspaper scribes were up to date and on their toes about Club happenings. In the 1960s and later, Donna Anderson and Ann Barling of the *Sun* also kept us in the news with many cheery articles. So even if the Club was not a major ingredient of society, it and its members were certainly watched by society. 'Twas a great flavour.

Carolyn Swartz, 1927 — Get that leg up!

47

 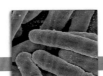 

1920s

Georgia opens. **1928** RCMPs. St. Roche launched. Nat Bailey's White Spot. Crystal Pool. Percy Williams wins at the Olympics. Fleming discovers penicillin. Walt Disney's Mickey Mouse, Al Jolson's "Jazz Singer," Gershwin's "Rhapsody in Blue." "Showboat."

CHAPTER 4

1931-1941 • Our Halcyon Years

The Neighbourhood, Our Badminton and Tennis Stars, Our Secretary, Finances, the Outbreak of World War II, and the Benevolence of the CPR

Many long-time Club members look on this decade as the glory days of the VLTBC, notwithstanding the distress of the longest, most severe, and most widespread economic depression in history, one which brought the Club to the brink of financial ruin. The times were tough for everyone, but our members could still laugh — claiming that one of the benefits was to be able to wear shorts instead of more expensive trousers or skirts!

During this period the Club had the strongest male and female badminton players in the country. Our tennis players reached almost the same level, and the standard of play by visitors at our tournaments was better than at any other time. The Western Canadian drew stronger entries than ever before — all were amateurs, although a few received modest out-of-pocket expenses. Spectators filled the stands and bleachers at the big tournaments, which were always great social events. From the broad, shaded veranda of our Tudor-styled McLure clubhouse, Club members enjoyed a splendid vista while enjoying a leisurely tea — all in an unhurried and gracious atmosphere. Jean Milne, who in her career journeyed to such hallowed sites as Wimbledon and Forest Hills, said that no club possessed the ambience of VLTBC. We were also very proud of our excellent new six-court badminton hall, completed just as the sport was becoming popular both in Canada and the United States. With our Club and B.C. soon to emerge as Canada's badminton powerhouse.

On the occasion of the VLTBC's 40th birthday celebration in 1937. In elegant turn-of-the-century dress, from left to right are: Mrs. K. Muir, Mrs. W. Gordon, Vess O'Shea, Mrs. Lorna Ross, Mrs. Mary Haggart.

> **Nearby schools were a source of lots of juniors taking the No. 7 streetcar to the Club to learn and to play tennis and badminton.**

The Neighbourhood and Night Life

During that time, Club members frequently visited the South Granville neighbourhood. The Big Chief service station was at 15th and Granville — and yes, they did have mechanics! Next to it was the Blue Boy Café with its double cones and three scoops of ice cream, 5¢ lemon coke floats, and individual juke boxes belting out the tunes of the day. Clarks' Grocery was a little further down — in those days supermarkets didn't exist. In the next block was Rosenbaum's delicatessen with its smoked beef, pickled beets, cole slaw, and kosher dills. North of that, between 12th and 13th avenues, was a huge marble-tiled ice cream parlour serving enormous ice cream sodas, and just across the street Thompson & Page's Furniture, which kindly donated the Club's first TV set in 1954. Of course the Stanley Theatre was in full swing, with its 10¢ matinees for youngsters — the evening shows were for the adults. Tom Mix, Roy Rogers, and Trigger were ok, but the older folks didn't much cotton to the kids' kazoos. Apart from the Stanley, now flourishing with live theatre, the neighbourhood today is characterized by specialty shops, antique dealers, art galleries, and excellent restaurants — but no gas stations and no mechanics!

Just east of Granville lay the majestic estate of Senator McRae, Canada's largest mansion this side of Toronto and today home to the University Women's Club. It was, and still is, an eye-stopper, with its spectacular view, excellent gardens, swimming pool, tiled showers, steam room, and spacious ballroom. Their lavish parties were the talk of Vancouver — society at its zenith.

Horse-drawn Chinese vegetable wagons plied the streets — a Mr. "Ping Pong" owned one. And milk trucks, bread wagons and bellering junk men toured the alleys.

Also the schools of that era. Private — Crofton House, York House, Convent of the Sacred Heart, Vancouver College, and St. George's. Public — Prince of Wales, Point Grey, Magee, and Lord Byng were a source of lots of juniors taking the No. 7 streetcar to the Club to learn and to play tennis and badminton.

50

1920s

Laurel and Hardy. Iron lung. Ravel's "Bolero." Mae West's "Come up and see me some time." Kurt Weill's "Threepenny Opera" opens in Berlin. **1929** Ballatyne Pier. Stock markets crash. Great Depression starts. Privy Council rules that women are persons

Hotel Vancouver c. 1902.

Also Shawnigan on Vancouver Island, where members Doug Maitland, Corney Burke, and Tom Ladner attended. During World War II, they became known as "The Three Musketeers" — Canada's three most decorated naval officers for their outstanding service in motor torpedo boats.

Dancing was very popular and the city had no end of good bands and dance halls where you could always have a great evening. Vancouver attracted its share of big names, such as Rudy Vallee and Lena Horne. Mart Kenny and his Western Gentlemen held forth at the picturesque Spanish Grill in the "old" Hotel Vancouver. Later Doug Kirk's big band swung at the Commodore Cabaret — its bouncy dance floor being the best one west of Toronto — with his "Hawaiian War Chant." The tune "Always" was often his last piece, during which you sure got to know your girl friend! And then there were all sorts of formal affairs — UBC's Mardi Gras and the Police Ball were two of the most popular.

Dal Richards took over at the "Roof" of the "new"

Hotel Vancouver and held forth from 1940 until 1965. At first liquor was not permitted and whenever the Vancouver Police "Dry Squad" came to inspect, the Bell Captain phoned the Roof to warn them. Dal then started playing wartime's most popular tune, "Roll Out the Barrel," and out the barrel came, with everyone flinging their bottle or flask into it — to be retrieved once the cops departed.

Big Time Badminton Champions

Jack Underhill, Dick Birch, and John Samis — each one a giant — dominated the decade. Between 1928 and 1942 they won six Canadian singles titles and no end of mens and mixed, and with the exception of 1930, when Noel Radford triumphed, they won every Club tourney plus hosts of provincial championships. Birch's record of three Canadian singles titles was eventually matched by David McTaggart in the 1950s. However Samis surpassed them both by winning it four times.

In women's singles, three members excelled

and can be Magistrates. Commodore Cabaret built. Prohibition, speakeasies, mobsters and Al Capone. Winston Churchill visits Vancouver. Ballet Russe's Sergei Diaghilev dies; Pavlova, Nijinsky and Balanchine are stars. **1930** Marine Building opens. Men

> **❝Anna Kier Patrick… was the finest Canadian female badminton player of her time, or perhaps of any time.❞**

— Eileen (George) Underhill, Anna Kier (Patrick) and Eleanor Young (later Stonehouse). Young never won a Canadian title but captured various provincial ones. Between the three of them — with one exception in 1938, when Elizabeth Fleck (Brown) triumphed— they won every Club singles from 1928 until 1942. Each of these players was top flight — agile, fleet-footed, quick thinking, and possessing buckets of stamina plus a remarkable array of shots. Each brought unique strengths to the game. Eileen Underhill, who was slight in stature, played an exceedingly clever game, winning 12 consecutive B.C. women's singles. Her husband Jack was remarkably unhampered by a clubfoot that required a special shoe, created by Vancouver's well-known boot-maker and Club member, Roger Paris. Both Eileen and Jack later became members of the B.C. Sports Hall of Fame and Museum, founded in 1968.

Anna Kier Patrick had a mighty smash nearly equal to those of the best men and this, combined with exceptional anticipation and great speed, put her in a class by herself. Those who remember watching her in her prime say that she was the finest Canadian female badminton player of her time, or perhaps of any time. Vivacious Anna was exceptionally attractive and Kay Staples of Duncan recalled her "red hair flashing as she swept around the court." For sure she broke many a heart.

Anna was also known for her modesty, exemplified when she gave accolades to Dorothy Walton from Toronto, whom she had beaten to win the Canadian women's singles. Walton went to England in 1939 to play in the All-England, where she won the women's singles. Badminton Canada refers to Walton's "domination" of the game at that time, but those who knew

ride the rods. Breadlines. Hobo jungles. Relief camps. Dust bowls. "Brother, Can You Spare a Dime?" Noel Coward's "Private Lives." **1931** Cornerstone laid for St. Andrew's-Wesley Church. Marlene Dietrich, Greta Garbo, Dagwood and Blondie, Rudy Vallee

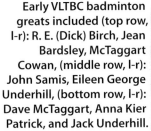

Early VLTBC badminton greats included (top row, l-r): R. E. (Dick) Birch, Jean Bardsley, McTaggart Cowan, (middle row, l-r): John Samis, Eileen George Underhill, (bottom row, l-r): Dave McTaggart, Anna Kier Patrick, and Jack Underhill.

both women disagree, feeling that Patrick and Walton were evenly matched.

Strong and aggressive Dick Birch was also a power player. His Duncan contemporary, Kay Staples, recalls, "He wasn't a leaper, but glided around the court clobbering everything in sight." When he and Anna Kier combined to win several Canadian mixed doubles titles, they blew their opposition off the court. During the 1934 Canadian championships, the question universally asked was, "Where have these people come from?" McTaggart Cowan, however, deplored their hard-hitting style. In a *Vancouver Sun* interview he, then the Canadian singles champion in 1923 and 1925, lamented that their game lacked "personality and science," and that "too much killing made it colourless." Most would question that.

Club members of the 1930s are divided as to whether Dick Birch or John Samis was our finest player. Jack Purcell, never a Club member, may have been the finest Canadian player, but his career as an amateur was relatively short-lived. Samis first drew attention when he won the under-16s at the B.C. championships in 1933. Ken Meredith — later Club president and holder of the Canadian men's doubles title, and a frequent opponent of elegant John — described him as being "so lithe, so smooth and so perfectly coordinated, with a style all his own which nobody could surpass." Velvet personified. One of his best shots was his serve — high and deep, always dropping almost onto the base line. Dave McTaggart was also in a class of his own — was "cat-quick and could get anything back." He reigned as Club champion for seven consecutive years, from 1952 to 1958.

✦
53
✦

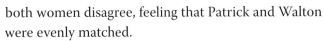

1930s

and Bing Crosby. New York's Empire State Building. Vancouver's $600,000 Municipal Airport. Vancouver Art Gallery, Kitsilano Pool, St. George's School. **1932** Burrard Bridge officially opened. First Christmas radio message by George V. Amelia Earhart solos

Dollar Shortages

Between 1930 and 1941, Club revenues and expenses for tennis and badminton were accounted for separately. The Club offered separate memberships — an arrangement that lasted until 1957 when family memberships were introduced. Our financial records indicate that the badminton sector was more profitable than tennis. However, those figures didn't allow for depreciation or taxes or for the apportionment of our capital indebtedness. So while the apparent "profitability" of badminton was somewhat illusory, the exploits of our badminton stars were not. Throughout the 1930s, the directors unsuccessfully struggled to get tennis membership and its revenues on a par with those of badminton, but there were many obstacles. They, along with those of the other major clubs such as Jericho and the British Columbia Electric, questioned the Vancouver Parks Board policy of renting taxpayer-funded tennis courts to groups or small clubs who otherwise might have joined a private club. A problem was our grass courts. During poor weather, they were unplayable and there weren't enough clay courts to accommodate all our tennis players. This was further exacerbated by the Club having separate dues for those who played on grass and for those who played on clay. During periods of extended rainfall — in Vancouver? Never! — the grass court members could only enviously watch those lesser mortals who were content to pay less to play only on clay.

VLTBC Tennis Greats — The Men

Although tennis was not a money maker, the Club was home to many outstanding players, the chief among men being Jack Brawn, who between 1929 and 1939 won nine Club championships and many provincial and city titles. Jack joined the VLTBC as a 13-year-old junior in 1924, when his father would bring him to the Club at six each morning to rally on the clay. At the age of 18, he won his first Club championship. Jack was a natural. No one who saw him play in his prime will forget how he "panthered" the court, hitting his hard, long-driving, flat strokes. He took the B.C. badminton junior championship twice and played highly competent squash on Vancouver's private courts. When World War II broke out, Jack joined the army as a private and saw action. After the war, he remained in the armed forces, eventually retiring with the rank of lieutenant-colonel. He then reactivated his interest in tennis and became president of the British Columbia Tennis Association from 1964 until 1966. In 1968, he was named "Mr. B.C. Tennis."

VLTBC Tennis Greats — The Ladies

Eleanor Young (later "Connolly" and later still "Stonehouse") was the daughter of North Vancouver's E.V. Young — a thespian and radio host on a late-night radio program on the Canadian Broadcasting Corporation (CBC). Mr. Young was long connected with the Club as a player, an umpire at important matches, and frequently as a tournament manager. He encouraged Eleanor to come to the Club from the North Shore to hone her skills at both tennis and

the Atlantic. World's largest single-span bridge opens in Sydney, Australia. **1933** Hitler becomes Chancellor. FDR's "The only thing we have to fear is fear itself." "It's Only a Paper Moon." "Easter Parade." Johnny Weismuller, "Me Tarzan, You Jane." CCF formed.

badminton. Her greatest achievements proved to be at tennis, where she walloped the ball and was especially noted for her powerful forehand. Kay Staples, who played with her in 1939 to win the Canadian women's doubles, remembered that she "hit her big forehand inside out" in a manner similar to Steffi Graf many years later. Eleanor's principal victories were the Canadian mixed in 1939 and the singles in 1940 when, after defeating Jean Milne, she paired with her to win the doubles. In the Western Canadian tournament, she took the women's singles in 1938 and 1939 and when competition resumed after the war, she also won in 1946. The Western Canadian tournament was discontinued in 1974 but during its history, no other Canadian player, male or female, matched Eleanor's record. In 1934 she won the Canadian junior girl's singles and was finalist in the senior women's singles against Vancouver's Caroline Deacon, who captured the trophy. They then combined to win the women's doubles.

On the strength of those performances, both were sent to Wimbledon in 1935 where they played in three events. Only Young won — a first round singles. However, the London papers highlighted her attire. This was when women players wore skirts, never shorts. Not so our Eleanor, who scandalized Wimbledon's establishment with her abbreviated shorts — preceding Gussie Moran, whose lace-trimmed panties in 1949 caused an even greater brouhaha, being reported in London that "lace curtains are for the sitting room." Hmm. Gussie played here in the 1939 Western Canadian and was a finalist in the under-18 singles. In 1992 Eleanor Young was voted into the Canadian Tennis Hall of Fame.

Now to Ashley Milne's three children, Colin, Susie, and Jean. Colin was a player of great promise, having won the Canadian junior men's singles before the war, but that was his last, for sadly he was killed in action in 1942 while serving with the Royal Canadian Air Force (RCAF). Susie's career, though notable, did not match that of her sister Jean, who was twice runner-up in the Canadian women's singles and also played at Wimbledon. Jean, with an American partner, won the Canadian women's doubles in 1936, defeating Eleanor Young and Caroline Deacon in a hard-fought match. Jean was ranked No.1 in Canada in 1936 and won many provincial and city events. She was very steady and noted for her spin serve and an excellent "flat" backhand. Her chop forehand was extremely effective on grass. She was cunning, very thoughtful, and always maintained excellent court positioning.

Unfortunately the relative merits of Eleanor Young and Jean Milne and their rankings led to many a tiff between their proud fathers. For several years, each of them went back and forth in the national rankings. In 1934, Eleanor was ranked second and Jean fifth. A year later, Young wasn't ranked at all, but Milne was second. In 1936, Milne ranked first and Young third. Then, in 1937, Young was first and Milne second. In 1938 Young ranked second and Jean was unranked, although her sister Susie was ranked fourth. In the following two years, Young was first and Jean second. After the war in 1946 and 1948, Young was again ranked first, followed in each case by Milne. Eleanor Young became

1930s

Men permitted to be "topless" on City beaches. Burlesque starts to fade. Canada's unemployment reaches 23%. **1934** First aircraft carrier. Vancouver Symphony's first performance. Sonja Henie. Dionne quints born. **1935** Alcoholics Anonymous founded.

The winners of a tennis tournament (c. 1935-40), left to right: Graham Verley, Jimmy Bardsley, St. L. Keith Verley, coach Phil Pearson, and Russell Hawes.

Canada's No.1 female tennis player for five years, a record matched only by Toronto's Carling Bassett 40 years later.

During these years at times, the two fathers carried on an acrimonious correspondence. Once Mr. Milne wrote a corker of a letter to the Canadian Lawn Tennis Association (CLTA), complaining that suitable recognition had not been given to his daughter Jean, which provoked Eleanor Young's father. One suspects that the mild-mannered Mr. Young didn't wish to be drawn into the controversy — nor did our board, which refrained from taking sides. Reflecting on the records of the two women, one can make a good case for the superiority of either. Eleanor Young was sturdier and stronger, yet Jean Milne had a greater selection of shots and was probably the craftier of the two. Yet it is impossible to overlook Young's more numerous rankings as well as her three successive and impressive wins against strong American opponents in the Western Canadian tournament. Young also excelled at badminton, a sport she took up because she said she felt it would improve her tennis backhand. As with her tennis, so with her badminton — she hit deep shots and went for the big smash. Her record of tournament victories in both sports wasn't eclipsed until Claire Lovett came along.

Tournament Starters, Umpires, and Billeting Visiting Competitors

The major badminton tournaments held at the VLTBC in the 1930s were limited to Canadian entrants. However, the major tennis tourneys drew large contingents of American players, which raised the overall level of competition. To encourage American players to come, the Club sometimes paid their travel and lodging expenses — if they weren't billeted by Club members, as was then customary. We also gave "free teas" to our visiting Americans, as long as they remained unbeaten!

In 1931 the Club hired E.J.H. Cardinall as tournament manager for the Canadian championships and, in later years, as manager for the Western Canadian. This didn't sit at all well with Ashley Milne, who wrote the directors demanding that he be "deposed." The directors replied that they were unable to break their contract. After the tournament was over, Milne again wrote to complain about Cardinall's conduct, but to no avail. Those who have run tournaments will appreciate that the tough job of starter (who ensures that the players are on the court on time) requires the dictatorial tendencies of Napoleon and the patience of Job. One suspects that with "Cardy" it was more the former that infuriated Milne. During one of their rows, *Racquet Hi-Lights* ran a little piece that Cardinall no doubt savoured:

> The starter may be lonely or bored, especially on the first two days of the tourney. Drop around for a chat and he'd be delighted to respond to questions as to whether a player came from Pasadena or Pouce Coupé in northeastern B.C.

The Club enjoyed a raft of experienced, well-attired, and fair-minded but firm umpires. Colin Walker and Jim Macken excelled. It was considered an honour to be called upon to act as an umpire (and to be a ballboy — no girls then), and they brooked no nonsense.

57

1930s

"Naughty Marietta" with Jeanette Macdonald and Nelson Eddy. Mayor Gerry McGeer reads Riot Act in Victory Square. Severe snow and ice storms isolate the Fraser Valley. Sliced bread 9 cents a loaf. Margaret Mitchell's "Gone With the Wind" starring Vivien

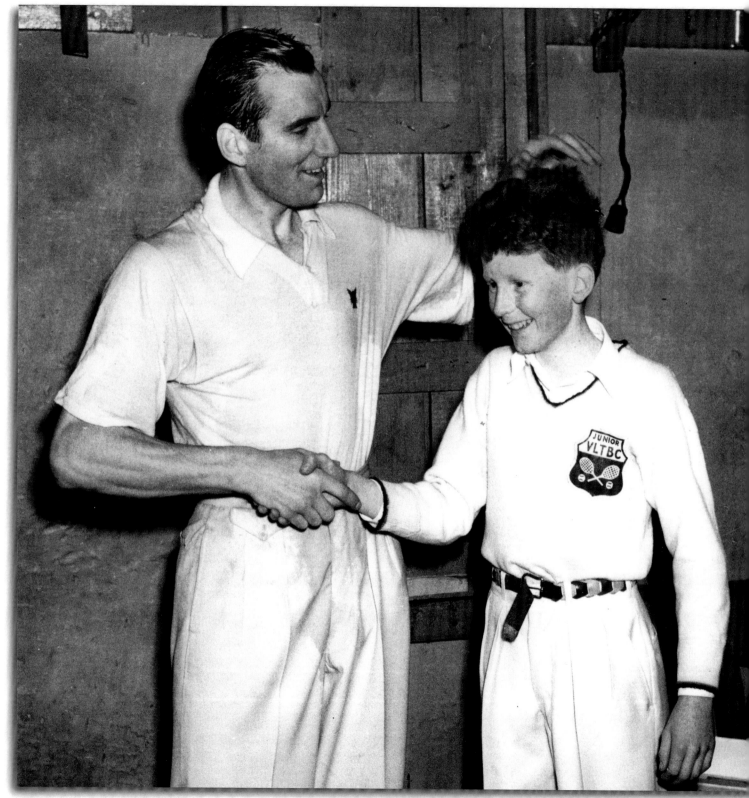

Fred Perry congratulates Art Jeffery, 1937.

Art Jeffery and Jack Pedlar were 1938 City Junior Champions.

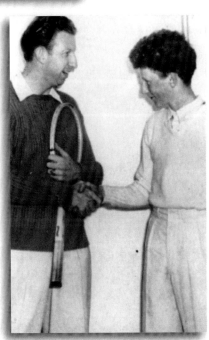

Don Budge and Art Jeffery, "the Redheads," in 1939.

Trash talk was verboten and correct decorum was the order of every match. While the job was a serious one, it was not without its lighter moments. One time an irate player, having just lost a match, passed the umpire in a narrow corridor. Refusing to yield, the player remarked, "I never give way to an incompetent ass." The umpire stepped aside, caustically replying, "Oh, I always do." On another occasion during Cardinall's tenure, the best umpire of a tournament was presented with a flask. He commented, "It's not so much the prize but the spirit with which it comes." It must have been full!

Our umpires were a talented lot and were often called upon to officiate in Duncan, Washington State, and Victoria. In 1973, the Empress Hotel in Victoria laid out a court on its front lawn where, with much merriment, Club member Alex MacDonald, then the New Democratic Party (NDP) government's Attorney General, played a well-known hustler, Bobby Riggs. I was the umpire, Alex's political opponent, and eventual successor as Attorney General. Needless to say, Alex was no Billy Jean King. Riggs easily whipped him, with Alex jokingly blaming his loss on "Gardom's biased umpiring." But I said, "Bobby's strip was immaculate and if that constituted favouritism, I'm guilty — *mea culpa.*"

Badminton didn't have such contumacious characters who were always in a state of impending conflict. Cardinall, with his bristling appearance and brusque manner could easily have been taken for a Senior Regimental Sergeant-Major in the British Army. In fact, he had served as a captain in a highland regiment in World War I. Yet his contribution to racquet sports in B.C. is incalculable. And Milne, although not as

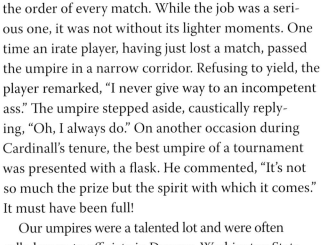

◆
59
◆

Leigh and Clark Gable—"Frankly, my dear, I don't give a damn." **1936** Olympics in Berlin. Rudyard Kipling dies. Mao Tse-tung completes Long March. Spanish Civil War starts. Germany and Italy ally. Seaforth Armouries officially opened. Lost Lagoon

managerial as Cardinall was, also played a major role in putting tennis on the map in our province. Both were characters, both were tenacious, both were irascible, and both were good. Memories indeed are made of this.

Visiting Fireman

At the 1931 Canadian championships, the Club persuaded the CLTA to pay for some of the costs of Canada's premier male contestants, Dr. Jack Wright and Marcel Rainville. It was money well spent — Wright won the singles and the two of them won the doubles, beating the well-known American Hank Prusoff and his partner. Prusoff had won the Canadian singles in 1928 and was to win it again in 1932. In 1941, he walked onto the court with a tennis press holding five racquets! To many spectators who felt lucky to own one racquet and an old one at that, this left an indelible impression. Would that they could see what tennis players lug about today!

The year 1941 also marked the first and only appearance in an open event in British Columbia by Don Budge, one of the greatest players of all time. Budge beat Colin Milne in straight sets to win the juniors under-18 title. In 1937 another international star, Jack Kramer — who later became the original promoter of the professional men's tour that ran from the 1950s until the 1970s — won the same

event. He also won Wimbledon in 1947 over his fellow American Tom Brown, who had also played at the VLTBC. That was the first men's final match to be played at Wimbledon by two Americans on July 4 — U.S. Independence Day. Both Budge and Kramer played exhibition matches at the Club and during

60

THE VANCOUVER SUNDAY SUN, VANCOUVER, B. C. JULY 25, 1926

SEEN AT THE MAINLAND TENNIS TOURNEY

PHIL BETTENS OF SACRAMENTO JUNIOR BAY COUNTY CHAMPION, AND OREGON DOUBLES CHAMPION.

IRVING WEINSTEIN OF SAN FRANCISCO INLAND EMPIRE DOUBLES CHAMPION.

G.D. HOLMES OF WINNIPEG.

HENRY STEVENS CALIFORNIA

H. STL. K. VERLEY VANCOUVER LAWN TENNIS CLUB CHAMPION.

BEVERLEY A. RHODES B.C. MAINLAND CHAMPION

PHIL NEERS CAPT. STANFORD VARSITY TEAM & OREGON STATE SINGLE CHAMP ON

THE HIGH ONES ARE EASY FOR MR. A.S. MILNE. V.L.T.C.

WALLACE SCOTT OF TACOMA — INTERNATIONAL SINGLES CHAMPION. LOTS PEACEFUL ENOUGH BUT HAS A TREMENDOUS SERVICE

CH. MERCER B.C. HARD COURT CHAMPION.

fountain. Interventionist monetary theories of John Maynard Keynes. Tampax. Life Magazine. Oil discovered in Saudi Arabia. Edward VIII abdicates to marry Wallis Simpson. **1937** George VI crowned. Monopoly invented. L'il Abner, Shirley Temple, Fred

Budge's 1939 visit, he was introduced to our then youthful Arthur Jeffery. Later, in a charming letter to Arthur's mother in which he declined a dinner invitation, Budge described Arthur as "a nice boy," which he was, and soon became our No. 1 player.

Before World War II, the July 1939 Western Canadian tournament garnered two famous Australians, Jack Bromwich — their 21-year-old star — and the much older and renowned coach, Harry Hopman. Al Stevenson considered Bromwich to be "rather timid and eccentric," while others thought he was "a funny bloke." Nonetheless, he was an amazing player, possessing great placement and a very deft touch — essentially left-handed, but completely ambidextrous. He was one of the first stars to hit two-handed shots — a technique pioneered by fellow Australian Vivian McGrath. In the singles, Bromwich encountered no serious opposition until he met Hopman in the finals. They then paired in the men's doubles final to face two brothers, Jerry and Jim Evert — the latter became the father of the famous Chris Evert. The Aussies won, but it wasn't easy. Umpire Jack Brawn declared it a "tremendous match," even though he had to ask Hopman to control Bromwich, who more than once walloped balls into the stands. Bromwich played in the mixed final with the Club's Eleanor Young and they won handily. Eleanor later said that her only job was to serve and return serve — Bromwich took care of the rest. He could, and he did. (I was one of the ball boys, clad in a plastic neck brace, having earlier broken my neck playing lacrosse. No paralysis — I was lucky — but that was the end of contact sports for me.) 1940 was marked by the appearance of young Budge Patty, another upcoming American. His final match in the under-18 was rained out so it was completed in California, where he lost.

In 1950 Bromwich planned to revisit us and play some exhibition matches as a member of the Australian Davis Cup team. However, as he was terrified of flying, he refused to fly from Los Angeles to Vancouver and returned by ship to Australia. The Western Canadian was held in 1940 and 1941 but was then suspended for the duration of the war.

Directors and Secretary Managers

Among the Club directors during the 1930s, two stand out for very different reasons. W.H. Malkin, president of the Club between 1930 and 1932, set the remarkable record of missing more directors' meetings than anyone. The Minutes reveal that he didn't attend any meetings, not even the AGM. One possible explanation may be that he was the Mayor of Vancouver during half of his term of president. This at a time when the Club couldn't afford to pay the municipal taxes. It was poor form, but we were broke.

Hubert Haines, who succeeded "Cardy" as secretary manager, served as president until 1933, when a director resigned from the board to take on the job. This didn't work and he was eased from office in 1935 to be replaced by still another colourful member, Harry Monk. He too was British — also autocratic, but not nearly as short-fused as Cardinall, nor as abrasive as Milne. His enthusiastic welcome for prospective members was legion. David Strachan asked him what he had to do to join and Harry replied, "Got ten bucks and you're in."

✦
61
✦

1930s

Astaire and Ginger Rogers. Mark Kenny and his Western Gentlemen at the old Hotel Vancouver playing "The West, a Nest and You." World Heavyweight champion Joe Louis. Edgar Bergen and Charlie McCarthy. "Snow White and the Seven Dwarfs." Ronald

Harry N. Monk, the secretary of the VLTBC from 1935 to 1947.

Monk's long suit was the playing welfare of our members, and many recall how adept he was at arranging matches. If you wanted to play but lacked an opponent and didn't know anybody, you saw Monk and he'd get you a game. It was not uncommon for members to be cheerily greeted by Monk, standing on the porch of the clubhouse at the 16th Avenue entrance, inquiring if they'd like a game. Not so lucky was Andy Carmichael. A strapping young lawyer and new member, Andy was sitting on the clubhouse steps one day, immaculate in his new whites with a new racquet, new press, and new white balls in a new green net. He approached Colonel Leader and said, "My name's Andrew Carmichael. I'm a new member. Would you like a game?" The Colonel rebuffed, snorting as he imperiously strode away, "I don't care who you are, and I wouldn't play with you if you were the last man on earth!" And he didn't.

Monk knew all of the members and their skills and as Ken Meredith said, he was a "real mixing factor."

H. N. MONK.
SECRETARY-MANAGER

PHONES BAy. 8181
BAy. 2084

Vancouver Lawn Tennis and Badminton Club

16TH AVENUE AND FIR STREET
VANCOUVER, B. C.

Court Rules

1. Singles are not permitted to be played if other players are waiting for a Court.

2. No rallying on the Courts if other members are waiting to play.

3. Two consecutive Sets are not permitted to be played by the same players on the same Court if other players are waiting for a Court.

4. The Court must be vacated at the end of the Set to give other players the opportunity to play.

5. Advantage Sets are not allowed to be played when other players are waiting for the Court.

6. Tournament Matches have the first claim on the Courts and are not governed by the foregoing Rules.

7. Members must play in white flannels, shorts or dresses.

8. Members must play in flat rubber-soled shoes without heels or ribbed soles.

9. Children and dogs are not allowed on the Club Premises.

10. Consideration is asked for other players in the Club, and members, while playing, are requested to refrain from making unnecessary noise.

11. Members taking bottles, etc., on to the Courts must return same to the Club.

12. Make use of ash-trays and containers.

"KEEP YOUR CLUB TIDY"

1935 Court Rules.

Mel Scott recalled Harry asking him to play badminton with a very cute and athletic young lady from Mission. Scott agreed and won the first two points and lost all the rest. That perky and pretty young woman, a track star and all-round athlete, was Jean

Coleman stars in "Lost Horizon." Dal Richards at the Palomar Supper Club. Benny Goodman swings at the PNE, next year at Carnegie Hall. **1938** Nazi's Kristallnacht. Neville Chamberlain's "Peace in Our Time." "Doing the Lambeth Walk." Nuclear fission,

Eckhardt (later Bardsley), who distinguished herself in badminton, and in tennis — which she first played on a wooden court in Mission. Harry's matchmaking sometimes extended beyond tennis and badminton to romance. More than one couple got married as a result of his introductions, Jack and Margot Brawn among them.

Being of the "old school" of Englishmen, Monk addressed those he considered to be his social equals by their surnames — à la barristers. He would use "Mr." only when addressing or writing his "inferiors." At one point one R. Forsyth, a member who didn't understand the nuance, complained to the directors about Monk addressing him in a letter as "Dear Forsyth." In the future, Forsyth wrote, could Monk address him as "Dear Mr. Forsyth." Harry also had a stint as secretary treasurer of the British Columbia Lawn Tennis Association.

Financial Woes, Near Disaster, and the Ever-Helpful CPR

Lurking in the background during these 11 years of sporting social activities — the tournaments, the sockhops for juniors, the gala balls, the New Years' parties, the bridge and bingo for seniors — was the gathering gloom of financial ruin. It dominated the board's discussions as the outlook became increasingly pessimistic as the decade wore on. An examination of our financial records revealed that the Club was in a state of undeclared bankruptcy. However, almost miraculously it didn't fold, largely because of our long-standing cordial relationships with the CPR and the Royal Bank. The old boy network between our members and the officials of these two corporations created an informal, interlocking directorate that was to ensure the Club's survival.

As early as 1930, before the Depression had hit with full force, it became evident that the Club couldn't repay the debentures that we'd sold in 1928. To make matters worse, the Club was also unable to sell all those which had been authorized. Because of the shortfall, the Club was forced to borrow $10,000 from the Royal Bank, secured against $15,000 of debentures, of which $6,000 remained owing. This was still not enough to build the badminton hall, so a kind member, W. Bailey, generously lent the Club $6,500 by way of bridge financing, to be repaid once the debentures were sold. However, they weren't, and by 1930, we still owed Mr. Bailey $2,800.

Our land and buildings were valued at $62,000, which, after total debts, produced a paper equity of about $24,000. A year later the Royal Bank reduced the interest rate on the Club's loan and also agreed that for every $100 paid on the principal, it would release $200 of the debentures that it held as collateral. The Toronto General Trusts Corporation, ever mindful that the debenture holders whom it represented were all Club members, also wished to be helpful and agreed to purchase the released debentures. The Club managed to lodge some cash into a sinking fund and this too was used to purchase debentures, with the money going to the bank. On paper all of this appeared to be admirable, but in reality it was all smoke and mirrors and we continued in a downward spiral. As if these problems weren't enough, the Club also owed the CPR $29,000, having paid only $1,000

63

fibreglass, nylon, instant coffee. "Jeepers, Creepers" Nazis march into Austria. **1939** The 25¢ toll $5M Lions Gate Bridge opened by King George and Queen Elizabeth. Germany Blitzkreigs Poland. Britain, France and the Commonwealth declare war. Holland,

on the deferred balance of the purchase price of the property, plus arrears of interest of $1,300.

Various cost cutting measures were introduced, including reducing staff salaries to $40 per month per person. However, the Club was still unable to pay any principal or interest to the CPR and nothing to the debenture holders. Even more worrying, the Club's equity, as shown on the balance sheet, was down to $6,000 and by 1933 the accumulated deficit had risen by $5,000, effectively wiping out that $6,000 equity. The directors then gave thought to trying to sell some of the property, possibly to the department stores David Spencer's or the Hudson's Bay. To make matters worse, for the first time a debenture holder threatened to foreclose if his interest wasn't paid. The directors instructed the secretary to tell him he could foreclose if he wished, but it was impossible for the Club to pay him anything.

By 1934 even the CPR, which was reluctant to take the property back, became increasingly alarmed after learning that the Club showed a profit of only $124 in 1933. It insisted that two CPR representatives — Newton Ker and Michael Greaves — sit on the Club's board of directors. By early 1935, the trust deed was so badly in arrears that the trustee, the Toronto General Trusts Corporation, called a meeting of debenture holders. Virtually all the holders of debentures attended in person or by proxy and heard the gloomy news from Club president, Leonard Read, that the Club's liabilities substantially exceeded its assets. At this point Michael Greaves, speaking on behalf of the helpful CPR, came to the rescue and informed the debenture holders that the CPR wouldn't foreclose.

Nice. The Club could therefore continue to operate, provided all income in excess of operating expenses be applied to City tax arrears. The debenture holders, for their part, passed a series of resolutions authorizing the Club to continue operations until January 1940, despite the default under its trust deed. They also waived accumulated interest and sinking fund payments until 1940. The times were tough for both the Club and the country, but how fortunate the Club was to be blessed with such compassionate and understanding creditors.

Late in 1935, the CPR's Newton Ker was elected president of the Club, and R.G. Phipps — of the Royal Trust Company, the nominee for the CPR in its land dealings with the Club — the vice-president. There was little doubt what forces lay behind these elections. Our accumulated deficit had risen to $27,000, including unpaid city taxes of $6,500. The Club was trying to pay enough to keep the property out of tax sale, but even that wasn't enough, so in early 1937, the CPR ponied up the $1,100 to take care of that, which it treated as a donation. However, every expenditure over $100, apart from wages and taxes, had to be approved by the CPR. Nor could we replace our secretary manager, Harry Monk — who the CPR obviously had confidence in — without its approval. The other two loans to the Royal Bank and Mr. Bailey were still outstanding, and interest on both was still badly in arrears.

The Club continued to struggle financially through 1938. Paradoxically, while the executive worked furiously to stave off disaster, there didn't seem to be much sense of alarm or dissatisfaction among

Belgium and Luxenbourg taken. Mussolini joins Hitler. Judy Garland's "Over the Rainbow" in "The Wizard of Oz." Glenn Miller's "Chattanooga Choo Choo," "Tuxedo Junction," John Steinbeck's "Grapes of Wrath." Sigmund Freud dies. Nuclear fission demonstrated.

the members — no requisitions for special meetings, no expressions of outrage, and no attempts to remove directors. The social vibrancy of the Club, it seemed, transcended its precarious financial position. However, by 1939 there could be no further pretence.

President George McCrossan — an elegant dresser, and at major tennis engagements, he'd always wear a marvellously Saville Row-tailored white suit, along with a handsome cane and Panama hat — was also the City of Vancouver's solicitor, and he told a meeting of the debenture holders on November 27, 1939, that "the Club is in a hopeless financial condition, that it is bankrupt and that the CPR could foreclose at any time, taking all our assets, not just our land." Earlier that year the Royal Bank — also a sympathetic creditor — agreed to settle its longstanding loan, which stood at $2,300, for $800 cash plus a deferred note for $1,500 at 6% interest. By virtue of the Club's prior arrangements with the CPR, the Club was obligated to continue to consult it re any financial restructuring. It did. And the CPR agreed — provided the Royal Bank assigned to it the debentures held as security for its loan. This was done too.

At that same meeting, McCrossan announced more bad news — that the Club had absolutely no prospect of paying off its debt to the CPR, let alone the balance due the debenture holders. However he also relayed some good news, namely that the CPR would — if the ownership of the land was returned to it — grant the Club a lease with an option to purchase, provided that the debenture holders gave up their rights under the trust deed, all of which would allow the Club to continue. Sighs of relief everywhere. So the debenture

holders, all of whom had held their securities since 1928 and not received a penny of interest, willingly placed their bonds on the guillotine and by a unanimous vote agreed to let the blade drop, eliminating their investment. As consolation for their loss, those who had invested $500 or more (later reduced to $200) were granted life membership in the Club.

And so in April 1940, the CPR once more became the legal owner of our property and granted us a lease together with an option to purchase. The term of the lease and the rent were at first undefined. However, after long negotiations, the CPR agreed in November to a 10-year lease, expiring in 1950. The CPR also gave the Club the option, if exercised before March 1, 1945, to purchase the property at a price to be negotiated. Huzzah! Goodbye darkness! Hello dawn!

September 1939 — World War II Starts

The outbreak of World War II in September 1939 was a hammer blow. After 1941, all tournaments but Club fixtures were suspended as many members went off to war — we don't have a precise count but it would be close to 200. And, sadly many didn't return; yet during by what seems a somewhat perverse set of circumstances, the Club prospered. The rearrangement of its relationship with the CPR, and the retirement on an orderly basis of its loan to the Royal Bank allowed the Club to move forward without being hobbled by the shackles of the past. On 26 January, 1942, the first meeting of the Club as a society was held and later that year, on December 21, its first AGM was held. The president, R.D. Peers, made the obvious comment that war service had reduced the male

65

1940s

Our Aquarium and the new Hotel Vancouver open. TCA flies to Montreal. **1940** Victory Ships built in False Creek. Boeing employs 5,000 in Richmond. Vancouver Sun's first Salmon Derby. Stanley Park's Theatre Under the Stars. Hemingway's "For Whom

membership but that the Club financially was now satisfactory. What a difference that year made!

The Club Becomes a Society

The rearrangements with the CPR and our debenture holders coincided with the Club's plans to restructure itself. In 1928 the Club was incorporated as the Vancouver Lawn Tennis and Badminton Club Limited. Over the years there had been much discussion about switching from a limited company, which implied a commercial activity, to that of a non-profit society. The obvious concern was that if the Club operated as a corporation, government tax agencies might conclude that the Club intended to make a profit (which it never did), and therefore be subject to taxation. But as a non-profit society, the Club would be exempt from taxation.

To make that switch involved a voluntary dissolution of the existing limited company and the transfer of its assets to a newly–to-be-incorporated society. However, existing corporate law forbade the voluntary dissolution of the Club's company if it was insolvent — which it certainly was. To circumvent these obstacles a new entity, the Vancouver Lawn Tennis and Badminton Club Society, was incorporated in September 1941. The somewhat meagre assets of the Club's former limited company were then transferred to this new non-profit society. And our limited company, which held the lease from the CPR, sublet to our new society, which effectively became the CPR's tenant.

All of these arrangements were approved at the AGM of the Vancouver Lawn Tennis and Badminton Club Limited on December 9, 1941. Probably due to the Japanese attack on Pearl Harbour two days earlier and the entry of the United States into the war, not to mention a local blackout, only three people attended: Club Secretary Harry Monk, Vice President R.D. Peers, and one unnamed shareholder! Not even a quorum! The magnitude of those events diverted the members' attention from the Club's plight and no one ever questioned the absence of a quorum as a reason to invalidate the decisions made by those two people — the secretary being prohibited from casting a vote!

1940s

the Bell Tolls." Wurlitzers. "Roll Out the Barrel" and the equally famous "Lili Marlene." The Andrews Sisters "Don't Sit Under the Apple Tree With Anyone Else But Me." Chamberlain resigns. Winston Churchill takes over. "You Are My Sunshine." Swastikas fly

Saviours

This lengthy account of the Club's financial difficulties during the 1930s and the early 1940's, along with the directors' attempts to avoid disaster may seem tedious, but it provides an understanding and appreciation of the challenges the Club weathered just to exist. For years the problems persisted, ever-present and seemingly ever insoluble. Only the extraordinary forbearance and leniency of the CPR allowed us to continue. What motivated the CPR's generosity? No one knows for sure. It was still selling its lots in Shaughnessy and perhaps it saw the Club as an inducement to its buyers. It probably would have made good financial sense for the CPR to foreclose — especially when the value of the Club's land exceeded the money it was owed — and reclaim the land and turn it into lots, along with its other lots in Shaughnessy. Perhaps the CPR decision-makers held back for sentimental reasons, as they had a long connection with the Club going back to the turn of the century. Perhaps it was good public relations. All we do know is that the CPR's actions exemplified outstanding corporate citizenship and as a result, the Club owes its existence to the CPR.

Credit must also be given to the Royal Bank of Canada whose Vancouver manager, W. Boucher, was a Club member. Although the Royal Bank was not nearly as financially involved as the CPR, it too could have shut the Club down, but also chose not to. In looking back, one must feel sorry for the debenture holders as most probably purchased them with the expectation of eventual repayment. W. Bailey probably lost the most. In 1928, he lent the Club $6,500 and subsequently received some principal payments, but no interest, and in 1940 he wrote off the $1,300 that the Club still owed him. Once more most generous of him.

1940s

over Paris. British Army cornered at Dunkirk—most cross-channel rescued. R.A.F. Battle of Britain—Spitfires and Hawker Hurricanes whip the Luftwaffe. "Never have so few done so much for so many." HMCS Hood, world's largest battleship, sunk by the

Club members on the steps of the McLure clubhouse on an early summer evening in 1948.

CHAPTER 5

1942-1956 • Building & Transition

Money Shortages, We Fire Our Secretary, Ever-Helpful Members, Archivist Al Stevenson's Racquet Hi-Lights, Our New Facilities, Movie Stars, U.S. vs. Japan Davis Cup, and Lady Directors

Dollar Problems Continue

There is little reference in the Club's records to the extent to which members participated in the war effort, whether in the Armed Forces, the Merchant Navy, or other endeavours on the home front. Also little reference to the privation that everyone was subject to — rationing and the difficulties in obtaining supplies and replacements for equipment.

While our Club membership declined during this time, our financial situation slowly improved during the last three years of the war. We were free of long-term debt and began to accumulate surplus funds which were invested in Victory Bonds against the day when we would negotiate with the CPR to exercise our option to purchase. There is no record of which Club directors dealt with the CPR, although W.G. Murrin, president of the British Columbia Electric Railway Company and former Club president, appeared to have had a hand in the affair, as did the CPR's purchasing agent, S.V.T. Jeffery, who became Club president in 1946. When the CPR took back the Club's property in 1940, we still owed them $29,000 from their original sale price of $40,000. In November 1944, the CPR forgave $9,000 of that sum and agreed to sell the lands back to us for $20,000 with a down payment of $8,000, with the remaining $12,000 to be paid in six annual instalments of $2,000 at 6% interest. By 1945, the Club had the necessary $8,000 down payment in hand, and the deal was struck — a deal which was most fortunate and most fair. How did it come about? Again, the speculation is that the same considerations were present as they were three years earlier — the CPR's corporate goodwill, its history of good rapport with the Club, public relations, and its view of its investment in us complimenting its larger and more important commercial endeavour to develop Shaughnessy Heights.

1948 – Exeunt the CPR

Apart from our down payment of $8,000 to the CPR and the $12,000 we still owed it, by 1946 the Club recorded an accumulated surplus of $14,000 — a first! By the end of that year, we paid the CPR another $6,000, leaving only $6,000 outstanding on the option to purchase. In order to ensure that the remaining payments were made on schedule, the Club instituted an austerity program, deferring all but the most necessary expenditures for maintenance. In February 1948, right on time, the Club paid the final $6,000 and again took full possession of the property. A banner day! Fred Bolton enjoyed the distinction of presiding over this the most significant event in the Club's history — far more important than the CPR's rescue in 1940, because by 1948 the value of our land had substantially increased. So, no longer did the CPR have to be consulted for every decision, and no longer did a request for $100 for new showers in the ladies' locker room have to be approved in a CPR boardroom in Montreal. It had taken 50 years, but the Club was no longer dependent on the CPR. The Club had finally come of age, could act on its own, and no longer needed a benevolent shepherd to oversee it.

Farewell Secretary Monk

The most divisive and turbulent personnel issue during this period was the removal/resignation of Harry Monk as secretary manager. His managerial shortcomings and his autocratic and imperious style, along with his too-often imbibing on the job, had alienated many members, and a movement to topple him gradually gained strength. Had his behavioural failings been his sole weakness, he may never have been ousted. But he wouldn't adopt acceptable accounting procedures, preferring to conduct his bookkeeping in a "fly-by-the-seat-of-his-pants" style.

Monk joined us in February of 1935 at a salary of $75 a month. He worked for the Club for 12 years and was compelled to tender his "resignation" to President S.V.T. Jeffery on 24 July, 1947. At an August 1 meeting at Jeffery's home, the directors discussed many related issues, going far beyond the obvious issues of severance pay for his long and loyal service. The following excerpt from the Minutes of that meeting shed further light on the day's events.

> This meeting was called for the purpose of endeavouring to arrive at an amicable understanding with regard to the secretary-manager of the Club. Mr. Jeffery advised that Mr. Monk had tendered his resignation to him personally on July 24, and that Mr. Monk had telephoned his house, confirming his action. It was mutually agreed that the many difficulties that we and others were involved in with the secretary-manager may have been caused by strain through over-work, and in view of the services he has rendered, we would suggest to him that he take a complete medical checkup at the expense of the Club; it being considered that it would not only be good for him but in the best interests of the Club. It was furthermore agreed that we would discuss this question with Mr. Monk privately on Saturday, August 2. It was also agreed that we would call a private meeting, to be made up of ten well-known members of the Club, who we considered would be favourable to Mr. Monk, and ten members who had

70

Bismark—three survivors. Wolf pack submarines devastate the Allies' merchant marine. Churchill's plea to America—"Give us the tools and we'll finish the job." Roosevelt hands over 50 mothballed destroyers. P.M. Mackenzie King's "Conscription if

registered complaints with regard to his actions, and to sit down and discuss the problem in a gentlemanly manner for the purpose of securing their views.

There was no question that Harry Monk had both his admirers and his detractors and both factions were very vocal. Jeffery pencilled an addition to the Minutes: "Spoke to Mr. Tom Reid to head the pro-Monk committee. He declined. Spoke to Erwin Elliott, on behalf of anti-Monk. He agreed." The latter forces prevailed and Monk's resignation stood, with the Club deciding to pay him an additional two months' salary. His departure triggered the resignation of the Club's auditor. Upon hiring a new auditor, his first task was "to A.S.A.P. devise and install an adequate system of accounting." Jeffery didn't stand for re-election and was succeeded by Fred Bolton who, among his many accomplishments in tennis, became the non-playing captain of a number of Canadian Davis Cup teams. A succession of secretaries followed. The genial Harry Wilkinson served for three years and was succeeded by Arthur Cox in 1953. Both individuals brought much-needed stability to the post.

Do-It-Yourself-ers

During the Club's first half century, our members did just about everything around the Club — except court upkeep — on a volunteer basis and at their own expense. I revised our bylaws. Busy beavers, each one dedicated. They planned and managed matches, round robins, and badminton scrambles as well as umpiring and refereeing tournaments. They planned poolside open-pit barbecues, raffles, parties, and dances, did all the necessary decorating and cleaning up and also undertook the never-ending task of maintenance — cleaning, painting, caring for our plants and gardens, and stoking the wood, oil, and coal stoves to name but a few. This inevitably caused some outrageous conflicts, often over the most trivial matters. For example, if Erwin Elliott didn't agree with any committee's decision — such as waxing the badminton court for dancing at the New Year's Party, he'd resign. Which he did many times!

Our members also made their views known in the *Racquet Hi-Lights* with articles such as "Court Manners," and how and how not to return a ball from a neighbouring court. They read about proposals to red-top (*En Tout Cas*) our clay courts (too expensive). About making "combination" locks compulsory, instituting a Suggestions Box (universally welcomed), and considering removal of Clay Court 1 for squash. Plus paying for the Archivist's film, agreeing to the Club keeping the 2¢ refund on soft drink bottles, and its etiquette for Sadie Hawkins Day and Leap Year. Members also rented movies — the likes of *The Lavender Hill Mob*, *Great Expectations*, *Henry V*, and *Oliver Twist*. Little wonder they felt that no racquets club in North America offered comparable operations and facilities for such low dues as did we. And no one did. In addition, our people considered their first duty was to ensure that no stranger and no new member was neglected. They weren't. And to mix. Which our members for a fare-thee-well did. Also to keep their "home away from home" refreshing, wholesome, and *the* place to be. This they did too.

71

necessary but not necessarily conscription." Rommel's Afrika Corps winning in the desert. Vancouver shipyards build Corvettes and Mine sweepers. Unemployment insurance introduced Commonwealth Air Training Plan initiated. **1941** Day of

Problems with Social Events

As usual, the board attended to all sorts of matters. In 1949, social events were thought to be getting out of hand, resulting in the establishment of a roster of directors to attend each one to make sure order was maintained and at their conclusion to ensure that the clubhouse was locked up, that all fires were extinguished — including the stove — and that all lights were put out. Each needed and each good.

Proposed New Facilities — Their Planning and Financing

It wouldn't be fair to say the Club went on a spending spree once the deal was struck with the CPR, however our austerity program was jettisoned and extensive repairs, alterations, and refurbishing started to take place.

In 1951 Colin Walker, our resident Aussie, became president. Born in Toowoomba (great name) on the Gold Coast in Queensland, west of Brisbane, Colin came to Calgary during World War II for the Commonwealth Air Training Plan and subsequently served with great distinction in the Royal Australian Air Force (RAAF) as flight lieutenant and captain of an anti-submarine *Sunderland* aircraft based in England. He and his crew of 10, whilst patrolling in the Bay of Biscay and searching for the downed movie actor Leslie Howard, were attacked by eight *Junkers 88*. They shot down six, were riddled themselves but managed to fly to Penzance in southwest England for a ditched landing at night. Later during the war, now Squadron Leader Walker, D.S.O. was appointed the RAAF's Western Canadian Liaison Officer stationed in Vancouver, where he met and soon married our talented Doreen Ryan and joined the Club. He was a fierce, never-give-up doubles player with Himalayan panache, and partnered Art Jeffery for many a title.

Naturally, all of our "down unders" were very proud of their country's accomplishments — rugby, swimming — but most especially cricket and tennis. Everyone knew of cricket's Don Bradman, the tennis whiz kids Rosewall and Hoad, their constantly-coaching disciplinarian Harry Hopman, Roy Emerson, and Rod Laver — who many consider probably the best all-round tennis player of the century. Rosewall and Hoad, as 19-year-old kids, broke all sound barriers when they won the Wimbledon men's doubles in 1953. Previously, a good singles player didn't reach his peak until around 23 years of age and in doubles, which allegedly took more brains, it was 26 at the earliest. Nowadays those folks are described as "veterans" — how times change!

In 1951 the Club paid Bennett & White Construction $5,719 to remove two clay courts and install two cement ones. By 1953 Walker and the directors concluded that the Club could not survive financially simply by offering tennis and badminton. The Club had suffered an operating loss of $6,600 on the tennis operations, which was partly offset by a profit of $2,800 from the badminton section. In May the board struck a committee, headed by director Jack Shakespeare, to consider large-scale renovations to the McLure clubhouse. Specifically, they studied the feasibility of installing three new locker rooms in a newly built basement, a 54-seat dining lounge with a

1940s

Infamy—December 7, Japanese attack Pearl Harbour. U.S. enters the War. Bob Hope, Bing Crosby and Dorothy Lamour in the "Road to Zanzibar." Glenn Miller's "Sun Valley Serenade." Vera Lynn's "There'll be Bluebirds Over the White Cliffs of Dover." George

Colin Walker (left) and Art Jeffery — formidable doubles partners.

modern kitchen, an upstairs lounge with a bar, plus an outdoor heated swimming pool. Coupled with this was a spirited campaign for family membership.

Planning proceeded and at a special meeting chaired by Walker on 19 January, 1954, the proposal was overwhelmingly approved. This set in train a complicated set of procedures reminiscent of those of 1928. A holding company — Vancouver Tennis and Badminton Holdings Ltd. — was incorporated for a friendly fee by Ken Meredith and all the assets of the Club were transferred to it. As the new legal owner of the Club's assets, the holding company could sell shares to members who had held shares or debentures in the now defunct Vancouver Lawn Tennis and Badminton Club Limited as well as to new members. A prospectus was filed with the Registrar of Companies, which stipulated that a member could only own one share, and that being a shareholder was a new condition of membership. The shares sold for $90 cash or $100 payable over six months. Once the

holding company had sold a minimum of $50,000, it could proceed with and pay for the renovations, and borrow additional money when required. The holding company then leased the land and the premises to the Club on a 99-year lease from 26 August, 1954, at a rent sufficient to retire any indebtedness resulting from the cost of the proposed renovations and municipal taxes. In short order the holding company sold about $70,000 worth of shares, well exceeding the planned minimum. This encouraging news was quickly offset by a much more discouraging development which surfaced at the first formal meeting of the holding company in September 1954. The anticipated costs of renovation had risen from $75,000 to $191,000. The consensus was that this was much too costly and so the board voted to scrap the plans — for a while.

A few months later the directors unanimously agreed to build an entirely new clubhouse instead of restoring our stately McLure. Their decision was partly influenced by the discovery that it sat on a huge

1940s

Formby. CBC's first National news service with Lorne Greene. Hitler invades Russia. Gracie Field sings at the PNE. Victory Ships built—24 hours a day, seven days a week. **1942** Singapore surrenders. Siege of Stalingrad. Turning the tide. Battle of Midway

Sod breaking ceremony for the new VLTBC clubhouse in 1956 (L-R): E. Kemble, C. Walker, W. Dring, R. Paton, P. Morris, W.G. Murrin, P. Lyford, K. Verley, D. Meakin, K. Meredith.

74

Second Mortgage Debenture, issued in November 1956.

On the VLTBC lawn in 1956. Back row (L-R): Eric Beardmore, Keith Verley, Sid Harold, John Leader. Front row (L-R): Mildred Jeffery, A.P. Horne, Jean Beardmore.

1940s

in the Pacific. General Montgomery's victorious Eighth Army Desert Rats at El Alamein. "Waltzing Matilda" Bing Crosby's "White Christmas". Humphrey Bogart and Ingrid Bergman in Casablanca. Butter rationed. Canadians of Japanese descent interned.

rock outcrop that would be too costly to remove in order to build a basement. Unlike today, talk of tearing down such a "heritage" building was not considered an outrage! An Extraordinary General Meeting was held with 157 members attending, and by a vote of 133 to 24 — the required 75% — the board received permission to proceed on a cash basis. If a mortgage was required, the directors had to return to the membership for approval.

Board member Wyn Madden interviewed four architects and Davison and Porter were chosen. They didn't charge for their sketches and their final fee was $3,050. Marwell Construction was awarded the contract and they got under way in 1956 during the presidency of hard-working Ken Meredith. To pay for the new clubhouse, the holding company borrowed $125,000 from the Bank of Nova Scotia, secured by a 6% Demand Debenture that was to be repaid from its rental revenues from the Club. The relationship between the Club and its own company was perhaps somewhat incestuous, but it followed the same pattern as when earlier the Denman Street grounds were held by the Vancouver Lawn Association and leased by it.

Mrs. Moo Furney

The imposing and regal Mrs. Moo Furney joined the Club as Secretary in August of 1954, during the twilight of the McLure clubhouse. She came with eons of experience, having worked at the Overseas Service Club in London, and the prestigious Jericho Country Club in Vancouver, which had closed in 1942. Moo really knew her food and Club members were treated to scrumptious buffets and smorgasbords. She lived in the second floor of our clubhouse, behind curtained-off quarters to the south of the men's showers and locker room — where no doubt she saw more of some members than she cared to.

A sense of humour was almost a requisite for the job, and fortunately Moo Furney possessed one. One evening "Doggy" (David Strachan) and Cy Craig, having imbibed a few cups, peeked over the curtains at Moo, who quickly remonstrated, "Oh you silly, silly boys." During her short tenure, the Club increased her salary to $325 a month. By August of 1956 she had left, and Mr. Vossin assumed the post of Club secretary.

1957 — Our Brand New Facilities and Our Spirited Staff

By the time the construction was completed, costs had risen to $295,000 — largely as the result of costs for the pool — with most to be paid from borrowed money. However we now had a brand new clubhouse, up-to-date sports facilities, an outdoor 60-by-25-foot swimming pool, a modern kitchen, plus a bar staffed by our ever-amiable Irish connection, Patrick O'Shaughnessy and Tony Finnerty. A member's Decor Committee was struck, with a budget of $18,500, which decided on everything from the drapes, settees, tables, flooring, lighting, colour, wood finishes, and tables to the glassware and silver. Paintings were borrowed. Going, and dedicated, people they were. We also purchased 285 steel lockers at $20 apiece. A good buy, and all are still in use. But there wasn't enough money for more parking nor for improvements such as storage and tool sheds.

75

1940s

1943 Tide more turns. Rommel knocked out of Africa. Penicillin becomes big time. Broadway's "Oklahoma". Commandos train at Kits Beach. SNAFU "Situation Normal All Fouled Up". Vancouver shipyards build 34 Victory Ships in 26 months. Six Emily Carr's

However, no badminton courts were taken away. Good. Prior to this construction we had nine clay courts in the lower section — four doubles and one singles with a practice board — plus four upper ones. Our present clubhouse sits where those lower courts were, and in 1959 we cemented the four upper ones to the west — which vanished when we built our indoor tennis facility.

In April 1957, with 250 attending, we had a cheery springtime opening. The need for a minimum monthly fee and more members became quickly apparent. Appropriately, in view of his role in negotiating our highly favourable 1944 arrangement with the CPR, W.G. Murrin, together with his wife, officiated. Also present was our founder, A.P. Horne; former president F.G. Crickmay, who had laid out our 16th Avenue grounds in 1914; and Jimmy Farquhar, who had donated our men's singles trophy when we were still at Denman Street.

Although the directors had envisaged that new facilities and more families would be the solution to our declining revenues, such proved not to be the case, at least not immediately. At the AGM in November 1957, the treasurer reported an operating loss of $6,600, due mainly to under-utilization of the dining room and bar. An on-going problem.

The transition from the old days to the new had its amusing moments. When the proposed project was but a gleam in the eye of director Jack Shakespeare and his colleagues, he called on the Forans — a delightful Irish couple who presided over the antiquated kitchen in our original McLure clubhouse, but nonetheless produced delectable meals on its massive wood-fired stove. Shakespeare peered at the ever-greasy stovetop and told Mr. Foran, "This has to be cleaned right down to the steel, and now." Foran, somewhat offended, responded in his Irish brogue, "Faith, Mr. Shakespeare, ye can't cook on a clane stove." Your call, ladies.

Our Incorrectly-Sized Swimming Pool

Unfortunately, when the pool was built in 1957, with precisely regulated hours for its use (we've always been sticklers for time), no one took into account its precise dimension to enable it to qualify for recognized swim meets and records — it wasn't long enough and its corners flared. This was most unfortunate, because there were hosts of great swimmers in B.C. — the likes of "Mighty Mouse" Elaine Tanner and our Club's own Bruce Robertson (son of Sandy). Bruce gained international fame with firsts, seconds, and thirds in world events such as the 1972 Olympics in Munich (where he was second to Mark Spitz), the 1973 World Aquatics in Belgrade (where he was first in the 100 metre butterfly), the 1974 Commonwealth Games in New Zealand, and the 1975 Pan American Games in Mexico. Also Leslie Cliff, who with Bruce learned to swim at Crescent Beach, with her three golds and two silvers in the 1971 Pan American Games, her silver in the 1972 Olympics, and her two golds in the 1974 Commonwealth Games. Just think — we too might have garnered some officially recognized swimming records here. The pool was upgraded, together with some court work in 1998 to the tune of $200,000, but it still doesn't qualify for Olympic recognition.

1940s

sell at $50 apiece. Eisenhower, Montgomery, Alanbrooke, Patton. **1944** V-2 rockets hit England. June 6, D-Day "Operation Overlord" invasion. Battle of the Bulge. Anne Frank diaries. Paris liberated. International Monetary Fund created. 11 year-old

But none of that worried most of our members, because for us in 1957 our pool was the "in" thing. Initially there was a diving board, but in the interests of safety it was soon removed. Sue Elliott was our first lifeguard and instructor, to be followed by the likes of Lyn Pomfret and Doug Weese, who got $1,200 a year plus fees from his private lessons, which cost $1.25 an hour. We had all sorts of swim competitions, including family races on Sundays, with Laurel Osler always exhorting her tribe. However children under three couldn't use the pool, much to Laurel and Lois Keenan's annoyance, as their kids, once they'd foregone their prams, could swim. However, our toddlers did get a 12-by-12-foot fibreglass wading pool.

Racquet Hi-Lights — *Al Stevenson*

In 1946 a monthly newsletter, *Racquet Hi-Lights*, was launched. This was only a year after the end of World War II. Wartime regulations were still in place and a greyness still lingered, particularly as so many Club members had been killed, such as Colin Milne. It was against that background that Al Stevenson inspiredly produced an irreverent publication, the stated object of which was to inform, but the real intent was to entertain. As he put it:

> If our editorials are less preferred than those of *The Atlantic Monthly* and our humour is less sparkling than that of *The New Yorker* we are not overly concerned. We aren't competing with them.

So, with the help of several talented contributors, Al set out to produce not merely a bulletin but a creative work. He requested humorous pieces and asked his writers to pick their topics. He did the editing. And in 1947, thanks to the generosity of Sid Winsby, our *Hi-Lights* became mimeographed on legal-size paper with a circulation of 1,000. And it was newsy. Covered marriages, births, deaths, hospitalizations, and the whereabouts of our members. Everyone seemed to know what everyone else was doing. And, they were interested. It even printed a letter from a tennis instructor in Cologne, Germany, requesting used balls because theirs "were several years old." One wonders if we complied.

Al (aka R-Kives) Stevenson, the VLTBC historian for more than 50 years.

However, the journal's hallmark was a sort of Monty Pythonesque whimsy, which also happened to be Stevenson's distinguishing characteristic, and his contributions were under the soubriquets of "Aunt Harriett" or "Clovis Pooty." Pooty was a roving reporter. On one of his assignments, he identified himself to a *haute couturier* as a "customer," with the *couturier* frigidly responding, "Sir, we do not have customers; we have clients." In one piece Al's Aunt Harriett gave advice to a female member who wrote, "I am going out with one of the swellest guys in the Club, but he won't play badminton with me. Hence I decided to take coaching and I mastered the 'smash,' but still he won't play with me. What should I do?

1940s

Elizabeth Taylor in "National Velvet". Frank Sinatra, teens' new rage. Glenn Miller missing. Fourth term for FDR. Gas and liquor rationed. CKNW on 24 hours a day. Doukhabour unrest in the Kootenays. Gas rationing increased. HMCS Discovery opened on

VANCOUVER LAWN TENNIS AND BADMINTON CLUB

1630 West 15th Avenue, Vancouver 9, B.C., Canada, Telephone: 731-2191

HOW TO BE UNPOPULAR IN THE TENNIS SEASON:-

1. Go to the Lounge for a drink just as the rest of your four takes the available court.

2. After your game, always be late into the Lounge so that you will never have to buy the tea.

3. Between points, assemble at the net for a friendly chat; and above all, lean heavily on the net. You can easily depress it or with luck you can break the net cord.

4. Protect your uneasy status as a player by never inviting those you consider inferior and always asking those whose ability is far greater than yours.

5. Never return a ball from the next court, especially if it is much newer than your balls; and get your own ball back by walking onto the next court in the middle of a spirited rally.

6. Never return a ball on the bounce to your partner when he is serving. With your back turned, roll it along the ground as far away from him as possible.

7. Whoop, yell and converse loudly when you are playing. Earnest players on the next court may find your conduct very entertaining.

8. NEVER produce new balls, even though the ones you carry are ready for the archives.

9. When the grass courts are full, stand in one of the opened gates and study the foursome playing. With luck, a ball may go into the pool and be the beginning of a beautiful friendship with the owner of the ball.

10. In the Haggart Cup, complain about the flagrant injustice of your handicap and the downright favoritism of the handicaps of the others.

11. If anything upsets your tennis, rage violently and blame it on the Tennis Director and the General Manager.

(If you can prove you are guilty of none of the above, you may approach the Directors to be fitted for your halo).

VANCOUVER LAWN TENNIS AND BADMINTON CLUB

HANDY GUIDE TO BEING HATED IN THE TENNIS SEASON

Reprinted by kind courtesy of our Club Historian, Al Stevenson

(Careful observance of these rules will not win you a popularity contest. If you are guilty of none, the Tennis Committee will provide you with a halo and wings).

1. Return balls to the server between points by hitting them anywhere in the general direction of the back fence - if possible when the server has his back turned.

2. Know that you have a chronic foot fault and do nothing to correct it.

3. Seldom produce any tennis balls and never put out new ones.

4. Preserve your uneasy tennis status by sidestepping all invitations to play in an inferior four.

5. Moan to the Haggart Cup Committee about the favouritism shown to others and the flagrant injustice of your own handicap.

6. Stand in the open gate leading to the grass courts so that a ball can go into the swimming pool.

7. Walk behind the court when the ball is in play.

8. Continue your singles game serenely while a hungry foursome hovers behind the court.

9. Show up at 3 o'clock for a 2 o'clock foursome, or better still don't show up at all.

10. Keep your next court neighbours amused by whooping, yelling and carrying on a spirited conversation while you are playing.

11. Go right into another court to recover a ball when a point is being played there.

12. Never return stray balls to the correct court, but ignore them, or keep them as a gift from heaven, especially if they are new balls.

13. Take a generous warm-up period each time you get on court when other fours are waiting.

14. Be the last to enter the players' lounge so that you will not have to order the tea.

15. Aim all smashes at your opponent's midriff.

16. Complain bitterly about juniors and women monopolizing the courts.

17. Adopt a patronizing attitude towards those who are still using the antique wooden racquets rather than the new metal ones.

18. Ignore the signs on the gate and make for the grass courts an hour before they are to open.

19. Try to have three of your foursome hold a court while you finish your coffee and sandwich.

20. Blame everything including the weather, on the Club Manager.

21. Play in bare feet on the grass courts.

Al Stevenson's two edicts, humorously identifying unacceptable behaviour both on and off the courts.

Signed, 'Worried and Puzzled.'" So Aunt Harriett replied: "Have you thought about your badminton coach? As he works on your game, why don't you work on him? Add another string to your bow and perhaps at the same time add another beau to your string."

Stevenson had a marvellous love of words and their origins as well as their effective use and quotations. Robby Robinson, nicknamed "Dicey," then a law student at UBC, also possessed a droll manner. One of his pieces described going to his first "Scrambles," clutching his ticket plus a 26-ounce bottle of Seagrams, hoping to "find a girl,"

> Having looked the field over, I ran upstairs to my locker and poured myself a shot, then another, and then ran down to check the crop, which was enchanting but disinterested, so I returned and poured a couple more — one for me and one for the lucky girl I hoped to land. But since she didn't know how lucky she was going to be, I gulped hers too." Overly self-served, Dicey abandoned his quest and passed out. The adage? If you drink too much, forget about the girl. She'd prefer that too.

More Writers — More Characters

Another regular contributor and one of the few who wrote under his real name was Lieutenant-Colonel John Leader, a retired British Army officer and one of the Club's most colourful characters. Born in Ireland, he immigrated to B.C. in 1916 after serving as an officer in the regular British Army. At the outbreak of World War I, he was called up to take command of the Royal Irish Rifles — a regiment of the ill-fated Ulster Army, which before the war had been mustered to fight the British on the Home Rule issue, but now found itself fighting the Germans to help save the British.

The Ulster units were annihilated in the Battle of the Somme in 1915. Leader, though badly wounded, survived. In 1916, the United States asked the Irish Rifles to send one of their officers to Eugene, Oregon to instruct their National Guard how to repel a potential invasion by Germans from South America! Leader was chosen. At the end of the war he became an instructor at the University of Oregon where, as he said in one of his pieces for Stevenson's newsletter, "By sheer brutality I forced a program of games on the campus." Leader was no pussycat at tennis, having played for Ireland in the Davis Cup. In 1949, he and Club member Oliver Lacey reached the finals of the Veterans' doubles in the Western Canadian tournament.

Leader's articles in the *Racquet Hi-Lights* were characterized by high-class nonsense masquerading as fact. In one issue he recounted his attempts to teach a couple of young ladies to play tennis, both of whom were in "great condition" — a play on the Victorian euphemism for being pregnant. So both, he observed, had to be "good at other games." His eye for good-looking women — who he referred to as "Wenches"— was well known, but he always kept his distance. When women began wearing short skirts on the courts, he was asked, "Should skirts be dropped?" He replied, "Yes, to the last drop."

Colonel and Mrs. Leader were exceptionally gracious. Guests recall being invited for a Sunday game

1940s

Deadman's Island. **1945** Auschwitz liberated. Churchill, Roosevelt and Stalin at Yalta. August 14—VJ Day, World War II ends—55 million killed, 20 million of whom in the USSR. Hitler poisons himself. Mussolini hung. FDR dies—Harry S. Truman elected.

Lieutenant-Colonel John Leader.

when serving because of his wretched ball toss) wrote an article about an urban hayseed who visited the Club, dressed to the nines, to learn about bridge. Three players, among them Erwin Elliott, asked him to make a fourth. The newcomer accepted, sat down, picked up the deck and asked, à la whist, "Gentlemen, shall we cut for trump?" Erwin Elliott fainted.

In a Christmas contribution to *Racquet Hi-Lights*, Hayden revealed he'd bought 24 Christmas cards, but only had 13 friends. "Ah well," he said, "there's always next year." Stan was sort of a Damon Runyon character. He revealed that the only Yuletide present he gave to his wife Ruth was a coalscuttle, explaining, "I hated to see her bending down and picking up the coal with her bare hands." For Stan there were two classes of people: "Givers and takers." He was a giver.

David Savage, Duncan-born and a school chum of Dick Birch, was the only contributor to *Racquet Hi-Lights* who made his living by writing. In 1940, after studying at McGill University, David settled in Vancouver where he wrote and produced a daily serial — *The Carsons* — for CBC Radio. After serving in the RCAF during World War II, he returned to the program, where he worked until it went off the air in 1965 — the longest running radio serial in the world. Savage then joined Simon Fraser University to teach English and contributed hundreds of articles to periodicals in North America — even one to *Playboy*! In 1946 David joined the Club and shortly afterwards, Stevenson, who was godfather to David's son Richard, enlisted him to write for the newsletter as "Anon."

In an early issue of the *Racquet Hi-Lights* David wrote about bridge, asking Club member Erwin Elliott,

at their home where they'd meet lots of "Wenches" and have a short chat with Mrs. Leader, who quietly whistled to herself as the Colonel tended to dominate the conversation. Afterwards, guests enjoyed one of her traditional English teas with all its trimmings — cucumber and watercress sandwiches; caraway seed, pound, and fruit cakes; hot scones with strawberry jam; and gobs of Devonshire cream. Delicious, and always plenty for seconds.

Stan Hayden, a steady tennis player (apart from having to tape two fingers of his left hand together

1940s

Enola Gay A-bombs Hiroshima, 140,000 killed; later in Nagasaki—80,000 killed. September 2—Japan signs surrender aboard the USS Missouri. United Nations Charter formed in San Francisco. "Granville Park" explodes in Vancouver Harbour. David Lean

a leading player, for the name of the standard work on the game. "The Bridge of San Luis Rey," replied Erwin.

"Anon" liked to enliven conversation. Too often, he said, a tennis conversation might start as follows:

Joe: "Hello Mike."

Mike: "Hi, Joe — Want a game?"

Joe: "Not tonight. Just before I left home I was splitting wood and I cut my hand off."

"Anon" then pointed out how more appropriate it would be if Joe, on entering the lounge, waved his remaining hand and apologized for his delay by saying, "Hi, Mike. Sorry I'm late, I was giving someone a hand."

However, truth is stranger than fiction. In the 1980s, Richard Raibmon was playing with Dr. James Sandilands, a rugged rugby enthusiast. Raibmon fell, dislocated his thumb and broke both his wrists. "Jim," he howled, "take me to the hospital!" Sandilands replied, "No, I'm ahead, let's finish the game first." So Richard's wife Shirley (The Blond Bombshell) carted him off to the Vancouver General Hospital for repairs.

For the first anniversary of *Racquet Hi-Lights*, Stevenson wrote a series of congratulatory messages that purportedly came from major newspapers. *The New York Times* said, "We understand *Hi-Lights* is given away for nothing, which is far more than it's worth." In 1951 Club member Miss Dixie Commerie volunteered to publish it. The board said, "Fine, providing you pay for that." Anticipatedly that didn't come to pass, for Dixie's product only lasted for three

Al Stevenson participated in the Denny-Cardinall Competition in August 1970.

81

years. Later its format became letter-sized, and in 1973 it assumed its present style.

During his brief tenure as assistant manager in the 1970s, Jan Lapinski contributed a monthly article, "Food for Thought." Touting an upcoming oyster feast, he wrote, "From a moralist's point of view, the oyster leads a scandalously uninhibited private life, changing sex periodically and spending alternating periods on each side of its conjugal oyster bed!"

For the past few decades the renamed *Racquet Hi-Lights* has been devoid of articles by members, humorous or otherwise. It features news about the Club's activities and operations, contains a menu or two — all well-designed and presentable, but with

directs Dickens' "Great Expectations". Family Allowance introduced. Double chair on the Cut on Grouse. First microwave. Jitterbugs, Hep Cats and Zoot Suits. Abbott and Costello—"Who's on First?" **1946** U.S. and U.K. initiate division of Jewish and Arab

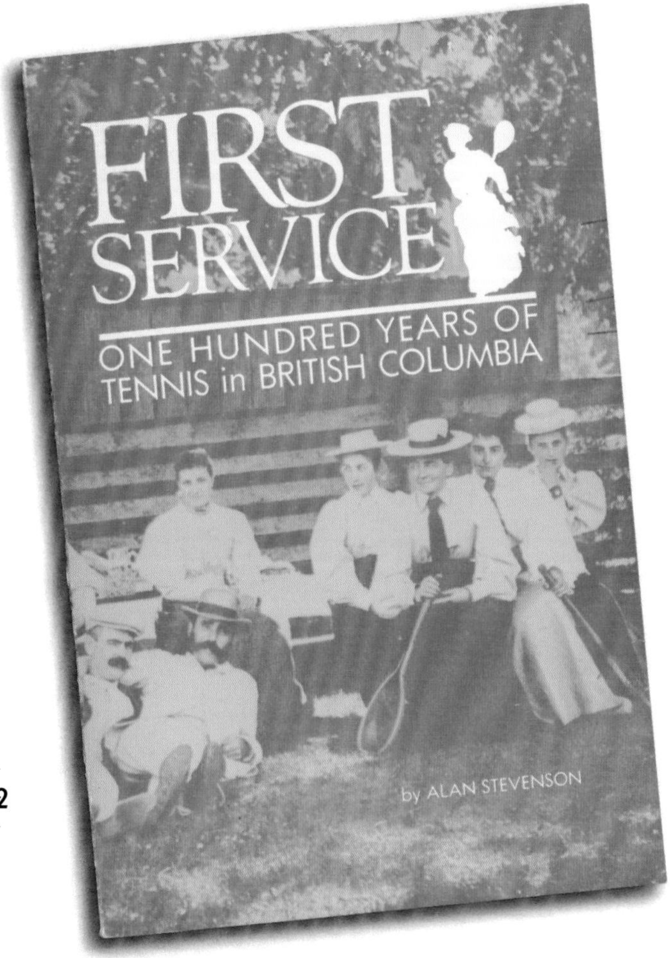

In collaboration with Bob Moffatt, Al Stevenson wrote and edited the above in 1981.

little literary pretension and somewhat sterile. In August 2006, the Club advised members that they could receive *Hi-Lights* by e-mail. Technology.

More About Al Stevenson and the Club Archives

Much has been said and much should be said about Al Stevenson. Midway B.C.-born, studied English history and language, received his B.A. from UBC in 1928, taught school until 1938, then tutored and handled a correspondence course for the B.C. Department of Education. In 1950, Ken Meredith asked him to assemble a history of the Club. He did — and that's how our archives got under way. And, apart from playing tennis, "R-Kives" became Al's most time-consuming love.

Al laboured for hours on end — took pictures, showcased our artefacts, and wrote tons of stuff. His guide, "How to Be Hated in the Tennis Season," is spot on. He was not well off. Was a bachelor. Lived alone. Had sparse belongings. Could barely boil water but was always on tap and could dig out just about anything about tennis and badminton, and all this without pay. However, during his last three years the Club ensured that he always got lunch and dinner. This he needed. He collated the history of tennis in B.C. from 1887 to 1981 and wrote *First Service* in collaboration with Bob Moffatt — another Paul Willey protégé and then the director of Tennis BC. Al was named "Mr. Tennis" in 1970. He died in 1994 and since then Joan McMaster has ably kept our archives going.

More About Badminton

Apart from our financial turmoil in the 1940s and 1950s, Club life was not significantly affected. And badminton continued to flourish and almost invariably turned a profit. Also there was a higher percentage of juniors playing badminton than tennis. They played with inexpensive plastic shuttles and used feathered ones from our seniors. Plus there are always fewer difficulties with it than tennis — it was immune from

1940s

states in Palestine. US. builds nuclear powered submarines. Nurenburg trials. Goering poisons himself. 30-ton computer invented. Dr. Spock's book on baby care. Bikinis arrive in Paris. "Annie Get Your Gun" with Ethel Merman. Irving Berlin's "There's No

Badminton Greats! L-R: Claire Lovett, Jean Bardsley, John Samis, Daryl Thomson, and Ken Meredith.

✦
83
✦

the ravages of weather — also tennis seemed to attract more temperamental personalities and prima donnas. Whatever.

However, until 1957 there were still separate fees. Many who played badminton wouldn't be seen during the summer, though they could use the clubhouse at any time. So, when the 1957 clubhouse came into being, these dues were replaced by one set, and playing members, except juniors, could use all the facilities at any time. The "Family Club" concept had arrived. Also we'd frequently made our badminton courts available without charge to groups such as the Vancouver City & District Badminton Association for junior tournaments, and to Crofton House School for its championships.

The amenities in the badminton hall were, and still are, sparse. Then there were drainpipe ashtrays — painted green to be less conspicuous. Cigarettes could be purchased from a vending machine in the club-

house and as you puffed a cig you could stay warm by bundling into one of the Club's Hudson's Bay blankets, which we're told more than occasionally were spirited away by ardent couples for warm-ups of their own. At all of our tournaments we always saw the methodical, dependable, and dour Bill McIntosh, blazered and long-white-flannelled, steaming the "birdies" to moisten their feathers. Also, Jericho's Jimmie Dexter skittering about with a four-inch brush, brooming the courts. They too were fixtures.

Our Leading Badminton Ladies

Among the female badminton players of this period, three were in a class by themselves: Claire Lovett, Jean Bardsley, and Lois Reid. Lovett was in her prime in 1947 and 1948 when she won the Canadian singles. She was a tall rangy lady and played a power game. Two of her frequent opponents were Bardsley and Reid and

1940s

the three of them shared the Club's singles championships for 10 years from 1947 until 1957. From 1958 to 1968, Claire won eight consecutive Club titles, a record unmatched by any other member, male or female. She was a natural athlete. As was Jean Bardsley who excelled in any sport she chose, especially racquets and track and field. She never won a Canadian singles but she took the doubles twice, playing first with Claire Lovett and then with Lois Reid and four mixed doubles with Daryl Thomson, plus numerous provincial and local championships. She minced about the court, was deadly at the net, and vivacious to behold.

Lois Reid was a physical education teacher at Lord Byng High School from which she had earlier graduated. David Williams was one of her classmates. Most affable Lois, although not slim, adroitly moved about the court, walloping her left-handed smash. Following many local and regional titles, she reached the pinnacle of her career by winning the Canadian singles in 1950, the last female Club member to win that event. She and Grace Leader also reached the finals of the women's tennis doubles in the 1949 Western Canadian.

At this time our most promising lady badminton junior, the winsome, demure Dee Edgell, came to the fore. Together with her pal Julie Coppens (now Julia Levy of Quadra Logic fame), both from Magee High School, she won the High School doubles. Then along with Daryl and Jean in 1951, she CPR'd east to play in the first Canadian junior singles at the Quebec Winter Club, to lose in the finals. Upon her return to Vancouver she took the City junior girls' singles. Dee, also excellent at doubles and mixed, was delightful and a joy to play and to be with. As was Sidney

Shakespeare who was a member of the B.C. team that won the Canadian juniors and later married Rhodes Scholar John Madden, also a Club member.

Our Leading Badminton Men

Amongst the male players, two dominated: John Samis and Dave McTaggart. Not far behind were Daryl Thomson and Ken Meredith. Daryl was our singles champion in 1950 and 1951, and took the Canadian doubles first with Ken Meredith in 1940 and later with Bert Fergus. He also won the Canadian singles in 1951 and the mixed in 1948, 1949, 1951, and 1952 with Jeannie Bardsley. He twice played for the Thomas Cup and was non-playing captain in 1964. In 1977 he also became president of the B.C. Lawn Tennis Association. Daryl, who died in 1980, was posthumously inducted into the B.C. Sports Hall of Fame and Museum (BCSHFM) in 1984 for his long and outstanding contribution to the promotion and organization of badminton. His wife Jean attends the BCSHFM's annual banquet. And it's fun to mention that Daryl and I in 1943, as students at Magee High School, won the Vancouver and District High School doubles, with Darry instructing me "to stay at the net and hit everything down. I'll do the rest." Good advice. He did, and I tried to. Don "Nick" Anderson, father of all our male member Andersons, also gained honours for Magee.

Daryl's good friend, A.O. "Effortless" Bert Jones, also really knew his doubles and captured many trophies — a thoughtful, never rushed, and marvellously positioned player. If you mucked anything up, he'd quietly cough and say, "Clear only to the back line and if we make three errors, we'll lose the match."

1940s

Louis Mountbatten presides over the end of British rule in India and the division of Hindu India (under Nehru) and Muslim Pakistan (under Jinnah). Polaroid camera. Polio virus isolated. "Streetcar Named Desire" with Marlon Brando. Princess Elizabeth

He carried me through to the B.C. "B" doubles. Daryl and Bert were also high-tech pioneers. Their accounting firm, *Mail Me Monday*, was the first in Canada to use computers, which they then rented in San Francisco.

Ken Meredith, who won our Club singles in 1948, was an A-1 doubles player too, winning the Canadian doubles with Thompson plus capturing many local and provincial events. Though both were excellent, they didn't match Samis in singles. In 1947 the B.C. championships were held here as a sort of run-up to the Canadian to be played in March. Samis, in the final of the men's singles, played Meredith, who had earlier disposed of Eric Leney — the last of the still-playing Duncan "greats." Samis won handily. Afterwards the soft-spoken Ken said, "Anybody who plays John has to be an iron man. He crucifies you on the base line, crosses you up at the net with drops, and leaves you badly out of position in the forecourt." In 1972, Samis was admitted to the BCSHFM. Its trustees consider six categories: Outstanding Athlete, Builders of the Sport, Pioneers, the Media, Team Accomplishments, and the W.A.C. Bennett Award for those who otherwise have significantly contributed. Samis won the Outstanding Athlete Award — a great honour.

In the Canadian singles finals, Samis played his archrival Dick Birch and regained his earlier titles of 1938 and 1940. *The Vancouver Sun* reported that he won because of his "condition and great fighting spirit. Birch didn't have it left in his legs." Birch avenged his loss to Samis in 1947, when he beat him to win the Canadian championship for his third and last time. However Samis' record of four national singles titles

surpassed that of David McTaggart's three, who won in 1956, '57, and '58, but McTaggart's string of seven consecutive victories in VLTBC singles stands alone.

One could endlessly discuss the relative merits of Underhill, Birch, and Samis who, when in their prime, compared with McTaggart. But insofar as the record of Club members, no player was as dominant as was McTaggart from 1952 to 1958, although John Samis' record extended over a longer period — from 1938 to 1949. Interestingly, neither of them was as great in doubles. Their styles sharply contrasted. Samis hit fluid strokes using long and graceful backswings, and Bill Keenan said he was "poetry in motion." McTaggart, on the other hand, hit short, sharp shots and could return anything from anywhere, at any time. With his speed and seemingly unlimited stamina, Dave would go out on the town yet the next day play as if he had been under his own covers all night. Unbelievable staying powers. He was our last male Club member to win a Canadian singles and later achieved greater notoriety in an altogether different endeavour from his early association and activity with *Greenpeace,* the international environmental organization. He played an important role in the organization until 1991. In 2001 he was killed in a car accident in Italy.

Another stalwart is Trail-born Bert Fergus. He too played in Canada's first junior singles and his star has risen ever since. Bert enjoys an over 50-year record touched by few, if any, insofar as support and promotion for badminton is concerned. In 1966 he conducted the trials for entry into the Commonwealth Games, and more recently chaired its badminton in Victoria in 1994. He managed Canada's Thomas Cup

85

Team in 1967 and chaired our participation in 1986. From 1988 to 1992 he was president of Badminton BC plus has managed Canadian teams in major tournaments through the world for just about forever. Bert received much recognition from his peers and his community, including being made a Life Member of Badminton BC in 1986 and recently receiving the prestigious International Badminton Federation (IBF) Meritorious Service Award. Prior to joining, he was many times an honorary member of the VLTBC and has won all sorts of major events — Canadian men's with Daryl Thomson and Wayne MacDonnell; fifteen golds in singles, men's, and mixed in the Canadian Masters; and earlier silvers in Internationals with David McTaggart and Eddy Choong. Gulliver busy.

Dave McTaggart and Bert Fergus, winners of the gold in men's badminton doubles. Mexico, 1959.

The Thomas Cup and Exhibitions

In 1948 we staged trials for the Thomas Cup — badminton's equivalent of the Davis Cup. It was named after Sir George Thomas, an Englishman and first president of the IBF. Sir George came to Vancouver for the matches to select western representatives for the team and was highly complimentary about Canada's calibre of play. John Samis was named for singles and Daryl Thomson for doubles. In the first match against India, played in Eastern Canada, Dick Birch, the captain, and Samis played both singles and doubles, and they each starred. The Canadians swept the series by seven matches to two but lost in the next round to the Americans in Pasadena. The pinnacle player then was American Dave Freeman, who was later described by Jack Underhill as probably the best singles player the game had then produced. Playing in peak form, Freeman whipped Samis by scores of 15-1, 15-5.

Early in 1954, two Malaysians, Eddy and David Choong, the top-ranked doubles pair in the world, came to play exhibitions against McTaggart, Thomson, Bruce Benham, R. Phillips, and John Bouck — who later became a judge of the Supreme Court of British Columbia. The brothers Choong put on a display of agility and dexterity the likes of which had not been seen here before. They were at the forefront of Asian players who soon came to dominate the game.

The Grass, the Clay, and the Cost of Maintenance

We've always had lawn and clay courts, but the directors questioned the maintenance of the clay,

1940s

Vancouver's first TV signal—from Seattle. Fraser Valley flood. Eatons purchase Spencers. **1949** Mao's People's Republic of China. NATO established. Arthur Miller's Death of a Salesman. Japanese and Native Indians enfranchised. Kerrisdale Arena opens.

which were playable sooner than grass after a rainstorm but were still prone to mushiness. However even more they questioned the continuance of our labour-intensive grass. Heresy! But were they worth the expense? This was a mite compounded by the fact that until 1957, our fees for playing on the lawn were higher than for playing on clay. But grass's higher fees still didn't cover its costs of maintenance, nor, to a lesser extent, the costs for the clay, which fell onto our members as a whole. It took a few bucks (guilders) for Frans Hals to do the Laughing Cavalier, but it was worth it. Likewise was the grass, although discussions with the membership about taking up the grass, and/or the clay, and putting in an all-weather surface, were generally welcomed — however the more than difficult resolution of these issues lay some years ahead.

In reviewing the records of our tennis and badminton players who were at the top of the heap from, say, 1920 until 1958, there is no doubt that our badminton side was the stronger and amassed way more Canadian titles than their tennis counterparts. After 1958 however, the Club was no longer the badminton powerhouse it once was, nor to a lesser extent was its tennis.

More of Our Lady Tennis Greats

We had many outstanding tennis players. Jean Milne might head the list, but she gave up competition in 1942, though after the war she played the occasional tournament and won a City singles against Claire Lovett. Mel Scott recalled her playing with her sister Susie in the finals of the 1947 Western Canadian doubles — a match that he umpired. During play, the Queen's representative — the Lieutenant Governor

— and his entourage entered the grounds. Jean and Susie stopped and stood respectfully to attention whilst the viceregal party proceeded to their seats. Their American opponents were bewildered, so, after explaining to the Americans the propriety of the occasion, umpire Mel declared a let and play resumed.

Mrs. Lovett was also great at tennis. Although not able to win an open national title as she did in badminton, she won a number of Canadian titles in seniors' events. She won our Club's women's singles first in 1945 and thereafter another 11 victories up to 1965 and stands among our members in a class by herself. In 1972 she was elected to the Canadian Amateur Athletic Hall of Fame as an all round athlete — a recognition not only of her badminton and tennis careers but also her earlier stardom as a basketball player in Edmonton. Four years later she was inducted into the BCSHFM for her badminton and tennis achievements. Other female players of note during that period include Jocelyn Pease, Grace Leader, and of course Susie Milne and Jean Bardsley.

More of Our Male Tennis Greats

In men's tennis, Arthur Jeffery unquestionably dominated. He was well trained — but not weight trained— from 1937 by our Club pro Gerry Clute, who received $90 a year and an occasional tea. Art was also supervised by his parents, his sister, Al Stevenson, and every guest of the Jeffery family. A lot of pressure! Redheaded Artie, who looked like a younger version of Don Budge, is a lefty with a two-handed backhand, an excellent return of serve, crisp cross-court shots, and a game exceptionally well-adapted to grass — a familiar-

✦
87
✦

1940s

Nancy Hodges first female Speaker. Australian National Airways—to become Qantas—first scheduled flights to Vancouver. David Williams and Garde Gardom graduate in UBC's second Law class. Couples first get married then live together and a human

Not pushovers! (L-R): Jim Skelton, Artie Jeffery, and Jim Bardsley prepare for Wimbledon, June 1971.

ity which he might have cultivated in 1948 as assistant Club groundskeeper. For 25¢ an hour he'd cut the grass, mark it, and in the evening water the grass and clay courts and then drag and roll them in the morning.

Between 1942 and 1961, Arthur won 13 Club men's singles, seven of them consecutively between 1949 and 1955, as well as being successful in countless other competitions. He garnered more Club tennis singles titles than any member and for two years he was ranked in the top 10 male players in Canada.

While Jeffery was our top singles player, Jim Skelton rivalled him in other pursuits. Skelton joined us in 1955. Prior to this, he was a member of Jericho and the B.C. Electric Club, where he became ranked first in B.C. in 1946 and '47. From 1946 until 1955, he was also among the top 10 players in Canada. After joining the VLTBC, he twice captained Canada's Davis Cup team, won the Club singles seven times, was president of Tennis Canada in 1974 and 1975, and took many seniors events. His graceful style of play, excellent backhand, and gentlemanly manner contrasted sharply with the unfortunate deportment of some contempo-

rary players. In 1948, Jim, Ron Sidaway, Russ Hawes, and Phil Pearson — a great but wild athlete who, to his subsequent regret, once played on a clay court in bare feet! — played a charity match opposite the old Post Office on Hastings Street to raise money for relief for the enormous Fraser Valley flood. The match was a success, and they raised some money. Skelton also excelled at handball, playing during the 1950s at the YMCA, where he was twice City handball champion.

Bill "Stick" Duff was another outstanding player. He was a long drink of water. As a student he beat Perry Jones to win the Los Angeles City championships, but lost the following year in the finals to Ellsworth Vines. He played in the All England at Wimbledon and subsequently published, along with Bill Tilden, *The Shooting Stars,* a book about Wimbledon. Too late they discovered that they couldn't sell it because someone else held exclusive rights for writings about Wimbledon. The Club obtained a copy, which is on long-term loan to the BCSHFM. Later Duff played with Fred Perry and they won three times at Wimbledon. "Stick" traveled to China, then to Manila in the Philippines,

being answers the telephone. Everyone dances the samba. **1950** China invades Tibet. Korean war starts. Churchill's "Iron Curtain" speech. HST okays superbomb—500 times more powerful than the one that flattened Hiroshima. Charles Schultz's "Peanuts".

where he was imprisoned by the Japanese during World War II. He arrived here in 1954, joined the Club, and often played with Al Stevenson — keeping him facing the sun and rarely winning a point!

Jim Bardsley was no slouch either. He was an excellent basketball player. Before the war he played at the VAC — Vancouver Athletic Club — south of False Creek near Hemlock, where baseball's Athletic Park was and which is now all condominiums. Yuck. In badminton he was so-so, had a mish-mash smash, but yelled at Jean a lot. Good at tennis. Never gave up. "When the going gets tough, the tough get going," kind of a guy and with whatever racquet he had on hand — usually an old beat-up one. And if his opponent blamed his game on his racquet, Jim would always say, "Try mine." As for calls — A-okay except he did recall a bad one on a match point in a VLTBC mixed final vs. Claire Lovett and me, when he called a close ball out. It wasn't. Later, at a party, well into his cups, he remorsed, "You know, that ball was in, but if you ever give a bad call, it's got to be at a vital point."

Jack Pedlar has been one of B.C.'s most durable and competitive doubles players. The younger brother of George and Will Pedlar — Will had been a Davis Cup player and was killed in action with the RCAF in World War II. Jack never asked for quarter and certainly gave none. For him, every point is match point. In the 1950s, he and his compatriots Albert Zein, Alec Walker, Bill Lees, Gordon Walker, and Jack Braverman played at their Stanley Park Tennis Club winter and summer, especially on Sundays. They always drew a crowd and called themselves "The 20 Club" — being Alec's locker number. Cold water. No heat. No showers. Brr. Their

club, sometimes called Lion's Gate in the early 1950s, was the first public courts club to win the Vancouver and District League. Jack was named "Mr. BC Tennis" in 1976 and continues to do battle here as a Club senior.

Our honorary member Lorne Main, a two-hander, was in a class by himself. And now, as an unbelievably spry 75-year-old, still is. He, with his sister Delores, started on a couple of public courts off Oak Street. In 1946, '47, and '48, he won the Canadian juniors and in 1947 also became the U.S. junior hard court cham-

Lorne Main, the world's most winning senior player!

89

1950s

First credit card—Diner's Club. Burns and Allen on TV. Nat King Cole's "Mona Lisa". New passenger terminal at VIA. First diesel train to White Rock. Road to Mount Seymour. **1951** Truman fires Douglas McArthur. UN becomes headquartered in New York.

pion. As a tad he partnered Art Jeffery to win the Western Canadian doubles in 1951. He was a member of Canada's Davis Cup team from 1947 to 1956 and captained it for three years and was ranked No.1 in Canada from 1951 to 1954. He won the Monte Carlo tournament in 1954 and played, and still does, just about everywhere. From 1957 to 1975 he didn't compete, but as a senior once more took off, becoming the World senior singles champion eight times (a world record), from 1986 to 2003. Also he won the World senior doubles nine times — another record — plus taking the Austrian Cup four times, three Crawford Cups, the Von Cram, and the Britannica Cup. The world's best senior player! Truly remarkable. Lorne could, and still does, return everything, and unlike a lot of hot shots, he'll play with anyone.

Then not a member, Lorne won the Western Canadian men's singles in 1950 — the first Canadian to have done so since Jack Wright won it 20 years before. Main and Art Jeffery, awesome serve returners, captured the men's doubles — the first Canadians in many years. The tournament was plagued by rain and the mixed final was played on a floodlit court in Stanley Park, to be taken by Claire Lovett and Jeffery.

Big-Time Tennis Visitors

Maureen Connolly, "Little Mo," started her phenomenal career as a 14-year-old dynamo. In 1948 she won the B.C. women's singles and, playing in the subsequent Western Canadian, reached the finals of the women's singles only to lose, but took the under-18 singles, plus the women's doubles.

In 1950 we sponsored a series of exhibitions by the Australian Davis Cup team at the Kerrisdale Arena. The Club guaranteed to pay the Australians' airfare from Los Angeles and return, their hotel accommodation and meals, plus split whatever profits there were. This led to controversy as to whether the costs of flying should be charged against revenues before the division of profits, or whether the Club was to pay for them in any event. The Club left it up to the Australian captain, Harry Hopman, to make the decision and agreed to abide by it. What precisely happened we don't know, but in any event we netted a highly satisfactory $1,200. Frank Sedgeman and Ken McGregor were standouts. They each had bullet serves. I was a line-caller, and one serve nearly took my head off. They each got $1,000. In those days the amateurs did better than the pros! Sedgeman had won the Australian singles in 1949 and was to repeat that in 1950. Playing with Jack Bromwich, he also won the United States Open doubles. McGregor was just coming into his prime and in 1951 he and Sedgeman won all four Grand Slam doubles titles.

The Davis Cup

The renowned Davis Cup, donated by American Dwight F. Davis in 1900, is for team competition between countries. And apart from the Olympics and the Commonwealth and Asian Games, it's the only trophy that is globally competed for. Mr. Davis' objective was that it would "contribute to mutual goodwill and understanding between sports-loving people of the world." It has. It does. A host country is decided by a coin toss and the "Tie" consists of four singles and one doubles.

1950s

Rogers and Hammerstein's "The King and I" starring Yul Brynner. Rock and Roll in. Lougheed Highway completed. Postal zones for Vancouver. "Top of Old Smokey." Princess Elizabeth and Prince Philip visit. **1952** Eisenhower elected. George VI dies. Britain

Presentations to American and Japanese Davis Cup team members at the VLTBC, July 1953. (L-R) Mrs. Clarence Wallace, wife of British Columbia's Lieutenant Governor; Tony Trabert and Hamilton Richardson (U.S.); Jiro Yamagishi, Masanobu Kimura, Atsushi Miyagi, Kosei Kamo (Japan) and S.V.T. Jeffery.

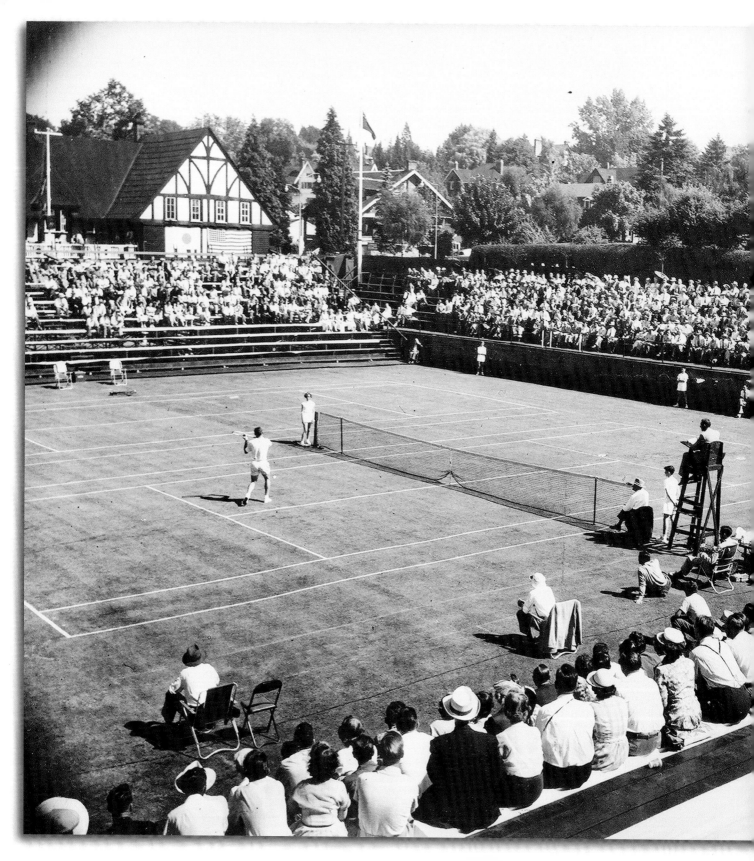

And a handsome and world-recognized trophy it is: 13-by-17½ inches, sterling silver, weighing 217 ounces, and of Georgian design. Each year details of the Challenge Round — the venue, the names of the teams, the winners, and the score — are engraved in the language of the winning country. The Cup had enough space for 15 years, then a tray was added, and when that became full a solid base was provided. It grows and grows. At a Challenge Round the Davis Cup is always on view. All now an excellent and worldwide popular tradition.

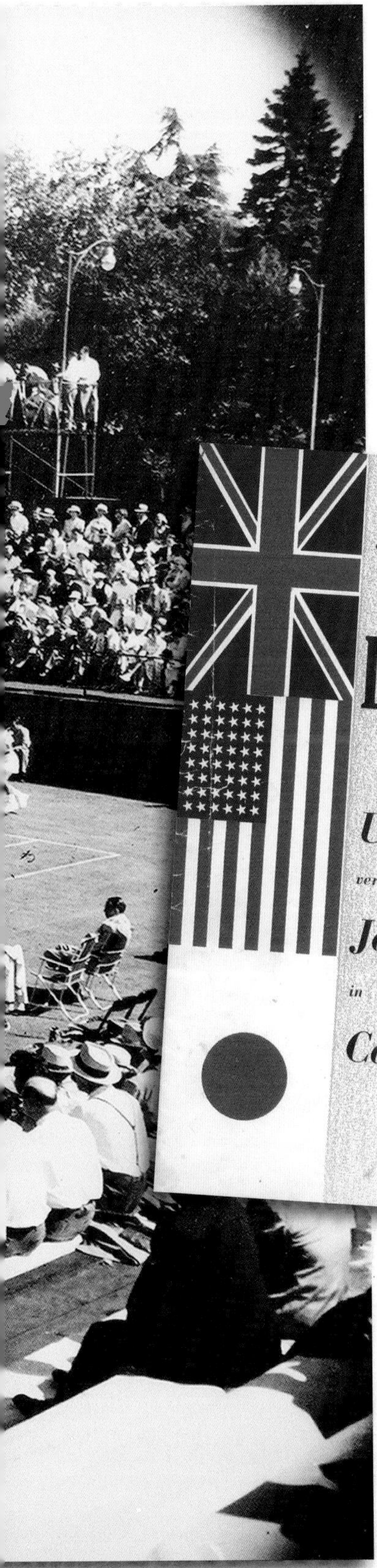

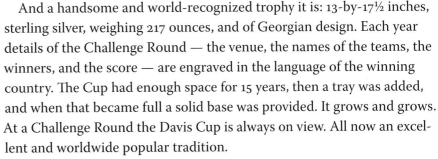

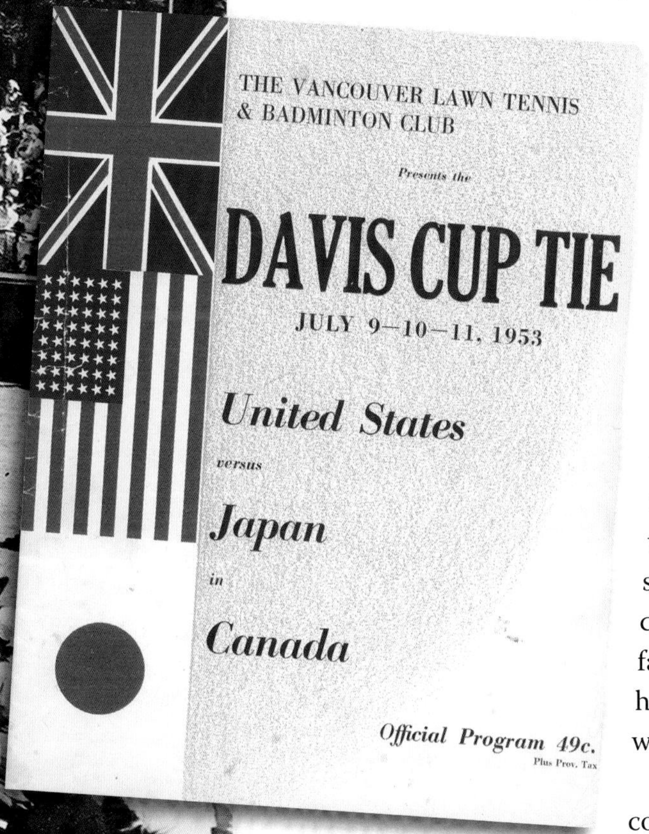

1953 — Davis Cup Tie — United States vs. Japan at the VLTBC

Davis Cup competition first came to British Columbia in July 1953 when the Club hosted Japan vs. the United States. It was only the second time in Davis Cup history that opposing teams had met on the courts of a neutral country. Originally, it was scheduled to be played on hard courts at the Seattle Tennis Club, however the Japanese team wanted to play on grass and the Cup rules stipulated that both teams had to agree on the surface. The Americans agreed to play on grass and as the VLTBC was the only suitable venue on the West Coast with lawn courts, so we were chosen to host the event. The fact that Canada was neutral ground may also have been a factor, as anti-Japanese sentiments were still running high in the United States.

To prepare for the match, the Club closed one court for a month and others were set aside for the Japanese players to practice on, following the head of the Japan Lawn Tennis Association's letter to the Club, explaining, "by virtue of Japan's special climate, we haven't a single grass court here." A large

A few of the VLTBC courts on July 9, 1953 during the Davis Cup Tie when the Club hosted Japan vs. the United States. Above: the cover of the 1953 Davis Cup Tie Official Program.

THE VANCOUVER LAWN TENNIS & BADMINTON CLUB

Presents the

DAVIS CUP TIE

JULY 9—10—11, 1953

United States

versus

Japan

in

Canada

Official Program 49c.
Plus Prov. Tax

93

committee was struck, co-chaired by Club President Colin Walker and S.V.T. Jeffery. The Honourable Clarence Wallace, Lieutenant Governor of B.C. and great-uncle of Club member Chris Wallace, served as honorary referee. Victor Denny, the president of the Pacific Northwest Lawn Tennis Association (PNWLTA) was appointed as official referee. The umpires were all well known B.C. players — Oscar Roels (Club champion in 1940), Jim Bardsley, and Colin Gamlin.

94

The Davis Cup

famous four-minute-miler John Landy at the 1958 Empire Games with our Pamela Rose.

A surprise visitor to the event was the Right Honourable Louis St. Laurent, Prime Minister of Canada — the only prime minister to attend a match in British Columbia. The event was formally opened by the Lieutenant Governor. Our president Colin Walker escorted him and Mrs. Wallace down the steps to the courts. Mrs. Wallace was wearing a long, flow-ing gown and Walker recalls, with mortification, step-ping on its train so that they both tripped. Only the quickest reaction by Ruth McLean, Mrs. Wallace's aide, prevented a dreadful fall. The Americans were subsequently beaten by the Australians, who cap-tured the trophy. The matches were well-attended — Mildred Jeffery handled the highly successful publicity. However, our records are sparse and merely record a profit of $332.

The formidable American team took all five matches. Its tremendously fit 23-year-old Tony Trabert was captain. He, like many of the U.S. stars, regularly exercised. I recall an American player in the Pacific Northwest who the day he won the sin-gles, the doubles, and the mixed, then proceeded into our sauna for some push-ups! Later that year Trabert went on to win the U.S. Open singles and after that, Wimbledon. The other members were Ham Richardson and Tom Brown, who as a junior had played here in the Western Canadian. The Japanese Team consisted of the up-and-coming Kosei Kamo, Jiro Yamagishi, Masanobu Kimura, and Atsushi Miyagi. While the U.S. team was in B.C., Tony Trabert much enjoyed a date with our Lola Gunn, as did the

1956 — Davis Cup Tie — Canada vs. United States in Victoria

The first Canadian Davis Cup Tie in British Columbia — Canada vs. the United States — was held at the Victoria Lawn Tennis Club in 1956. The Canadian team consisted of Bob Bedard and Don

develops atomic bomb. U.S. tests hydrogen bomb. W.A.C. Bennett becomes B.C.'s premier (serving until 1972 - BC's longest-serving premier). Bye-bye streetcars, hello buses. Eva Peron dies. "Dragnet". No-cal ginger ale. British Property lots sell for

> **❝The first female honorary life member was Mrs. Lorna Ross, a wartime widow and long-time companion of Erwin Elliott, who often echoed his sentiments like, 'You're the first in a long line of weak presidents.'❞**

Fontana from Eastern Canada as well as Larry Barclay and Paul Willey from the Jericho Tennis Club. The non-playing captain was Jim Skelton. The United States won 4-1. Twelve-year-old John Fraser worked as a ball boy. A few years later in 1961, he became Canada's junior champion and much later our president.

Lady Directors

Progress towards gender equality in the governing of the Club was slow. For several decades women members were well-represented on Club committees, but our directors were exclusively male. The first attempt to elect a woman director was in 1945, when Miss A.E. Scott was nominated, but failed to be elected. It was not until 1952 that Miss Doris Betchley was successfully elected and served for five years. A further period of male-only directors ensued until the election of Miss Mildred Jeffery in 1960.

The first female honorary life member was Mrs. Lorna Ross, a wartime widow and long-time companion of Erwin Elliott, who often echoed his sentiments like, "You're the first in a long line of weak presidents."

She was an enthusiastic supporter of the Club, loved her tennis, and won the Club singles in 1925 and 1926. Thirty years later, two male members proposed her for honorary membership and she was unanimously elected. She said that her innate modesty forbade her from wanting the award and that it had to be due either to "her tennis, her personality, or her longevity."

If Lorna liked you, terrific. If she didn't, duck. She was a lively, feisty lady deeply involved in Club activities, and never hesitated to voice her opinion on each and every aspect of our operation. Doris Belchley recalled how during her time as a director, Lorna, complaining about something, followed her into the ladies' locker room, hectoring all the way. Also, some said Mrs. Ross was awarded her life membership in the hope that the conferment of that honour would somewhat subdue her because she wouldn't be able to vote at annual meetings! If that was the plan, we seriously doubt if it succeeded. But Lorna was a good sort, of great support to Erwin — prepared most of his dinners — and was an unrelenting player and Club booster.

✦
95
✦

$2,000-$3,000. **1953** Elizabeth II crowned. Korean war ends. Chiang Kai-Shek flees to Taiwan. Hillary and Tenzing climb Mount Everest. Marilyn Monroe centrefolds Playboy" "Doggie in the Window". Little Mo Connolly grand-slams. CBUT-TV starts.

Squash Jesters, 1965. Back row (L-R): Don Leggatt, Barney Lawrence, Harry Bell-Irving, John Nicolls, Dave Foster, Hilary Wotherspoon, Bill Burk. Front row (L-R): Bob Wade, Bud McKay, Ted Tilden, Eric Beardmore, Ed Kemble, Ian Stewart, Jim Macken. Missing from the photo: Jack Larsen, Sandy Robertson, Nigel Williams, Lorne Webster, and Mitch Hiddleston.

CHAPTER 6

The Evolution of Squash

Its Arrival in B.C. and at the Club
More Facilities, Indoor and Rooftop Tennis, More Parking, the Badminton Hall Blazes, Members' Other Pursuits, More Stars, Coaches, Canada vs. Mexico Davis Cup, Bottle Games, and Social Fun

Squash has it origins in the 1820s at Harrow, one of England's famous public (i.e., private) schools, where it was a knock-about activity for boys waiting for a court for the more ancient game of Racquets. Some claim it was also played by upper-class prisoners at London's Fleet debtors' prison, when they weren't occupied trying to avoid a beating or scrounging a meal. A softer ball was used for squash than for tennis, soft enough that one could "squash" it by hand, and that's probably how squash got its name. By the 1860s it had blossomed in the wealthier parts of England where the upper and upper-middle classes built courts at their country estates and London clubs.

Between the two world wars, squash was taken up by the British Army. Following its introduction to their bases in India and later in Pakistan, the game became popular in both countries, which subsequently produced no end of world-ranked players. Also

the Royal Air Force built courts at many of its bases around the world. And in 1929 the Squash Racquets Association was founded in England to become the arbiter of squash both there and in its dominions. The United States Squash Racquets Association came into being in 1907. However in the United States, where they so often wish to do their own thing, squash evolved differently. As the result of a multi-country decision, the International Squash Racquets Federation was created in 1967. It's now known as the World Squash Federation and is the governing body for squash — which is not yet an Olympic sport.

Squash Comes to B.C.

As in England, our well-to-do residents were the first to play the sport here. In 1912 the eminent Vancouver lawyer E.P. Davis constructed an English-sized court at his huge McLure-designed estate in Point Grey, which is now Cecil Green Park. Captain

Massey Goolden built one at his residence, The Knoll," on the corner of 57th and South West Marine Drive, and Ernest and Irenée Rogers had a fine one at their home on Angus Drive. The Jericho Country Club was the first club to build a court in Vancouver. A few courts also sprung up in Victoria and Duncan.

Squash — the English, the American, and the Canadian Game

The English court, although the same length, is wider than the American, the wall markings differ, and the "tin" on the front wall is higher. Only the server can win points and a game consists of nine points, whereas the American game goes to 15, with points being won whether one is serving or receiving. Also the ball isn't the same. The English game uses a soft ball. And even that varies: there are "slow" soft balls and "fast" soft balls. The Americans used a hard 30-gram hollow rubber ball — not as hard as a golf ball, but getting there. To get a decent bounce, it had to be warm. A hot tap was helpful. Also the American game favoured power hitters, whereas with the English one it's finesse that counts more and, with its softer ball, longer rallies, and a wider court, it calls for more stamina.

Compromise eventually came about by using a ball that was midway between the English soft one and the American hard one. But Canada had trouble making up its mind which game to adopt and what size courts to build. Needless to say we were leery about building courts which could become outmoded. Decision was reached. Our first courts for singles were built to the American size, and play was governed by their rules. However in 1964 the English game also came to the VLTBC. For singles the softer ball is the order of the day and for doubles, the harder one. And since the mid-1980s, the popularity of the English game on an English-sized court — the "International Court" — has markedly increased both in Canada and the United States.

We Build Our Squash Courts

The year of 1957 was a landmark one for the Club. We did ourselves proud by completing our first major rebuilding since the construction of our McLure clubhouse way back in 1914. Prior to 1957, we had our badminton, our grass courts, and the clay — five of which were slightly more elevated than the others, and one was a singles — each being lined with stapled cloth tapes. You could slide on the clay but sometimes sliding over a cloth tape was another thing, and more so at the Kelowna Tennis Club, which had metal tapes. Many a sprained ankle, including mine. There were lots of diversions in the Okanagan — once a bull snake latched onto a foot-faulter's foot. He F-F'd no more. However in 1957 we lost our clay singles, its backboard, plus three doubles.

Squash, the third in the trilogy, didn't arrive until 1961 although active planning started three years before, when the board once considered sacrificing a badminton court to make way for it. Fortunately that didn't happen. So we had first class facilities — a new clubhouse, modern equipment, and a heated swimming pool — however, our tennis courts were still outdoors and subject to the whims of the weather. It was an exceptional year if the lawn was still playable

1950s

Edmonton-Vancouver Transmountain pipeline. **1954** Roger Bannister beats John Landy in the 3.59.4 Miracle Mile at Empire Stadium. B.C. Lions first game vs. Winnipeg. Sports Illustrated. Colour TV—$1000 per set. "Elvis "Blue Suede Shoes" Presley.

Squashers in the Snaker, c. Christmas, 1962. Back row (L-R): David Strachan, Vladimir Plavsic, John Nicolls, Art Stilwell, Tim Hugman. Front row (L-R): Ron Newcombe, Werner Forster, Garde Gardom, and Bob Wade.

by mid-September when the leaves fell, and the dew and worms took over. So even though our clay courts could go on somewhat longer, effectively there was no tennis after October. Badminton players had no such worries, so increasingly we thought of squash to add another indoor winter activity, plus some covered courts to ensure year-round tennis. The provision of those facilities formed our major building projects over the years to come. But, for all three activities, paying spectators continued to be sparse. We don't

do good at the gate. Nor, apart from tennis, do they televise well. And publicity, at this time if any, was hard to come by. And still is.

1961 – Squash, the Tudor Room, the Pub, and the Private Dining Room Arrive

Impetus for construction of our squash courts sprang from a coterie of members from the Racquets Club who'd joined the VLTBC in 1957. Amongst them

1950s

Vancouver's first cocktail bar opens in the Sylvia Hotel. Six day shopping week. New Granville Street Bridge opens. **1955** Bill Haley's "Rock Around the Clock". Salk polio vaccine. Kentucky Fried Chicken. Reverend Martin Luther King's bus boycott in

Bette and Merton Lechtzier — prepping for more fun.

were Bill Crawford, Bob Wade, Sandy Robertson, and Ron Weber. VLTBC's Eric Beardmore, also an ex-Racquets Club member, led the charge. Talk about zest. "Beardie" could start a party at the drop of a hat with his "Brown Velvets" — champagne and McEwans ale. In 1959 he became our president and in 1960, under his unrelenting and dedicated leadership (for him the Club was *the* thing), the directors gave the go-ahead for the Tudor Room, the pub, a new bar, a private dining room, two singles squash courts, a juniors' lounge and snack bar, plus an open and covered parking lot — all to be up and running in 1961. Wing-Commander Beardmore was something — piloted Hawker Hurricanes during the Battle of Britain, was wounded, shot down and bailed out over the English Channel. A spirited survivor who could party like no one else.

Elegance, Innovation, and Fun

The theme was Tudor. The theme was elegance. Club member Art Stilwell was our architect (and remained so until 1984), Read

1950s

Montgomery, Alabama. 18 hours CP Air Vancouver-Amsterdam. TV's $64,000 question. Vancouver's first Grey Cup—Montreal Alouettes beat Edmonton Eskimos. Provincial Government buys Lions Gate Bridge for $6 million—half its value. Annacis

L-R: A.P. Horne, Eric Beardmore, and Colin Walker.

Jones and Christopherson the engineers and the talented decorator was Gordon Willerd of Chelsea Shop — all shepherded by Eric Beardmore (and we're sure by Jean too). They worked wonders. Overnight the graciously panelled Tudor Room, the dining room and the pub became *"the* places to be." Not ostentatious, although extremely fashionable, with a marvellous but laid-back, somewhat "Elizabethan" formality. Merton Lechtzier laid some excellent Club-monogrammed carpet and his loving wife "Beebs" (Bette) — who named his car "the Flying Horse Bun" — produced a first-class 1890s cover for our dining room menu. The food was good. The service A-1. The atmosphere warm and inviting. And, we became very much *the* eating place and watering hole north of the downtown core. And on Saturday nights, it was close to SRO. Excellent vibes. And societally once more we had arrived.

During this period our ever-innovative John Nicolls ("J.P.R.," as he was best known) came up with a brilliant suggestion — why not go for a high-rise where the badminton hall and east parking lot now stand? The first four or five floors would be for our athletic endeavours and the top five would contain suites for sale or lease. In those days zoning likely would have been no problem. But the Club, suffering as always dollar shortages, couldn't and didn't rise to the occasion.

John was chock full of fun. He initiated "The Mighty Arts Players" — assisted by Stuart Wallace, Mike Catliff, Harry Bell-Irving, and Irvine Clarke from Seattle. They were close to being professional. And John, with his Bob Newhart approach, more so. Skits included take-offs such as the one of Dr. Peter Bell-Irving — who left a match to answer a telephone

1950s

Island—Canada's first industrial park. **1956** Russian tanks roll into Czechoslovakia. Egypt takes control of the Suez. Crest—first fluoride toothpaste. Disposable diapers. Julie Andrews and Rex Harrison in "My Fair Lady". Grace Kelly marries Prince Ranier

Celebrating the opening of our new facilities. 1961. (L-R): Eric Beardmore, Gladys Meakin, Dudley Meakin and Jack Allan.

call (no cell phones then), forgot to return, had tea and went home, leaving his opponent on court, who was soon to be covered by fall leaves. A hoot.

A Squash Committee was formed, headed by Sandy Robertson — an all-round athlete , member of BC Sports Hall of Fame and one of B.C.'s best basketball players, and its best baseball player — and including Messrs. Wade, Crawford, Nicolls, and Harry Bell-Irving, all of whom worked wonders. And on 16 September 1961, these exciting new premises, plus our two brand new American-size squash courts, were officially opened by our Club's founder, A.P. Horne. I took a movie of it with a camera loaned to me by my father-in-law W.G. Mackenzie. I sure hope someone finds my movie. A spirited ceremony and exhibition matches were followed by tea, then by lots of "sauce," a sumptu-

ous buffet, and a lively band and dancing in the Tudor Room. An invitational tournament soon followed. Our new premises and new courts were an instant hit, exceeding all predictions and markedly increased our membership and, needless to say, greatly invigorated our bar. Our convivial squashers were a jolly lot and they spent their money — even on Sundays when our bar was closed, getting Tony Finnerty to preside at Bill Crawford's home or at Sandy Robertson's for their post-tourney bashes. Humungous!

The Club Purchases (and Sells) a House

The Club briefly dabbled in real estate investment. In 1964 it purchased a house at 1746 West 15th Avenue, across from the B.C. Electric Clay Courts. The Club bought the property for $12,874 and registered it in the name of Tom Marshall, one of Ken Meredith's law partners. In 1966 the Club sold it for $13,000. But in hindsight, if only we had kept it! In 2005, it was assessed at $985,000!

1970 — The Link Building and More Squash

In August 1966, a proposal to build a doubles squash court in the badminton hall was put before a special general meeting of the Club. Following fierce and understandable opposition from the Club's badminton aficionados, it was readily defeated. But the board's decision to outlaw black-soled shoes — which left awful marks — was welcomed.

Then, as part of the 1970 construction, with President Willy "White Shoes" Crawford presiding, our two American Singles Courts were converted to International and two doubles were built in the now-called "Link" building, between our indoor tennis courts and the clubhouse, under the direction of architect Art Stilwell and Robertson, Kolbeins, Teevan, and Gallagher as engineers. Doubles squash is unique to North America and is little played in England or in the Commonwealth. Here we play doubles under U.S. rules on a 45-by-25-foot court and with a ball bouncier than the American hard one. There was lots of opposition to the construction of our doubles court, for squash was looked upon by our non-squashers as "fun and healthy but somewhat of an esoteric activity," and for some years it was under-utilized. However now it's in frequent use, partly because many seniors find it easier on them than singles. Also, there's way more laughs. Ian Beardmore — son of Eric — Ken Mackenrot, Mike

"Dodsie" Dodds, Keith Clark, John Hungerford, and John Osburn are enthusiastic regulars.

Due to the speed, the pace, and the swinging of racquets by gladiators hovering beside each other, squash can be a mite hazardous. Vancouver's well-known philanthropist Joe Cohen lost an eye whilst playing at the Jewish Community Centre. Eye guards became mandatory for juniors and, as the result of a board decision in 2004, for all doubles players. And the American 30-gram ball — almost as hard as a golf ball — is a nasty piece of work and to get one on the leg or rump begets an almighty welt. Depart the "T" or else! Fortunately most could and there were few serious accidents, but no end of enormous bruises and many wounded feelings. Ask Weber.

Squash Tourneys and Squash Greats

In 1971 we hosted the first Canadian Nationals on the West Coast. In the Club tournaments of this era one name stands out — dour, hard-fit Martin Gibson. During the 11 years following construction of our squash courts, Martin won our Club singles eight times and the B.C. championship four times. Amongst his Club opponents was Sandy Robertson, the winner of our first Club squash tourney. In 1962 and 1963 Sandy also became B.C. champion and in 1965 won the Pacific Coast championship — not bad considering he didn't hold a racquet until 1955. Bruce Jaffary, a converted tennis player, won our singles in 1965.

Squash Visitors — The Talented Khans

In 1966, Mohibullah Khan, then ranked as the best player in the world, held an all-day teaching clinic

103

1950s

names changed to numbers. Elvis rocks at Empire Stadium. **1958** Kruschev becomes Soviet premier. Texas Instruments' microchip. Pasternak, author of "Doctor Zhivago", refuses Nobel Prize. B.O.A.C. jets London to New York. Thalidomide. Gene Kelly's

Lapham Cup Grant Trophy

Canadian Team

FRONT ROW: Richard Jackson (Vancouver), Bruce Jaffary (Vancouver), Ted Tilden (Montreal), Neil Desaulniers (Vancouver), Mike McBean (Montreal), Bill Crawford (Vancouver) Chairman, Mike Jackson (Vancouver) Captain, Jim Bentley (Toronto), Ritchie Bell (Montreal), John Hickey (Toronto), Barry Grant (Toronto), Bob Wade (Vancouver), Steve Jacobs (Vancouver).

SECOND ROW: Ted Trevor-Smith (Vancouver), Tom Watts (Hamilton), George Morfitt (Victoria), Joe Siegenberg (Edmonton), Jack Hoogstraten (Vancouver), Sean McDonough (Hamilton), Simon Dorey (Vancouver), Bruce Alexander (Vancouver), John Hungerford (Vancouver), Sandy Robertson (Vancouver), John Osburn (Vancouver), Michael Martin (Montreal), Fred Beasley (Calgary), Giles Fenn (Vancouver), Martin Kaffka (Vancouver), Allan Brown (Vancouver), Bob Puddicombe (Vancouver), Keith Clark (Vancouver), Tim Bale (Vancouver), Rae Godbold (Toronto).

BACK ROW: Eric Barclay (Vancouver), Ian Beardmore (Vancouver), Mark Heaney (Vancouver). Missing: Brian Covernton (Vancouver).

The Lapham Grant Championship.

at the Club, followed by an exhibition game against Seattle's Harry Conlon. Later that year Hashim Khan, winner of seven world titles and the progenitor of a host of Khans — each of whom became renowned squash players — conducted a four-day clinic. He returned the next year to play an exhibition game. For years Hashim and Mohibullah dominated both the English and the American game. Other notable visitors included Geoff Hunt of Australia, the top-ranked player in 1976, who in the same year played an exhibition against fifth-ranked Ken Hiscoe. Several excellent players also came from Seattle including Ted Clarke, Gene Hoover, and Tom Owens. Closer to home, skilled David Foster of the Racquets Club often played here.

The Lapham Cup and the Grant Trophy Matches

In March 1969, we sponsored the Lapham–Grant Matches, one of the most prestigious amateur events in squash. Both trophies are at stake during a gala weekend of competition. The Lapham Trophy, donated in 1922 by Henry Lapham of Boston, is for play by international singles players from Canada and the United States. English players are eligible, provided they play the American game, which few do. Traditionally the Americans have been the most frequent victors, with Canada next, and the English winning just once. The traditions surrounding the competition are rich — including elaborate black-tie dinners at which the Cup itself is brimmed with the best champagne.

In 1944, Alistair Grant of Quebec donated the

Jim Macken

Grant Trophy for similar competition in doubles. In 1969, the singles competition was played here while the doubles were held at the Men's Athletic and Recreation Centre in downtown Vancouver, since our doubles courts had not then been built. The Americans swept the Canadians in the Lapham Cup competition — Canada's only two wins were by Club members Jim Rogers and Larry Barclay. In the Grant tournament play, the Canadians fared better, narrowly losing four of seven matches. Bruce Jaffary, playing with a Montreal partner, won as did fellow Club member Hilary Wotherspoon, playing with Jim Macken. Jim, who possessed a canny court-sense and deft strokes, was a former Canadian Davis Cupper and another example of a player who could cross over from one racquet sport to another. However in badminton he sure had his problems — used tennis strokes, and seemingly never bent his wrist. But lots of tennis players had trouble with squash. They found the area too confined and the game too quick and rough. Wimps? No — but maybe so from a squasher's perspective.

The Canadian championships played at our Club

1950s

"Singing in the Rain". Maurice Chevalier's "Thank Heaven for Little Girls". Bogner's fancy ski togs. Supreme Court of Canada okays Sunday sport. Second Narrows Bridge collapses — 19 killed. Interurban ends. W.A.C. launches B.C. Ferries. Ripple Rock blocked

in February of 1971 were a big hit. Colin Adair from Montreal took the men's singles, having earlier won the same event in the U.S. Open, to become the only Canadian to win both titles in the same year. By 1971, squash had become firmly entrenched in the life of the Club and with the construction of our new indoor tennis, all of our racquet sports were away to the races.

The Jesters

"Jesters" could well characterize no end of our Club's raqueteers. But in this context we're referring to our squash elite. The Jesters Club started in 1920 in England. It is for men and by invitation only, although recently a few ladies in England have become members. Our province-wide "Nest," as they call themselves, was founded by Dr. Kemble Greenwood from Victoria (a British Army champion) and Ned Larsen from Shawnigan Lake. They were B.C.'s first members, together with Harry Bell-Irving, John Nicolls, Jim Macken, Jack Larsen, Ed Kemble, and Dr. Bob Houston.

From our Club today, 14 belong. Bill Crawford was Canadian president from 1989 to 1995 and our Jesters consider him to be the best in recent memory. During World War II, Bill flew with the Royal Air Force and as a 22-year-old proudly navigated Winston Churchill to the conference with Stalin in Yalta. They're a highly dedicated, well-travelled, ultra-social group, and with a Jester on their ties ever support squash all the way. And their wives do too. In honour of Bill's wife Richenda, who passed away in 1998, the Crawford family donated the Crawford Trophy for Women. Its first recipient was Ruth Castellino, Greg Desaulniers' wife.

1970 – Indoor and Rooftop Tennis with Tennis Quick Arrives

Planning for indoor tennis got under way in 1968 and construction began the next year. At first the directors planned a permanent structure to house three indoor courts plus put three all-weather courts on the roof for an estimated $600,000. However, a revised decision to build eight new tennis courts, four inside and four on the top, and to locate new squash courts in the Link building pushed the overall cost up to $1 million — of which about $800,000 was to come from a mortgage and the balance from the Club's surplus. The hope was that these new facilities would result in an increase in membership, also that the entrance fees would materially pay down the mortgage. But as events later proved, in the short haul there was no substantial increase in membership so our dues were increased instead. Such is life at the VLTBC.

So by January 1970, during the twilight days of Bill Crawford's presidency, we got a first-rate facility opened by President Ted Trevor-Smith following excellent work by the Building Committee chaired by John Nicolls — who later, whilst on holiday in Acapulco, was tragically killed by a shark. Our perennially professional, ever-helpful Bill Keenan, who chaired our Building Committee for the major renovations in 1961, again took over and was a member of it until his death in 1999. Outstanding.

Tennis Quick was used to surface the indoor courts. It was excellent. Porous. Easy to clean. One could slide a bit on it and not fall, plus it was acoustically

1950s

by 1237 tons of explosive—largest non-nuclear explosion in history. For B.C.'s centennial Princess Margaret opens reconstructed Fort Langley. Hula hoops. **1959** Alaska becomes 49th, and largest U.S. State—Hawaii its 50th. St Lawrence Seaway opens.

"Silver traying" Bill Keenan for his never-ending work on the Building Committee.

A-1. The same surface was used for the roof courts — both of them to be replaced later by *Plexi Pave*, a non-skid coloured emulsion applied over asphalt with none of those attributes. An unfortunate decision promoted *inter alia* by some "aging greats" who felt it would improve their play. Whether it did or didn't, who knows, but it wreaked havoc on the knees, and many fell. However, so much was the demand then for our new indoor courts that in 1972, the directors marked out a tennis court in the badminton hall for use during the summer months, leaving two badminton courts available for the few who played in summer. And there, not since play in the 1890s on the plank courts at the City Tennis Club — the forerunner of our Club — was tennis played, albeit occasionally, on a wooden surface.

1950s

Motown's Diana Ross. Temptations. Julie Andrews in "The Sound of Music". Deas Island tunnel, Oakridge shopping centre and Q.E. Theatre open. Lorne Greene stars in TV's "Bonanza". Dolly Parton launched. Castro takes over Cuba. **1960** JFK becomes U.S.

View of the Badminton Hall along Fir Street

Parking — Acquiring and Closing the East Half of 15th Avenue

The 1970 improvements did not include additional parking space. At that time, 15th Avenue still ran from Fir to Pine. With the cooperation of the Vancouver Parks Board, the Club — organized by Sandy Robertson and myself — got the City to agree to close 15th Avenue and sell it to us, so that we could use the eastern half for parking and give the western half to the Parks Board in order to increase the size of Granville Park. We also agreed to resurface the four Granville Park hard tennis courts plus tear down our dilapidated perimeter fence, which had been propped up since 1914, and build a new one. The Club paid the City $4,500, constructed our fence, and kept the trees along 15th.

As part of the agreement, the Parks Board granted us exclusive use of two of those courts during April and May, before our grass courts were in play. Throughout these negotiations, Mr. Hec Roberts, the City Engineer, and Mr. Stuart Lefeaux, the Vancouver Parks Board Superintendent — both of whom Sandy knew well — were extremely helpful. How times have changed! Today it would be almost unthinkable that the City would close a street for the benefit of a private club, one often perceived to be a playground of the wealthy, although we weren't. Methinks it was the four courts in Granville Park and our new fence that persuaded them.

1971 — Fire in the Badminton Hall

In 1971 an early-morning fire seriously damaged the badminton hall. It started in its roof and only the prompt response by the Vancouver Fire Department prevented it from also destroying the Club's archival material and spreading to the clubhouse. Prior to the fire the hall had been virtually unaltered since it was built in 1928. However, as the result of the blaze and water damage, the floor had to be replaced and the roof repaired. Our insurance covered most of the costs, but not the much-needed improvements to the wiring and heating systems. For a while the City insisted that our badminton hall house only two courts, but eventually they relented and the five original courts remained.

Hence the present-day structure is essentially the same as it was in 1928. The spectators' gallery is still awkwardly placed, the fixed benches are uncomfortable, there are no toilet facilities — but the building does smack of history. And, notwithstanding the hall's somewhat drab and old-fashioned appearance, the courts are superb. Wayne MacDonnell, six times Canadian singles champion, member of the BCSHFM, and former president of Badminton Canada, said that our courts were "as good as any in the world." The high ceiling and good background make a shuttlecock stand out so players know where it is the moment it leaves their opponent's racquet. Some think the run-back is too short, but not MacDonnell. However, by international standards, there is not enough space between the courts. The solution is to either reduce the number of courts, or leave one vacant during major tournaments and play matches on either side — which is what we do. On every account, and obviously from the praise of many, we've a treasure where no end of badminton history has been made — and we're sure more will come.

109

1960s

President. Laser developed. Canada acknowledges that it was formed by our First Citizens Aboriginal Communities, by France and by England. Jean Lesage becomes Premier and modernizes Quebec. The Twist. Chubby Checker. The Pill. Soft drinks in

GALLERY OF PAST PRESIDENTS

110

The Presidents' Gallery

Billiards and the Past Presidents' Rogues Gallery

Amongst other amenities provided for our members during this period was a handsome billiard room — officially opened in February 1965 at a ceremony presided over by Mel Scott. It was well-utilized by our seniors for snooker and billiards, although there had been some outcry that it might turn into a low-life pool hall. It didn't. We weren't that sort of people.

In 1959 we located an array of photographs of past presidents following no end of effort by Al Stevenson. Dr. Theodore Boggs, a former professor of economics at UBC, sent a photo taken of him 20 years earlier, telling Stevenson that he had deliberately avoided

taking pictures of himself in the intervening years because "I wanted to avoid giving anyone the opportunity to suggest that I, like the dinosaurs and other prehistoric characters, ought to have disappeared from the scene, as they did when the appropriate time came." Also former president Leonard Read, tongue firmly in cheek, wrote, "I would suggest, in all modesty, that my photograph be placed on an illuminated easel in the foyer, and below my name in large gilt lettering, the title 'Brown Bomber,'" alluding then to the heavyweight boxer, Joe Louis. No dice. Mr. Read was treated the same as the rest, however he was still sore at whoever had earlier swiped his classy Panama hat.

1960s

aluminum cans. Garibaldi lifts at Whistler. B.C. Ferry's Tsawwassen-Schwartz Bay. Jack "the Golden Bear" Nicklaus starts his amazing golf career. **1961** Space trips. Yuri Gagarin and Alan Sheppard. JFK's "Ask not what your country can do for you, but what

Other Sports and Activities

Our members were also involved in loads of other activities. Many excelled in rugby — à la Bud Speirs, Ian Adam, Gerald McGavin, Chris Reynolds, Norman Lidster and his son Mark, "fleet-footed" Tom McCusker, the Chikites sons, Terry Lanigan, John Tennant, Gordon Love, the Keith MacDonald boys, and big Pat Claridge, who was also an offensive end for the Grey Cup-winning B.C. Lions football team in 1964. Hard-hitting and tough-talking George Puil starred at UBC, captained Vancouver and the B.C. Reps, toured Japan for B.C., the United Kingdom for Team Canada, and also played for the London Irish and for Ireland. Former president Andrew Bibby played at St. George's, UBC, and Oxford, where he received two "Blues" and in 1980 and 1985 battled for Canada in the Hong Kong Sevens. Rugby was big time then, and still is.

Also lots were involved in soccer (Dave Stadnyk at one time owned the Whitecaps), rowing, field hockey (the Leaders and Pam and Gordon Cooper), basketball, cricket, sailing, golf, plus our Olympic swimmers (more about them later). Ron Gunn was no Olympic champ and said that the only cup he ever won was at a girls' freestyle meet at Crescent Beach where, being the only boy, they gave him one. He much enjoyed his squash and was better at it.

Peter Bentley made a great mark in golf but his first love was tennis. As a VLTBC junior he reached the B.C. finals to be beaten by Lorne Main 6-4, 6-4. Then in the Pacific Northwest junior singles he won the semis against the California titleist and once more faced "Lorne the Great" in the finals, who took him 6-3, 6-3. Peter's dad, Poldi Bentley, saw that and said, "If you can't beat a guy who plays with both hands, you'd better quit." He did. And soon was on UBC's Golf Team, for 15 years had a scratch handicap, became his club champion, and was chairman of the Canadian Open for 10 years. Now at VLTBC are his four Hislop grandchildren who continue to do great things in badminton. Also Tom McCusker, with his sort of an Arny Palmer butcher-shop stroke, plunked in two holes-in-one at Point Grey.

We've had some authors, including the irrepressible Simma Holt, and artists like Valerie Brouwer and Nicolette MacIntosh. Eileen Churchill had a great vegetable garden. Plus our hunters and shooters (no, not "Hooters") in the likes of Jack Churchill, who every year got his moose, deer, and even bear. Also Chris Reynolds — a superb shot who hunts duck, geese, pheasant, and prairie quail when they were around, plus snared the occasional stray rainbow. Lots did this. And needless to say, the VLTBC put on many "game" dinners. Very classy. Very yum.

Our sailors were "Bravo Zulu" too. George William O'Brien, nicknamed "Oberon" by Stuart Wallace, piloted his *Endless Summer*, Australia's former America Cup contender, to win the Transpac — Los Angeles to Honolulu race — and locally also sailed Victoria's *Swiftsure*. Arnold "Arr matey!" Booth's eight-metre *Concerto* — purchased from Bob Ross — was the first to run a coloured Maple Leaf spinnaker. John Long's *Mary Bower* won just about everything. Philip Graham's huge *Troubadour* raced everywhere, and Vladimir Plavsic in his *Kanata* won the arduous

111

you can do for your country". Nikita Kruschev orders construction of Berlin Wall. 101 Dalmatians. First electric toothbrush. The Pill. B.C. Government expropriates the B.C. Electric—Gordon Shrum becomes Hydro's first chairman. **1962** Cuban missile crisis.

Garde Gardom, Tom Osler, and Dudley Meakin
*Blythe Spirit*ing. 1978

Victoria to Maui race. Quite a guy that Vlad. Came from Yugoslavia and apart from being an architect — he and Werner Forster designed UBC's stadium — he played Olympic water polo plus trumpet for Stan Kenton. He's also a long-standing close friend of Peter Newman, one of Canada's outstanding authors. Barry Downs designed Vancouver's architectural showpiece, Canada Place, with its cruise ship docks and Trade and Convention Centre. And we had boaters as well — Cam Wilkinson's *Lazy Gal*, Dudley Meakin's *Blythe Spirit,* and Al MacNeil's *Poppy*, which made the *African Queen* look good. A zesty lot.

Nor can we forget our "horsey" set. All sorts. Kathleen Madden. Marmo Shakespeare. Walter Koerner. Nan Hardy (Nicolls). Lots of Southams. Barbara Jeffery, Helen Mackenzie (Gardom), Sheila Ross, Deebo Andersen (Holden), Marianne Gell (Bell), John Nicolls, Ron Gunn, "Cowboy" Stu Wallace, and Garry and Gail Schell. Equestriana personified. They hunted, jumped, showed, drove, dressaged, and gymkhana'd for a fare-thee-well. Bob Ross did 'em all — plus harness and straight racing. Jimmy Forsythe also had a couple at the track.

A few played polo. Most skied. Dick Lyons was head and shoulders our most graceful. Lots figure skated — June Wark and Mildred Jeffery, who also judged. Mild-mannered Bill Thorpe was a black belt in judo. John Larsen and John Madden rowed. A few ten-pinned — Lechtzier and Churchill. Track and field and joggers too — shot-putter Hans Knut Waage, sprinter Joe Gilmore, Jean Bardsley, Jackson Sayers,

and Peter Cundhill. Tony Hugman flew floatplanes. Pretty Valerie Mahabir held ballet classes for our teenagers and our talented Bach-loving cellist Gordon Cooper played away, as did Norman Clarke on his organ and Tom Lavin with his professional Powder Blues. Norm loved his "Yaller" convertible and baseball with his pal Arch ("don't call me Archie") Bailey. Then there's our well-muscled cyclist — Jim Beadle — who thought nothing of an Abbotsford return prior to a set or two. Together with our cooking specialists Bob Sung, Lesley Stowe, and Cordon Bleu-trained Ginny Love, swift-skating hockeyist John Fairchild, and Anthony Windeyer — our fitness centre's fittest ballroom dancer. And, tanning — no one tans like Laurel Osler. She was a mighty fine wind-surfer, skier, and dragon boat paddler too.

Also highly community-minded were our members, various mayors—Philip Owen, then councillors, MLAs, MPs, senators, jurists, and on school, parks, and hospital boards, plus supporting every charity you can imagine. Volunteerism at its best. However the Club's never been noted for its philanthropy,

112

1960s

Pope John XXIII. Queen Elizabeth Playhouse opens. James Bond. David Lean's "Lawrence of Arabia" and later "Dr. Zhigavo". The Beatles' "Love Me Do". Johnny Carson's "Tonight Show". "West Side Story". Wilt-the-Stilt Chamberlain scores 100 points in a

although our members sure have and still are. Large and small. Among the many outstanding are Jeannie Southam, Bill and Marjorie-Anne Sauder, Maury and Mary-Margaret Young, Joe and Rosalie Segal, Enrico and Aline Dobrzensky, and the Bentley and McGavin families from whom our city and British Columbia have exceptionally benefitted. It's crystal clear that from our beginning we've been on the go all the time. Would that there were more hours in the day and more days in the year.

Finances and Entrance Requirements

During the late 1950s the Club's finances were robust. The opening of the new facilities in 1957 generated 100 new members as well as a small waiting list. For the next decade the membership remained full and the waiting list grew, so that when planning began in 1968 for our new tennis facility, the Club was enjoying a healthy cash flow and the directors were breathing more easily.

To maintain our financial stability, we always had to balance the need for new members to replace those who had resigned or died. Over the years various classifications were used. At one time applicants who were competent tennis players could be fast-tracked over duffers. Another time the directors authorized more female than male members. In later years references were required from supporters of the applicants and the directors sometimes fussed over who could be a supporter — a business associate, a relative, or only people who were totally unrelated?

Eventually the directors stipulated that those applying for membership had to be introduced to a director, who would decide if the applicant was "suitable." This was a variation of a longstanding Club practice of "blackballing," or screening out, those who faced opposition from Club members, often because of their unsavoury business reputations. In practice the Club loathed blackballing an applicant and so if it seemed sure that he or she would be rejected, the director involved would discretely request that individual's supporters to prevail upon him or her to withdraw the application. Sometimes, however, opposition was more personal. In one instance, a member learned that her ex-husband was planning to join the Club and mounted a tirade against him and, notwithstanding the Membership Committee's positive recommendation, the board of directors intervened and asked the chairman to inform the applicant that a blackball was likely. He withdrew his application.

Currently, the application process takes two steps. If on a first ballot, 10 adverse votes are cast, a second ballot may be taken and if the affirmative ballots are double the adverse ones, the applicant is accepted. Rules which happily are less stringent than before.

Collegiality Governs the Day

In one sense we're a mini-United Nations — people of every race, religion, colour, creed, political persuasion, economic circumstance, and first language. But thankfully different, because apart from a few passing spats about infrequent bad calls, or no-shows or whatever, we get along, don't gang up, and mix and play together. Also, as volunteers, lots put in many hours for the Club's many interests. Great. Keep it up.

1940s

single game. Grouse Mountain chalet burns. Typhoon Freida downs 3000 trees in Stanley Park. Trinity Western College opens in Langley. **1963** JFK's "I am a Berliner—Ich bin ein Berliner". Quebec's FLQ bomb mail boxes. JFK assassinated in Dallas. Laser

> **"... apart from a few passing spats about infrequent bad calls, or no-shows or whatever, we get along, don't gang up, and mix and play together. "**

Members, Juniors, Others, and VIPs

A subject most frequently discussed about membership over the decades has been the behaviour of some juniors — hopefully always appreciating that kids will be kids. Perhaps a far cry from those faraway days at Denman Street when the directors resolved that juniors were equal to seniors. There've been various complaints. In 1963 the secretary caught a couple of them red-handed rifling a locker. They were banned from the Club and the president and secretary got hold of their parents. However, thefts from locker rooms and elsewhere have probably been committed way more by outsiders and our adult members than by our juniors. Brazen thieves have even come in off the street, with one taking a nasty swing at our general manager, Graham Laxton. So, be vigilant. Be honest. Keep your locker locked. And general managers, please keep your left up!

Honorary Life Membership has been granted to a small number of outstanding Club devotees. At present we've only two — Ken Meredith and me. Honorary memberships have also long been a part of Club life. A few of the latter are annually awarded to people of distinction (e.g., B.C. Lieutenant Governors, premiers, and political luminaries such as the Right

Honourable John Turner, plus outstanding athletes like Nancy Greene, who twice won the World Cup in skiing). Courtesy members include presidents of the BC Tennis, Badminton, and Squash Associations and sometimes others who have rendered meritorious service to racquet sports, whom we've not included.

As mentioned in the preface, long lists of worthy members whom we've not included, for by implication all members are worthy. However between 1957 and 1972, the deaths of a few cannot be overlooked. W.G. Murrin, a former president, died in 1963. Former president of the B.C. Electric Railway and whose signature appeared on every streetcar ticket, Murin had been one of those responsible for the purchase of our property from the CPR in 1944. Another member we mourned was the Honourable Sherwood Lett, distinguished soldier and Chief Justice of the Supreme Court of British Columbia.

And then E.J.H. Cardinall, who to tennis players in Canada and the United States was without qualification "Mr. Tennis." Those eulogizing spoke of him as an "institution," the likes of which would never be seen again. Making allowances for funereal rhetoric, they were correct. As a player, tennis administrator, tennis entrepreneur, and devotee of the game — pug-

1960s

developed. First metal tennis racquet. Weight Watchers. Richmond Iona sewage disposal plant opens. Tolls come off Lions Gate Bridge. Liberal's Lester Pearson becomes Prime Minister. **1964** Nelson Mandela starts life sentence. Brezhnev becomes Soviet

nacious and pitying those less devoted to the sport than he was — he was unique. In November 1966, the Club extended its congratulations to A.P. Horne, the only surviving founder, on the occasion of his 98th birthday — his last. Throughout more than 70 years of Club membership, Mr. Horne maintained a keen interest in our fortunes. Officiating at the opening of our 1961 clubhouse renovations, he looked far younger than his years. His death severed the last link with those who had gathered at that first meeting at the Hotel Vancouver in 1897 to establish the Club. May he, they, and every member who has passed on R.I.P.

Role of the Secretary Manager

Neither the successes and prosperity of the Club, nor its incidents of failure and economic hardship can be attributed solely to the directors and members. For the secretary manager has probably more influence on the direction of the Club and its day-to-day administration than any board member. In the early days, Monday was the secretary's day off — with no kitchen and without its secretary, the Club was virtually closed! However, the role of the secretary changed significantly between the end of Harry Monk's era in 1947 and that of his immediate successors.

In Monk's day the secretary was as much a social secretary as a business manager — perhaps more so. Life though was much less complicated then — no worrying about union contracts, minimum wages, accurate accounting, deductions for income tax, pension, and health benefits, nor of having to abide by a plethora of government regulations. Since Monk's time, Club managers have become professionals. After Monk, a succession of managers served without distinction until 1958, when the remarkably capable, industrious, ever-present, and hands-on Tom Myring was appointed secretary manager. The nomenclature of the position best reflects the changing times. At first, the Club had a secretary, then a secretary manager, then a general manager, and now a chief executive officer.

Hard-working Tom Myring was the first of the new breed of professional managers. He provided an enormous and much-needed stabilizing influence and at all times had a firm hand on the pulse of the Club until ill health forced his departure in 1970. He is remembered among other things for installing closed-circuit TV to lessen thefts in the locker rooms and for hiring a mean Alsatian for nighttime security. And he meticulously made sure that people paid their accounts. Well do we recall the story about a pigeon landing on the balcony with Stuart Wallace saying, "No need to collect a guest fee, Mr. Myring, he's a member."

He returned as secretary manager in 1972 but, again dogged by sickness, resigned in 1974 and re-entered private business, buying and selling real estate, hotels, and shopping centres. He was highly successful and soon quietly became quite wealthy. He hadn't been to the Club since he left — and Mrs. Myring had never been here — so in June of 2006 President Bibby hosted a much-appreciated luncheon in their honour.

Professional Tennis Coaches

In the Club's early years, our most proficient players coached others graciously and without charge. In

115

1960s

Secretary. Martin Luther King awarded Nobel Prize. Cassius Clay "I am the greatest" beats Sonny Liston. The Beatles play Vancouver. Barbra Streisand's "Funny Girl". Port Mann Bridge opens. W.A.C. Bennett and Lyndon Johnson sign Columbia Treaty at

the 1930s, we secured Edward Kelter — a world-famous Danish gymnast, classy swimmer, diver, and tennis player to boot — to coach tennis. After that he joined the just-started B.C. recreational "Pro-Rec" program.

Professionals, or "pros," didn't surface until the later 1940s. And they weren't paid much, e.g., the likes of Bev Rhodes, Gerry Clute (whose wife also taught us bridge), and Keith Verley — who was elected a life member in 1957. Jimmie Bardsley started at $4 an hour and graduated in 1951 to $80 for the season — plus free tennis privileges for Jean. Jimmie's "Homers" were something. He home-brewed on Thursday and drank 'em on the weekend. It's a wonder he survived.

Our pros mainly coached our juniors. For the seniors some free tuition was provided by David Strachan and Modesto-tutored Bill Ledingham. From south of the line, California's David Gillamn, Ken Napier, and Fred Earl from Modesto occasionally appeared. And from the 1960s on it became a full time job. Paul Willey worked 1960–69, Lex Vinson 1970, Tony Bardsley 1971–73, Ian Pomeranke 1974–79, Roger Jarrett 1980–86, and Russ Hartley has been with us since 1987.

Paul Willey was hired in 1960, earlier having tennis scholarshipped at Modesto College in California. He was an excellent player, winner of many tournaments, with an enormous backhand, a great serve, excellent anticipation and was among the 10 top-ranked male singles players in Canada from 1950 to 1958. In 1956 he and Larry Barclay ocean-linered to Wimbledon and met Australia's Rosewall and Hoad in centre court. They gave them a good battle, but the Aussies were too good. In 1951, playing with the legendary Doris Popple, he won the Canadian Open mixed. Then in 1959 he won the Western Canadian men's singles at a time when American competition was very strong, and became

117

Paul Willey coaching a group of tennis aspirants. The VLTBC has been home to numerous top junior players, many of whom trained under Willey in the 1960s.

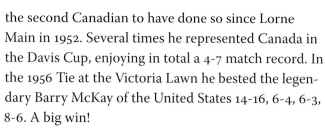

(L-R): Don McCormick, Bob Moffatt, Bob Puddicombe and Bob Bardsley.

Victor Rollins and Bob Moffatt; Richmond Men's Doubles Champions, 1965.

the second Canadian to have done so since Lorne Main in 1952. Several times he represented Canada in the Davis Cup, enjoying in total a 4-7 match record. In the 1956 Tie at the Victoria Lawn he bested the legendary Barry McKay of the United States 14-16, 6-4, 6-3, 8-6. A big win!

There had been many professionals before his time, but Willey's record surpassed them all. He coached tennis and ran the pro shop until 1971 — where he had his ups and downs. In 1962 the directors instructed him not to hire Club members for the pro shop, nor to permit juniors to use it as a meeting place. Moreover, he was not to address senior members by their Christian names, but only by their surnames with a "Mr.", "Miss," or "Mrs." There were no "Ms." then. Very different from

the time of Harry Monk. Willey was a promoter, not the world's best administrator, and his tennis theory was, "hit the ball as hard as you can and storm the net." But no question his junior tennis program was the best in the country and produced our Club's best-ever crop of juniors. He also did his bit for Werner "the Great" Khan, who later on in life became one of "Willey's Wards" when he played for the UBC tennis team.

Grass Court Nine Hard-Surfaced for the Coaching Court

Willey didn't have a much-needed coaching court. So in the mid-1960s, during my presidency, our members were solicited to express their opinion about closing grass court nine and building the Club's first

1960s

Peach Arch. Lions win Grey Cup. Deas Island Tunnel renamed Massey Tunnel—tolls end. **1965** Churchill dies. Miniskirts. Skateboards. Britain goes metric. Riots in California's Watts County. U.S. Blacks gain voting rights. Britain bans TV cigarette advertising.

1967 Collegial Diehards: Bruce Wark, Bill Keenan, Mert Lechtzier, Tom Osler, and Sid Winsby.

exclusive coaching court — a hard one. The support was overwhelming and it was built almost overnight. Grass court nine had never been popular. It was beside an odiferous compost bin — chock full of grass clippings, veggies, eggshells, fruit flies and their many companions, including an occasional resident rat. It stank. An opponent of Mark Tindle once complained, "What's that foul smell?" Mark replied, "It's my lousy backhand." The best letter I received contra eliminating any lawn court was from John Nicolls, who said, "There's every reason to take out the grass and that's the best reason to keep it."

Our VLTBC-Coached Tennis Greats

Willey's coaching program produced lots of stars. His Vicki Berner came to prominence by winning the junior ladies Canadian in 1961. She didn't win a National singles, however, she did capture the mixed and doubles — with Susan Butt in 1963 and later with Faye Urban from Windsor. Vicki won the Nationals four years straight, from 1966 until 1969. She was Canadian-ranked in the top 10 every year from 1964 until 1973 — often in second place — and in 1971 took top spot. Vicki also competed several times at Wimbledon. After reaching the finals of the Canadian

1960s

Tony Bardsley.

Closed singles in 1972, she turned professional and played on the Virginia Slims tour and became one of its directors in 1974.

Willey-trained Bob Moffatt and Alan Skelton won various provincial and regional titles and, in Skelton's case, the 1964 Western Canadian plus our Club championship in 1966. Alan later became the professional at the Golden Gateway Tennis Club in San Francisco and in 1983, Moffatt became the executive director of Tennis BC. He established the magazine *Match Point* and from 1988 until 2004 presided over Tennis Canada.

Other Willey protegés were Tony and Bob Bardsley; Janice, Mark, Kim, and Jill Tindle; and Victor and David Rollins — who were also the Club's most prolific salmon fishermen. However, let's not forget Jake Brouwer who hauled in a 81.5 lb Spring — "King" as our American friends call it — in July 1980 at the Kenai River in Alaska. Big Jake enjoys our all-time record! Nor forget Dudley Meakin, who could find a good Spring or a Coho or a cod anywhere. In those days we used to throw away snappers, but now they cost an arm and a leg.

Sadly, a couple of our top-flight juniors died early. The charmingly polite Steve Volrich from cancer and the charismatic Ed Siemens from burns suffered in a car accident. His car had run out of gas and was being pushed to a gas station. Close to a pump, the car's power steering seized and its bumper punctured the fuel hose. Ed tried to get the spilling gas into a pail while his friends pleaded with the attendant to shut off the pump. He did, but then turned it on again and a spark ignited the gasoline, engulfing poor Ed in flames.

1960s

AIR CANADA

Men"—Trudeau, Marchand and Pelletier. Pearson re-elected. Canada/U.S. Auto Pact. T.C.A. re-named Air Canada.

Paul-trained Bob Puddicombe undoubtedly had the most illustrious tennis career of any male Club member during the 1960s and '70s, as well as being outstanding at squash. In 1964 he won the men's tennis singles in the Canadian Closed. He played for Canada four times in the Davis Cup, against the United States, England, Finland, and France —although, as he somewhat ruefully mentions, he didn't win a match. Twice he played at Wimbledon, and in the mixed with Faye Urban got through the first round. He attained national ranking in 1965, as No. 10, and three years later was ranked first. He was last "nationally ranked" in 1976, as No. 10. In his prime, had Puddicombe not elected to study medicine, most felt he could have attained international status in any racquet sport he chose, for as one observer put it, though Bob never played badminton competitively, he could pick up a racquet and within five minutes be better at it than anyone else. He was a cool, smooth lefty — never rushed, and remarkably co-ordinated.

And of course the Bardsley brothers, Tony and Bob — good genes — sons of Jean and Jim. Of the two, Tony was destined to be the better player although Bob was nationally ranked in 1969 and 1974. Bob was the more graceful and best at mixed, which he often played with his mother. The brothers were fierce competitors but always made peace, especially at their parents' Sunday night dinners. They were and still are awesome doubles partners. Tony first showed up in the national rankings in 1968, in second place, just behind Puddicombe, and remained in the rankings with one exception until 1975. After he turned pro in 1968, he played professional tourna-

ments against stars such as Pancho Gonzales, Rod Laver, and Stan Smith. He also played Davis Cup for Canada for six years, won numerous titles in British Columbia, and was ranked No.1 three times. He won the Canadian Closed doubles in 1974, '75, and '77. In 1974 he reached the finals in the singles, and the following year returned to win it. In 1971 the Club hired Tony as tennis pro, succeeding his mentor, Paul Willey, and Tennis Canada awarded him its Distinguished Service Award for his long and outstanding involvement.

Another prominent tennis player of this time — though not a student of Willey — was Susan Butt. Sue grew up in Victoria, a contemporary of Sharon Whittaker (Bleuler) who played excellent badminton. Susan emulated fellow Victorian Marjorie Leeming, who in the 1920s was twice ranked as the No.1 in Canadian tennis. Butt placed second in the 1957 national rankings. A year later, while at UBC, she slipped to fifth place, but by 1959 and '60 was again top-ranked. During the next six years she down-victoried, but in 1966 regained her top ranking, just ahead of Vicki Berner.

Susan played all the major tournaments in North America — six times at Forest Hills — as well as in Europe, South Africa, and Australia. In 1961 she played at Wimbledon, where she advanced through three rounds of singles before being beaten by the first seed on centre court — one of our few female Club members to have played at that renowned site. Four times she played for Canada in Federation Cup matches — the equivalent of the Davis Cup for women.

It appears no male Club member ever won a

1960s

1966 Mao's Cultural Revolution. Indira Gandhi becomes Prime Minister of India. U.S. Catholics okay meat on Fridays. Mastercharge. Grey Cup riot in Vancouver. W.A.C. opens Centennial Fountain fronting Vancouver Court House. "Mighty Mouse" Elaine

Canadian Open. Our women were better, such as Eleanor Young, with her 1940 victory in singles. Yes ladies, *you* predominated.

Badminton Whizzes — Ours and the International Stars

Squash was vibrant in the early 1960s. However badminton went through a bad patch and the directors were often concerned about its lack of play. Nor did they dance around the maypole about tennis. There were, though, pools of talent in each. In badminton Wayne MacDonnell stood out — a non-fee-paying member from the Racquets Club who was granted an honorary membership by virtue of winning our singles in 1959 plus six successive Canadian singles from 1962 until 1967, a record unmatched by any other male Canadian.

Badminton got a huge boost from exhibition matches played here in 1961 by the world's No.1 player, Erland Kops, of Denmark, together with the World doubles champs Finn Kobero and Hammergard Hansen, who pioneered the upfront and back as opposed to the sides game. (One of them borrowed my only cashmere sweater, never to return it!) Robert McCuaig, the English champ, also took part. Then in 1963, President Jack Allan reported that badminton emerged from its doldrums, no doubt partly by virtue of another appearance by "Kops The Great," this time to play in the Canadian Open. He won all three events, and Denny Boyd, sports writer for *The Vancouver Sun*, reported, "Erland makes all the classic shots, moves his opponent around, studies him, tires him and bewilders him until he goes over

122

the horns for the kill." Ken Meredith recalls that Kops with his strong wrist could backhand smash cross-court from his baseline to that of his opponent. That was then new and he was strong as a bull.

MacDonnell, holder of the Canadian Closed, got through to the quarter-finals but lost to a Thai in a very tough match. In winning the mixed, Kops played with Claire Lovett. One recalls him pointing to the net

Claire Lovett.

1960s

Tanner wins four Gold medals at the Commonwealth Games. Start of Canada Pension Plan. Whistler's lifts and Grouse Mountain Skyride open. **1967** Israel's six-day war against Egypt. Thurgood Marshall, first American black appointed to U.S. Supreme

Badminton Team Canada 1967. (L-R): Rolf Paterson (B.C.), Ed Paterson (B.C.), Bruce Rollick (B.C.), Wayne MacDonnell (B.C.), Jamie Paulson (Alberta), Jim Garnworth (Ontario), Bert Fergus (B.C.).

Paul Willey coaching the badminton juniors, c. 1962.

and ordering her to "Stand there, woman!" In other words, "Get out of the way and leave it to me," which she did, reminiscent of Jack Bromwich playing tennis with Eleanor Young 25 years before. Kops was remarkably fit and was the first Caucasian to beat the Asians in their hot and humid home grounds.

Claire Lovett found Wayne MacDonnell to be a much more sympathetic partner when they played two years later in the Vancouver and District championships. In the finals they met and beat the reigning Canadian mixed titleists, Mimi Nilsson and Rolf Paterson. Wayne said it was one of his greatest victories and well recalls the match-winning point. Lovett served to Paterson at 16-all. Rolf let it go, thinking it was out, but it dropped on the line. Bad luck, Rolf. Way to go, Claire!

In 1964 we held the Thomas Cup Zone playoffs between Canada and Japan — Japan won handily. The only Canadian to win was MacDonell, who beat Japan's No.1. Bert Fergus who, with MacDonell, had won the Canadian doubles the year before, was also routed. The victorious Japanese followed the birds to Victoria to play the United States — a Tie that they also won.

Our Professional Badminton Coaches

Perhaps the biggest boost that the Club's badminton program ever received was in 1969, when we hired Abdul Shaikh as coach. Abdul had forged a distinguished career in India, his birthplace, winning the All-India Open men's doubles and mixed. He had also played for India in international competitions against Thailand and Malaysia, then the world's top-

Canadian Championships, 1966 — Mrs. J.R. Macken presents the trophy to Claire Lovett, winner of the Ladies' Senior Singles.

1960s

Court. Hippies. General de Gaulle's "Vive Québec Libre" in Montreal. First heart transplant by South Africa's Dr. Christiaan Barnard. Public Broadcasting Corporation starts. Microwave. Twiggy. Carol Burnett show. Canada's first McDonalds take-out opens

ranked team, where he and his partner won the men's doubles. After Abdul came to us he won a string of 18 gold medals in singles, mens, and mixed. Playing in the United States, he twice captured the World Masters doubles.

After starting as an assistant to Paul Willey, Shaikh later became our head pro for badminton and squash. Amongst others in badminton, Rex Moore well-acquitted himself in 1971 by winning the Canadian junior doubles as well as a key match between Canada and England. While working for us, Shaikh also found time to compete

Our renowned Abdul Shaikh.

internationally and playing with Yusef Khan, he won the Canadian Masters Open. He also coached the Canadian National Team in the Pan American Games, three Commonwealth Games, three All England Championships, the Thomas/Uber Cup Ties, and the Atlanta Olympics in 1996! He also took on our ever-popular fitness program. Since his retirement in 1999, Shaikh has continued training badminton coaches throughout the world. Yes, our Abdul is something. Our badminton hall has been named after him and he's received recognition upon recognition. Each earned. Each deserved.

1963 Davis Cup Tie – Canada vs. Mexico – and the Canada Lawn Tennis Championships at the VLTBC

In 1963 the Club hosted two major tennis tournaments — the Canada–Mexico Davis Cup Tie, chaired by me, followed by the Canadian Lawn Tennis championships. During the run-up to these matches, I caught chickenpox from my little daughter Karen. Concerned that I might have to step down, I asked Mel Scott to become 2IC. Not wishing to alarm an increasingly apprehensive Mel, I downplayed my ailment. "It's just a rash and will soon pass." I wasn't too sure, nor was he, but thankfully it did!

The Mexican team featured two exciting Wimbledon and U.S. doubles champions — the handsome, ever-graceful, cat-like Rafael Osuna, and Antonio Palafox. Juan Arredondo and non-playing captain Pancho Contreras completed the team. Canada's squad, captained by Jim Macken, consisted of Francois Godbought, Keith Carpenter, and Harry Fauquier. We salvaged only one point in the series — a singles win by Ontario's Keith Carpenter.

As anticipated, this Davis Cup Tie was a major sporting and social event, held under the patronage of our Lieutenant Governor the Honourable Major-General George Pearkes; Chancellor Zenakdo Munoz of the Mexican Consulate; the Honourable Sherwood Lett, Chief Justice of the Supreme Court of British Columbia; and the United States Lawn Tennis Association's Robert Caldwell of Seattle, who served as official referee.

The Hudson's Bay Company, the City of Vancouver, and the Club hosted functions for the teams. Press

125

in Richmond with 18¢ hamburgers. French language radio starts in Vancouver. Bath-tub races from Nanaimo. **1968** Pierre Elliot Trudeau elected leader of the Liberals. Apollo 8 orbits the moon. Nixon becomes President. Bobby Kennedy and "I have a

Davis Cup Tie, Canada vs. Mexico, 1963. Teams and committee.

DAVIS CUP TENNIS

Canada vs. Mexico

VANCOUVER LAWN TENNIS CLUB

15th and Pine

JULY 26, 27 and 28

★

See OSUNA and PALAFOX, World Amateur
Doubles Champions in Action!

ADMISSION: $2.00 per Day $5.00 for 3-Day pass

Tickets available at:
VANCOUVER LAWN TENNIS CLUB   RE 3-6116, RE 3-1710
HUDSON'S BAY COMPANY   MU 1-6211

Poster for 1963 Davis Cup tennis.

and radio coverage was excellent, although the hoped-for television income never materialized. Advance ticket sales constituted 40% of the gate — $2, or $5 for a three-day pass. However our overall revenues were not the best. Expenses came to $4,900 with the biggest ticket being $2,400 for temporary stands and 1,800 seats. All in all the Club lost $80, but thanks to a number of hard-working volunteers, the matches went well and were great fun.

Keith Carpenter stayed for the Canadian Lawn Tennis Championships and reached the singles and doubles and, with Club member Vicki Berner, won the mixed. In the doubles, Carpenter played with Tom Brown of San Francisco, who had last played at the Club as a member of the U.S. Davis Cup team in its match against Japan in 1953. However Brown and Carpenter lost in five hard-fought sets to a couple of diminutive and very speedy Mexican juniors — 15-year-old Marcello Lara, and 17-year-old Joaquin Loyo Mayo. Boy, were they exciting! We covered the expenses of the Mexican players to the tune of $1,200 with the expectation that they would all remain for the Canadian, however, much to our chagrin, Palafox and Osuna

dream" Martin Luther King assassinated. Arthur Ashe wins U.S. open. Water beds. "Laugh In". "Hair" on Broadway. Jacuzzis. Art Phillips founds "Team". Vancouverites parade for skier Nancy Greene—Rossland's Olympic gold medallist. B.C.'s Centennial

Canadian Championships, 1966 — Mixed doubles finalists (L-R): K. Carpenter, V. Berner, Al Stone, and R. Bentley. The winners were Carpenter and Berner.

left. Ann Barclay, then living in Toronto, took the womens and zany Whitney Reed, an American, won the singles. Reed had a buckets of bizarre but winning strokes and was a colourful character who showed up late for his singles final after being dragged from the bar of his hotel. Even so, he easily whipped Keith Carpenter in straight sets! Whitney, albeit a comic, was remarkably coordinated, used bewildering shots, and could toss four balls into the air and effectively serve one of them.

Unfortunately the Western Canadian tournament continued its decline throughout this era, and the Club questioned the wisdom of carrying on with it. In his 1950 Annual Report, Club President Sid Winsby advisedly grumbled about "the mediocre material sent up to us for our Western Canadian from our neighbours to the south." In 1958, Bob Bedard from Quebec — not a natural racquets player, but built like a fullback and an excellent, fair-minded athlete and took the Canadian Open at the VLTBC. He was

1960s

Museum, H.R. MacMillan Planetarium and Bank of B.C. open. Heli-skiing at Whistler. Inaugural Tokyo-Vancouver flight. Chargex (Visa) comes to Canada. **1969** July 20, Neil Armstrong lands on the moon "One small step for man, one giant leap for mankind".

ranked No.1 in Canada and played Davis Cup 1954–62. After 1968, professionals became eligible to play in all tournaments, but the Club directors were unwilling to join a satellite professional circuit in order to attract them. So the Western Canadian fell off, hastened by our decision not to let it any longer be played on grass, with its excessive wear and tear. In 1974 it petered out and became no more.

The Gordon Trophy

In 1949, G. Blair Gordon from Montreal donated a trophy for tennis competition between Canadian and American players over the age of 45. For the first 20 years, the U.S. won virtually every contest, but Canada enjoyed successive victories in 1991 and 1992. The Club held the first Gordon Matches in Western Canada, with Jack Churchill heading the organizing committee assisted by Don Maltby and Jim Skelton. Play consisted of four doubles and four singles with the Americans taking the honours by winning seven of the eight. The only successful Canadians were Jim Bardsley and Clare Irish, who won their doubles. Jim Skelton lost a hard-fought singles and, in doubles, also lost with the multi-talented but capricious Harry Miles. Genial Harry had an array of shots, but humorously used absurd drops, rather than smashes, to put away an opponent — a tactic that caused his various doubles partners many grey hairs.

Harry pulled everyone's leg — used to say that if his wife, who was an excellent cook, didn't have a can opener, he'd starve. Seeing a pile of strip on a bench, he'd ask, "Is that yours?" If you said, "Yes," he'd throw it on the floor. Harry was a jeweller. He could fix any watch at the drop of a hat, but it took him months, if ever, to return it. So we carried on with his loaners. And his Christmas present for his ever-understanding wife Helen? One earring from stock. Ample grounds for his murder or worse.

Bottle Games

Tennis players weren't big spenders — in fact, most were downright tight. In those days, playing for a bottle or a case of beer was high stakes, and among the high rollers were Norm Harris and Erwin Elliott — who were always on the lookout for a "couple of pigeons." They found them — most often Merton Lechtzier and Glenn Whitelaw! On one occasion they also whipped Ron Gunn — "Gunner" — and me. Attired as we were in boaters, long trousers, sashes, and fake handlebar moustaches, it was no contest! Playing Harris and Elliot was like a "friendly" in three-card Monte with a stranger on a train, and they led lots of lambs to the slaughter! They'd play for a jar, gulp it, drive to Chinatown for a something to eat, then to the Terminal City Club for some snooker.

After one of these evenings, Whitelaw, well into his cups, arrived home late, tripped, fell, and broke a bureau while trying to get his pyjamas on, remarking to his distraught mother, "It's alright, Mother, I was out with Walter Bell," which he wasn't. But all the mothers loved member Walter Bell, who shared digs with Jake Brouwer. Many a mother would invite the fastidious Walter for dinner. Unfailingly polite, Walter would always phone the next day, complimenting his hostess upon her dinner, gravy, and dessert, and asked for the recipes. Walter could do no wrong.

1960s

Joe Namath's New York Jets beat Baltimore. "Butch Cassidy and the Sundance Kid". "Raindrops Keep Falling on my Head". "Sesame Street". Britain abolishes capital punishment. Trudeau's Liberals beat Bob Stanfield's Tories. YWCA and Roberts Bank Causeway

George Carter and Rex Jackson often took on Andy Carmichael and Alex MacDonald. That bottle vanished in seconds. Most dear to me was a three-setter for a case of Molson's, with Colin Walker, Art Jeffery, and Deryk Leader. Walker partnered me and of the four, no question I was the weakest — not at all in their league. Jeffery and Leader had us one set down, 5-0 and 40-0 in the second with Leader serving when the ultra-competitive Colin trumpeted, "We've got 'em now!" And amazingly, we did! Deryk had an almighty rabbit's ear. The beer was great!

Visiting Celebrities

They usually played at the Cave Cabaret or sometimes at the Palomar or Izzie's to fine-tune their acts before they opened in Vegas. One rising star was the multi talented Earl Grant and his big band. Unfortunately, he was killed in a traffic accident a short time afterwards. Lots came to the VLTBC for a game, including the likes of Dinah Shore, Ed Ames of the Ames Brothers, Barbara McNair (good friend of the Keenans), Bill Cosby, and Elton John. They enjoyed B.C., Vancouver, our Club, and playing on our grass, for each of them was a treat.

Social Fun and Functions at our Home away from Home

Myriads of social activities were the order of the day following the construction of our 1957 clubhouse and its 1961 upgrade. Regular functions included New Years Eve, the Wassail Party, Easter Egg Hunt, Spring Balls, and special events like Hawaiian and Calypso parties around the pool which, clothed or not, many

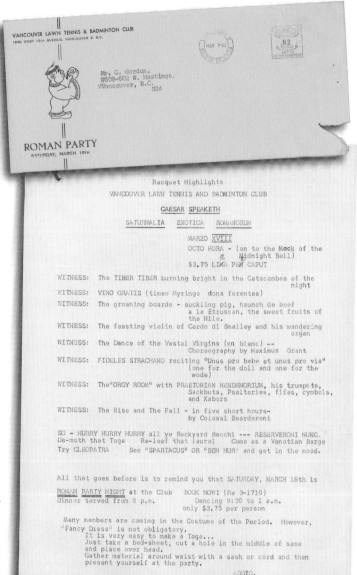

129

Invitation to the VLTBC Roman "Bacchanalia," 18 March, 1961.

ended in. Most functions were conceived and cheerfully run by our lady members. For our Luau, kindness of Brenda Cooper and her sidekick Marnie Sick (who drove a black Austin Healey, then the hottest

open. Vancouver gets NHL franchise. Boeing 747s arrive here. Swanguard Stadium built in Burnaby. **1970** "Ms" becomes popular. "Male chauvinist pigs" not. Cesar Chavez's United Farm Workers. "Bridge Over Troubled Waters". Mary Tyler Moore Show.

❝Sure the courts got crowded but you'd wait, have tea, a bite, or a drink, and chat about the news of the day, whose strokes or game was best or worse...❞

convertible in town), sweet-scented pikaki leis were specially flown in by Canadian Pacific Airlines. Then the Bavarian beer garden, Chuckwagon barbecue, Highland fling, the Dixieland Ball, Nights in Vienna, and an Italian festival. The Mens' Stag — gentlemen's party for $7.50 with "the Club being closed to all other activities — no exceptions," and the free (Is anything truly "free"?) Christmas Wassail were both enormously successful, especially the Wassail, where much merriment arose with Harry Miles and George Goode leading the pack, and John Pratt-Johnson not far behind.

For the young, for the old, and for those in between, the Club formed an enormous part of a member's life. They played here. They socialized here and they partied here. Some had their weddings, wakes, and birthday receptions here and went together to the football games at Empire Stadium. It was far from impersonal. Everybody knew everybody or soon got to, especially within their own age group or racquet interest. New members received the warmest of welcomes and soon they too were part of the mix. And mix we did. It was not only a home away from home, but for many a member almost a home unto itself. Homogeneity. Lots even met their spouses-to-be — among others the Lechtziers, the Scotts, the Keenans, the Taylors, and the Whitelaws.

Most everyone participated, contributed and helped, were hospitable, and also made their own fun with very little, if none of this "leave it up to the staff" stuff — an unfortunate price to pay for increased affluence. Life then was much more in the "slow" lane and much influenced by British customs. Rare roast beef and Yorkshire for Sunday dinners. Huntley & Palmer and Peek Freans biscuits, Lea & Perrins and Lyle's Golden Syrup, plus sawdust on the floors of all butcher shops. Few were well off. Then we were one-car families and without winter or summer getaways. Sure the courts got crowded but you'd wait, have tea, a bite, or a drink, and chat about the news of the day, whose strokes or game was best or worse or "basically unsound," as Ed Kemble said of Mel Scott's.

A lot was offered. Theatre dinner parties, including the show, for $5.50. Sunday menus from $3 to $5, for children under 12, half price. Costumed Gay Nineties dos. Ringing in the New Year 9–2 a.m., together with a Royal Buffet for $14. Friday night round robins and dancing. Gourmet and international dinners. A trencherman's delight. And who can resist that old saw about the two cannibals who were having dinner, with one saying, "I don't like your brother," and the other replying, "Never mind, just eat the noodles." Fashion shows, Valentine balls for those young at

130

1970s

George C. Scott in "Patton". A.B.C.'s Monday night football with Don Meredith and Howard Cosell's "Tell it the way it is". FLQ murder Quebec labour Minister Pierre La Porte. Canada goes metric. P.M. Trudeau introduces War Measures Act. First CPR Coal Train

The Mother's Day Menu from 1962 offered wonderful fare for the occasion.

heart, Christmas bingo, with Marguerite Campbell always winning something, Turkey Shoots, duplicate bridge, and barbeques for $2. Carnival parties 6–10 p.m. for our juniors. The place jumped.

And the Saturday night gatherings in the Tudor Room generated a warmth and glow of their own.

We enjoyed the songs of Eleanor Collins, Elmer Gill at the piano and once Woo-Woo Stephens and his banjo. Woo-Woo, a travelling entertainer, was quite a romantic — dearly loved his wife and had her picture in his wallet. I asked him when he last saw her. "Six years ago," he said! Ah well. Our Tudor Saturday night dances generated an enormous turnout, almost SRO. Huge fun. Live music was always the order of the evening — the likes of Brick Henderson and Claude Logan, but most often Doug Parker's Trio or Quartet. Everyone danced — the best ladies being Helen Miles, Gladys Meakin, Jo-Anne Brydon, June Wark, Betty Clasbie, Sonia Adam, and Barbara Jeffery. "Artie" did his forward rolls and scissor kicks and after they wrapped it up, Gerry Hamilton or Jack Churchill took over the ivories. Director Sally Carter belted out "When the Saints Come Marching In." The ballerina twirled and following closing hours, Tony Finnerty backdoored the bar until Al and Jen MacNeil decided it was champagne for everyone. And on their tab!

Irish Tony was *something!* During World War II, he'd been a batman in the British Eighth Army in North Africa — the "Desert Rats," and then a steward in a shipping line. When he came to us he brought along his cousin Patrick O'Shaughnessy. He became an instant hit — knew everyone by name and helped our members remember theirs after they had one of Patrick's "Walking-up-the-wall-and-across-the-ceiling" Spiders! Pat eventually left us to tend a bar in New York and after many years of service as our assistant manager, Tony went to work for Jimmie Forsythe at Denman Place.

Often our stamina was such that our "dos" didn't stop here — it was off to Vi's on Keefer Street for some well after midnight T-bones, fries, and hot biscuits. VLTBCers never tire.

◆

131

◆

 1970s

to Robert's Bank. Chief Dan George receives an Oscar. **1971** China attends its first U.N. meeting. U.S. bans TV cigarette advertising. Greenpeace founded. Archie Bunker's "All in the Family". Micro-processors, silicon chips, CATscans. Louis "Satchmo" Armstrong

CHAPTER 7

1972-1992 • Consolidation

1972 — We Celebrate Our 75th Anniversary

Our anniversary celebration was that year's social highlight, held on a slightly overcast but otherwise lovely June 17. It was enormous fun. The Lieutenant Governor, His Honour J.R. Nicholson, attended our VIP luncheon and kicked off the celebrations, which were presided over by President Ted Trevor-Smith.

Honorary life members Mary Haggart, Erwin Elliott, Al Stevenson, and Lee Boulter graced the occasion with their presence and almost everyone was fancily dressed. The Club's women's and men's A singles matches were played in the afternoon, with Jean Bardsley and Mike Bolton taking the honours. Ladies in period costumes served tea and refreshments throughout the afternoon.

◆
133
◆

Above. Opening of the indoor courts, 1972. (L-R): Lee Boulter, the Honourable Jack Nicholson, Bill Crawford, Ted Trevor-Smith, Colin Walker, and Sid Winsby.

Opposite (L-R): Betty Clasbie, Bill Whittall, Shannon Trevor-Smith, the Honourable Jack Nicholson, Bill Crawford, Ted Trevor-Smith, Richenda Crawford, and Ralph Clasbie.

KITSILANO GETS SET FOR SHOWBOAT (Pages 13-14)

An historic day for tennis buffs

Period costumes of the generations, such as these indicated by club historian Alan Stevenson of 1536 West 14th, will be worn for exhibition tennis matches during Vancouver Lawn Tennis and Badminton Club's Diamond Jubilee (1897-1972) celebrations this Saturday (June 17). Col. the Hon. J. R. Nicholson, Lieut.-Gov. of B.C., will attend a noon luncheon, then officially open the celebrations at 1:30 p.m. Finals of the club's men's and women's "A" championships will also be played during the afternoon, tea and refreshments will be served from 3 to 6 p.m.; and the best-dressed old-time couple will receive a trip to Europe during the dance that follows an evening "Royal Buffet".

—DON MATHESON PHOTO

THE COURIER
SERVING WEST-SIDE VANCOUVER

Tel. 266-7107
2265 West Forty-first

THE COURIER, VANCOUVER, B.C. 15¢ JUNE 15, 1972

Art group joins

Al Stevenson, the VLTBC archivist and historian, had much to do with the Club's 75th Anniversary Celebrations in June 1972.

134

The festivities were rounded off with an excellent dinner, a gala dance in the Tudor Room, and a well-attended bar.

Dick Hibbard — sporting Bermuda shorts, knee-length socks, and a handsome blazer — became the centre of great attention. During the celebrations there was a draw for a trip for two to Wimbledon — which included box seats for a couple of days. It was a reverse draw, and Hibbard, Merton Lechtzier, Don Maltby, Peter Cundhill, and Donna Anderson emerged as the five finalists. Soon the five were narrowed to three: Maltby, Cundhill, and Hibbard. Dick did his level best to "reasonably" sell half of his interest, but no luck. However, luck out he did! He won the whole thing!

A few days later a member wrote the president, complaining that since Dick was improperly dressed for the occasion — shorts rather than long trousers — he should have been disqualified from the draw! Lordy, Lordy. Hibbard was a stickler for spit and polish, even doing "Ship's Rounds" to ensure that our maintenance was up to par. And so, with the 75th anniversary behind us and imbued with a spirit of optimism, the Club moved forward into the next two decades, its period of consolidation.

Dollars, Cents, and Our Fiscal Gurus

The 1970s and 1980s afforded welcome relief from the financial vicissitudes of the earlier years. Challenges still presented themselves, but not on the

1970s

Exhibition at the opening of the indoor courts. (L-R): Bob Bardsley, Art Jeffery, Lieutenant Governor Jack Nicholson, Bob Puddicombe, Bill Crawford, and Larry Barclay.

less an accumulated depreciation of $600,000, resulted in a book value of $1,200,000. Adding that to the surplus of the previous year plus a modest 1972 profit resulted in a net asset value of $1,375,000 — the cash, or liquid assets of which were approximately $365,000.

Since we are not, and never have been, a commercial enterprise, the question as to whether depreciation should be claimed as an expense was a matter of judgement until 1996 when Generally Accepted Accounting Principles (GAAP) required that non-profit organizations record

135

scale of those of previous decades. New federal tax legislation had an impact on all social clubs — no longer could their dues be deducted as a business expense, and only 50% of business meals and business entertainment could be allowed. Also, the election in 1975 of a socialist government in B.C. had a dampening effect on business activity in general, and for the next 20 years or so our economy was plagued by varying degrees of uncertainty.

Profits, Losses, and Accounting Thereof

The AGM in 1972 reported a loss on operations of $63,000. This, offset by entrance fees of $57,000 together with other recovered costs, resulted in an operating profit of only $2,500. The Club's land, buildings, and equipment were valued at $1,800,000, which,

depreciation on fixed assets. i.e., not amortize them. Since then the Club has recorded the value of our fixed assets — land, buildings, and equipment as depreciated/amortized.

The expense of major repairs and / or renovations is charged to operations, while the cost of any new facilities is charged to the fixed assets. These procedures may seem arcane and unnecessary to the casual observer but for tax purposes, they aren't. Any private club has to be constantly aware of the temptation of the tax gatherers to assess it as a taxable business by virtue of its bar and food operations. In addition in 1959, when our holding company, as distinct from the Club, was still the legal owner of our property, our chartered accountants recommended that any cash advances from the Club to it should be secured

1970s

negotiations by Kissinger and Chou En-Lai, Nixon becomes first U.S. president to visit Beijing and (later) Moscow. Club member Robbie Burns' journalist son John acquires Nixon's chopsticks as a souvenir and is asked to sell them for $10,000. Bloody

by mortgage to more firmly ensure that the monies advanced were loans and not distribution of income.

Registrar of Companies — Bylaw Approval

In 1960 the Vancouver Tennis and Badminton Holdings Ltd. (VTBH) — the Club's holding company — approved the following amendment to its bylaws: "The Company shall not engage in the operation of any business for profit and the payment of dividends to its shareholders is prohibited." To become effective, this required the approval of the Registrar of Companies. However, he balked at the amendment insofar as it dealt with dividends — presumably on the grounds that payment of dividends to shareholders was the essence of a company's being and could not be barred. Two years later however, the VTBH, with the Registrar's consent, made an application to the court which approved the following: "The company shall not engage in the operation of any business for a profit."

Still unanswered was the question of how the VTBH surplus should be dealt with if the Club were ever to fold. In the 1980s a bylaw was proposed which provided that in the event of the winding up of the holding company, any surplus it had would not go to its shareholders but instead to an organization "with similar objectives." Amazingly, the 75% majority required to pass the bylaw fell short by 5%.

Following our auditor's advice that our holding company had outlived its usefulness and should be wound up, at the 1985 AGM a motion passed which approved the same amendment the Registrar had questioned 25 years before, namely, that dividends would not be paid to shareholders, and that if the VTBH wound up, any surplus would pass to the Club — which would become the legal owner of all of its assets.

Resolving the Outstanding Debentures

This still beset us. As earlier mentioned, in 1957 our holding company borrowed from its shareholders, i.e., Club members, $75,000 by way of non-interest-bearing debentures which were repayable only after all other indebtedness was retired. With the pending disappearance of the holding company, the problem of the debentures had to be grappled with — either to be paid out to every holder or have them agree to assign them to the Club, which would assume the obligation. Many of the holders had died or vanished so that option wasn't available, hence the Club called the debentures for redemption and the 1985 AGM authorized the board, if called upon, to borrow the necessary funds. In 1986 the holders were notified that they could claim payment, but as of 1993 only $20,000 had become redeemed. A few debentures were donated and from those proceeds two paintings were purchased for the clubhouse. By resolution in 2002, the holders finally forfeited their right for any reimbursement and gave the balance outstanding — which in 2004 amounted to $42,060 — to our Legacy Fund, amortized for payment in full by 2012. Nice gesture.

Rules Governing an "Unlikely" Dissolution

Under our present bylaws, should the Club become dissolved, after payment of debts, any accumulated income would be distributed to "non-profit or chari-

1970s

Sunday in Londonderry. U.S. Governor George Wallace shot. Munich Olympics. Mark Spitz takes seven swimming golds. "Grease". Liza Minelli in "Cabaret". NDP Government, Premier Barrett's, and B.C.'s first black MLAs Rosemary Brown & Emery Barnes

(L-R): Bert Fergus, John Fraser, Norman Hester, and Abdul Shaikh.

table organizations as selected by a Special Resolution of the members and any property remaining would be sold and the proceeds distributed to the Playing Members, to the Honorary Life Members and to the Life Members." It is extremely doubtful any of this will ever come about, although years earlier Jack Margach, one of our brightest lawyer wags, suggested, "I'll become so damned objectionable everyone will quit and I'll get it all." Didn't happen.

Entrance Fees — Surplus

In his 1958 Annual Report, President C.E. "Paddy" Morris questioned whether entrance fees should be treated as income or as capital for the acquisition of capital assets, for the repayment of long term debt, and partly to offset operation losses. They had been included in our revenue statements, but in his view they were "capital funds and should only be used for capital purposes." However, in the ensuing years our entrance fee income became co-mingled with our income from operations and is partly used to offset operation losses. Although this has been criticized at various AGMs, we continue to treat them that way and when there's a positive result, they are retained as an investment and show up on our balance sheet as accumulated surplus.

And it was that accumulated surplus which made it possible for us to embark on two significant renovations without having to borrow, viz. the upgrading of the dining room in 1985 and the much larger project in 1993 involving the construction of the fitness room and a completely renovated players' lounge together with its corridor access. From 1972, when the Club had cash on hand of $365,000, our surplus grew

1970s

elected. TV's "M.A.S.H." begins. Capital Gains Tax starts. B.C. minimum wage $2.50 an hour, highest in Canada. City of Vancouver Archives move to Vanier Park. **1973** Pablo Picasso dies. Telly Savalas is TV's "Kojak". Billy Jean King whips Bobby Riggs. WAC

John Brennan, David Strachan, Pat McGeer, and Dennis Molnar.

138

steadily and, not withstanding the 1985 expenditures on the dining room, when the 1993 renovations got underway we had some $1,300,000 cash in hand. That was progress.

Directors' Spending Powers

Procedures for payment for renovations were, and still are, contentious, because they call into question the directors' power to spend significant sums of cash without the sanction of a 75% majority of the members at a Special Meeting, as required by B.C.'s Society Act. This was formally considered by the board in 1983 and the following was recorded as policy: "Under the bylaws the Board has the power, without membership approval, to spend any amount of dollars on capital expenditures. However it has always been customary to inform the membership of such proposed expenditure, and this would continue to be our practice." That policy, however, applied only to cases where money was in hand and not to those where borrowing, accompanied by mortgage of the Club's assets, would be involved — that would require a 75% approval.

Treasurers

Throughout we've been superintended by watchful treasurers on watchful boards, and from the turbulence of the 1940s to the early '60s by the likes of Ed Kemble of Yorkshire Insurance, "Aussie" Ron Newcombe plus Ralph Carle of our auditors firm.

1970s

retires and Bill Bennett wins South Okanagan By-Election. Karen Magnussen wins World Women's Figure Skating Championship for the second time. Queen Elizabeth opens the spectacular Sydney Opera House. **1974** Britain joins the EEC. Watergate.

Ralph did a six-year stint as the treasurer and after that another two as social director.

Small Change

Our money managers were busy and during the first 70 years of our life the board made pretty well every financial decision, however small — and mainly small — and however big. Then, not like now, the directors considered the minutiae of money matters. Things like in 1916 setting the groundskeeper's salary at 25¢ an hour; in 1931 agreeing to spend $25 to partition the showers in the men's locker room; in the late '40s that we'd sell soft drinks for 7¢, pie à la mode for 15¢, and dinners for 60¢, unless it was steak, in which case it would cost between 65¢ and 80¢; also to refund dues from $3 to $15 to members who moved. This kind of decision-making continued into the '60s and '70s. Dinner for the Gay Nineties Ball was set at $2.50, International ones $6, fashion shows $1.75, and Sunday brunches three bucks, five for a steak, and for kids under 12 half price. Babysitting was 65¢ per child. The Haggart Cup, $10 a couple — cocktails included! What detail. What deals! For ease in accounting, in 1973 we switched from cash to chits.

In 1951, bonuses for two of our staff were set at $20 apiece. Three received a $5 box of chocolates. Later, in the '50s, a ticket for the exhibition by Lorne Main vs. Fred Fisher of Seattle was 50¢, weekly passes for the Western Canadian sold for $2.50, and Saturday night dances cost a dollar. In 1956, members were billed $5 for staff Christmas bonuses. The board gave the okay for an oil heater for the badminton hall, provided its coal stove was sold. Wonder who got that. And all of this at board level. Just imagine how long it took. Little wonder their meetings seemed to never end.

Our Biggest Bucks

Throughout you'll note I've referred to costs of the time. In today's dollars the fair market value of our

		Cost at the time $	2005/6 dollars $
1914	Purchase 16th & Fir	40,000	679,750
1914	Erect McLure clubhouse and courts	25,000	445,250
1928	Build the badminton hall	30,000	325,800
1957	New clubhouse and pool	320,000	2,265,000
1957	Furbish new clubhouse	18,500	133,940
1957	LayKold 4 tennis courts	12,758	87,500
	Tudor Lounge, pub and 2 squash courts	319,000	2,125,000
1970	Indoor tennis and more squash courts	1,011,000	5,205,000
1975	Eliminate grass courts, new outdoor courts and bubble	289,000	971,000
1978	Balcony	121,000	346,000
1984	Players' lounge reno	291,000	503,000
1986	Dining room reno	230,000	367,000
1993	Phase I reno, main floor	577,000	706,000
1996	Phase II underground parking, an elevator, new showers and a steam room	4,985,000	5,882,300
1998	Phase II upgrade pool and courts	200,000	240,000
2003-5	Recent consultant costs	337,000	337,000
2005	Bubble for clay courts (est.)	725,000	725,000
2006	Increased cost clay courts bubble	360,000	360,000
	Cost miscellaneous expansions, renovations	2,500,000	2,500,000
TOTAL:		**$12,391,258**	**$24,204,540**

139

Nixon resigns. Pattie Hearst kidnapped. Calculators become affordable. City buys Orpheum Theatre. St. Roch Museum opens. MacDonald Detwiler builds space shuttle's Canadarm. Royal Hudson—Vancouver to Squamish. **1975** General Franco dies—King

premises, by way of comparison and chronological summary, is an eye-opener. Have we ever grown from our four lots in 1898 to our multi-million dollar plant today!

And well you can imagine how much blood, sweat, tears, and money-finding all of this involved. W—H—E—W !

Our Auditors

Initially our bookkeeping was very much a "back-of-an-envelope" exercise, but the larger and more complex we became so did it and we've always been well served by our treasurers, Finance Committees, and chartered accountants. Since 1940, the firm Carter, Reid and Walden (Alec Reid was a member) — which in 1949 morphed into Clarkson and Gordon, then in 1980 into Ernst & Young — have been our CAs and auditors. Firm member Ian Adam, who joined the Club in 1953, shepherded our audit from then until 1990, except for two years when he was in Toronto. In 1992 he became and continues to be a highly-valued and most knowledgeable member of our Finance Committee. Ni Hao Ian.

The Annual General Meetings

Traditionally these have been held in November. The board often advanced Special Resolutions requiring 75% of votes cast, e.g., for matters such as amendments to our bylaws. But apart from our more technically involved members and those who were seeking specific answers to specific questions, few attended and sometimes it was tough to acquire our necessary 5% quorum. However, throughout our history our members have generally been satisfied with the actions of our directors — which speaks highly of each. Members often questioned the financial figures at the AGM. The "Miscellaneous item," small though

140

Bill Crawford's belles: Barbara Jeffery, Lola McCarthy, Donna Anderson, Helen Gardom and Valerie Brouwer. (the 1970s).

1970s

Juan Carlos takes over Spain. Helsinki Accord of Human rights. "Jaws". Margaret Thatcher elected. Premier Bill Bennett's Social Credit elected. Suez Canal opens after 8 years. U.S./Soviets dock in space. "Godfather" starring Marlon Brando. Max Ward's

it was, was always one of great interest to Harold Haggart. He unfailingly requested particulars and always got them.

In 2000, a new bylaw permitting proxy voting was approved. It was questioned in 2004 as a result of a legal opinion that proxies couldn't be used for the election of directors, which surely had to be the original intent. In order to increase member participation hopefully this will be reviewed and soon rectified.

The AGMs produced their share of laughs. During World War II, urbane Tim Hugman was a tank commander with the Governor General's Horse Guards, was wounded in the Italian campaign at the Battle of Monte Cassino, and later was promoted to colonel. After the war he became the senior pulp and paper salesman in the U.K. and in the Far East for the timber giant, MacMillan Bloedel. The Colonel got his suits, shoes, and shirts handmade in London, where he stayed at the likes of Claridges, and in Singapore at Raffles. He loved loud music, especially the William Tell Overture played in candlelight and into his sparkling Goode's crystal he poured an enormous three- or four-ounce Scotch.

And so invigorated at one AGM, he relayed a joke. "What's the difference between a caucus and a cactus?" and gave the answer. England-born Jocelyn Pease — prim, proper, and Protestant, was also in attendance. Jocelyn was a redoubtable tennis player — sort of a backboard in motion — but one would say not very "worldly." She lived alone on 14th Avenue and went downtown to office work, but the Club, as it was then for so many, was her *raison d'être*. However, possess a raging sense of humour she didn't. Nor did she understand the Colonel's joke and many times asked him to explain it. We wonder if he did.

Bill Crawford, Keith Verley, His Honour, and Richenda Crawford, cutting the cake at the opening celebration for our indoor courts (1972).

141

1970s

Wardair. "Sideburns" popular. Trudeau enacts Wage and Price Controls. False Creek Seawall completed. **1976** Jimmy Carter elected. Deng rules China. Sylvester Stallone's "Rocky". ABC's first female Anchor. Barbara Walters. Females become eligible for

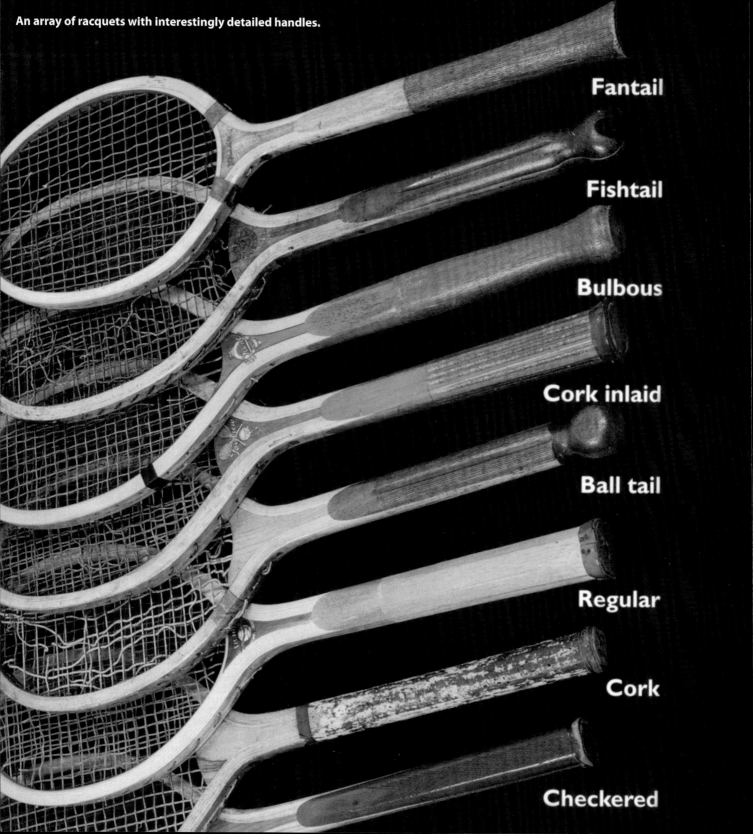

An array of racquets with interestingly detailed handles.

Fantail

Fishtail

Bulbous

Cork inlaid

Ball tail

Regular

Cork

Checkered

CHAPTER 8

Tools and Teachers of the Trade,

Etiquette, Prize Money, Table Tennis, Swimming, and Fitness

Tennis Racquets and Balls

Technology has regularly transformed the tennis racquet as well as the game. The racquet started as a fishtail handled affair, loosely strung with cat or sheep's gut. Then the excellent wood racquets appeared — Dunlop, Slazengers, Wilson, Bancroft, Wright, and Ditson, to name but a few — weighing between 12 and 14.5 oz. Today's racquets are even lighter — some as light as 8.5 oz. — and made of expensive metal, graphite, and ceramics, or their combinations. The frames have become much bigger, some even enormous, such as Head, Prince, and Yonex. The stringing has undergone several transformations as well, from gut to a variety of synthetics. Each change has caused a revolution in the game, even for duck bangers. Also, racquets seem to be a fashion statement at many clubs, with members rarely appearing without a plethora of large, high-priced racquets in an equally expensive and enormous bag. Hallmarks of affluence

An advertisement for Slazenger's Demon Fishtail racquet, c. 1900.

and no doubt big business for the suppliers.

The rules of tennis are silent as to the size, dimension, and weight of racquets, which over the years have taken on some strange shapes. Today's are all "wide-bodied," ranging from 95 square inches to the "oversize" of 115 square inches. This much lighter and more powerful weapon, combined with the new materials, has radically changed the

A flat-top racquet with a rare, beautifully inlaid handle, dating back to about 1885.

game. In times past, players used the classic "Eastern" grip with its graceful and sweeping strokes. Nowadays its the "Western" one to hammer and topspin the ball. From a spectator's perspective, those changes have enhanced the game, especially the men's, where play is characterized by longer rallies rather than by an overpowering serve followed by storming the net and putting away a volley.

Tennis balls, by contrast, have changed little from the early white felt English Spencer-Molton balls with their stitched seams. In 1925, Slazengers produced a white, rubberized, seamless ball that was sold in a six-pack cardboard box and became our first "official" ball. Since the advent of televised matches, several different coloured balls have been used — orange, pink, and the currently popular "optic" yellow. Wilson and Penn are today's favourites.

Tennis Coaching

The Club operates clinics for tennis, badminton, and squash. The junior tennis clinics, under the supervision of Head Pro Russ Hartley and his four assistants, are particularly well organized and popular. About 100 junior members are divided into five levels: the "Purely Recreational," the "Futures," the "Developmental," the "Competitive" for those demonstrating a strong commitment, and the "High Performance" group for juniors who show strong potential. Adult clinics are less aggressive and most are taught in groups.

And no, the best strategy is not, "lob short and storm the net." For as John Newcombe once said, "Tennis is hitting the ball when the other guy ain't." Those who lose can always seek solace from B.C.'s Gordon Shields' remarks after a doubles game in 1928, "They weren't better than we were, they just didn't miss as often!" or, "We lucked out." Losers are imaginative! The positive buzzwords are always changing — "Keep your eye on the ball, even to its seams! Concentrate! Never tank! Never give up! Keep in the groove! Focus! Play with intensity!" All good advice.

© Arnold C Buchanan-Hermit

1970s

Rhodes Scholarship. Romania's Nadia Comanesci gains first perfect score in Olympic gymnastics. Viking I lands on Mars. Parti Québecois founded. Summer Olympics in Montreal. Episcopalian church approves ordination of women. UBC'S museum of

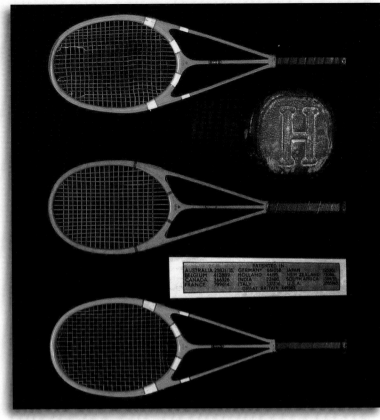

These Streamline racquets were made by Hazells of London, and date to the 1930s.

In his formative years, Russ Hartley played on grass at the Victoria Lawn Tennis Club. He later became pro at the Victoria Racquets Club and the Arbutus Club before coming to us in 1987. Under his tutelage, our Club juniors have excelled. Michael Levin was the Club's men's single champion from 1999 to 2001, and Stephen Kimoff in 2002 and 2003. Fifteen-year-old Kyle Sartorius won in 2004 and 18-year-old Ian Harvey in 2005. In the women's, Marina Levin triumphed from 1999 to 2003 and 13-year-old Rebecca Marino won in 2004 and 2005. Way to go, kids! Way to go, Russ!

The Club's coaching programs are supplemented and benefit from various league and inter-Club matches as well as all sorts of in-house competitions for all ages. The backboard and ball machines are in almost constant use and Hartley's observation that "the tennis program is jammed," especially on family nights, is spot on.

Tennis Serves and Etiquette

The Club's been blessed with many members who packed a powerful serve. Walt Stohlberg had the hardest of any, followed by Oscar Roels and Paul Willey (who in a match in the Canadian in 1952 smoked 21 aces). The most cunning ones belonged to our lefties, Bob Puddicombe and Art Jeffery. We had lots of colourful servers plus some of the goofiest, e.g., Erwin Elliott's almost backhand twist and twirl spun backwards, Sid Harold's behind-the-head, and Mel Scott's "boomer"— his convoluted windup rivalling Sikorsky's first helicopter! And mention has to be made of Fenner Douglas, wearing his black belt, and his sword-like pointing before he delivered. Unorthdox to be sure, but all were effective!

Frugal Mel Scott was quite a guy. He served several terms as a director — volunteered for just about any task, and working with Ed Kemble and The Yorkshire, he brokered all the Club's insurance. During World War II, he served as a lieutenant in the Seaforth Highlanders of Canada and was wounded by "friendly"

145

1970s

Anthropology. Jericho Beach's Habitat and Arthur Laing Bridge open. Welfare protesters storm B.C.'s Cabinet. **1977** Panama granted full control of Panama Canal. Alaska pipeline. Clog shoes. MRI. "Love Boat" on TV. Two 747s collide in Canary Islands—574

fire in Sicily, leaving him with a stiff right arm and a small pension. After the war during a tumultuous doubles game I bowled him over, causing more damage. "That's okay," Mel reassured, "Now I'll get my pension increased." He did. Also he's remembered fondly for consuming more peanuts in the Snake Room than anyone ever has or probably ever will!

Etiquette? Simple. Arrive on time. Properly call the lines. "Hmmph!" is acceptable, but give your opponents the benefit of a doubt, and keep quiet when they're serving. Al Stevenson's *Guide to Being Hated* was a hoot: "Never buy balls. Never promptly or directly return them to the server, nor those from a neighbouring court. Never correct an outrageous foot fault. And, blame everything, including the weather, on the Secretary Manager."

✦
146
✦

Tennis Prize Money — Odlum Brown — Hollyburn

In 1978 some money appeared for tourneys — $75 for B.C.'s Grand Prix Circuit. However three years later, Nike, Bekins Moving & Storage, and Penn Balls donated $30,000. B.C. was on a roll.

In 2004, Tennis BC, Tennis Canada, the brokerage firm Odlum Brown, and the Jericho Tennis Club, secured B.C.'s first Women's Tour Association Tournament. The resulting Odlum Brown Vancouver Open was a $100,000 event involving many top and upcoming female players from around the world. In 2005 The International Tennis Federation, along with the United States Tennis Association, Tennis BC, and Tennis Canada sponsored a 200-entry tournament at the Hollyburn Country Club in West Vancouver from July 30 to August 7. The prize money at stake was substantial — US$100,000 for the men and $25,000 for the women.

Directed by Hollyburn's miracle manager, former golf pro Ed McLaughlin, the tournament took place again in 2006 and was even more successful. Some 6,500 spectators went through the turnstiles and the club sold 40 boxes for $2,000 each. What a plant the Hollyburn Country Club is. It's the largest club west of Toronto and owns 49 beautifully vista'd acres, 20 of which are yet to be developed. The waiting list is long, and the 7,500 members enjoy indoor and outdoor hard courts, grass, and clay shortly to come. Badminton, squash, swimming, fitness, ice-skating, curling, and hockey are also available, not to mention fine dining.

The Women's Federation Cup — Hollyburn, 1987

The Hollyburn Country Club went on the world stage in 1987 when it hosted the Women's Federation Cup, involving two singles and one doubles team representing their countries. About 45 countries participated, with the Canadian contingent acquitting

die, worst aviation accident in history. Seabus inaugural run. **1978** Begin and Sadat sign Camp David Accord in the U.S. Disco. Test-tube babies. Diagnostic ultrasound. Coca Cola sells in China. "Evita". Gastown clock back to running on steam. B.C. develops

A display of Wilson racquets—all of them carry Jack Kramer's picture and/or autograph. Kramer started consulting for Wilson in 1947.

1992 Davis Cup Tie — Canada vs. Austria at Hollyburn

Buoyed (or "girled," to be more precise) by their success, Hollyburn took on the Canada vs. Austria Davis Cup in 1992. As host country, Canada decided to play on lawn courts, but Hollyburn didn't have any. Tennis Canada came to their rescue and at its expense, installed three courts. Lucky Hollyburn! The matches were spirited and Austria won 3-1. Pierre La Marche captained the Canadian team of Glen Michibata, Daniel Nestor, and Hollyburn's own Grant Connell.

Badminton Racquets and Birds

The evolution of badminton racquets has been less radical than that of tennis or squash. During the 1980s, players experimented with a "queen-sized" head, but it was clumsy, hence the egg-shaped model continues. As with tennis, the materials for its racquets have dramatically changed. First they were all wood and had to be kept in a wooden press when not in use to prevent buckling. They were gut strung — 12–15 lb. maximum. Nylon was tried but it was "flat" — didn't have the "feel." In the late 1950s a wood laminated head and metal shaft came into being, e.g., the 5 oz. Dunlop's Maxply. In 1972, racquets became yet lighter with the 3.7 oz. Carlton. Japan's Mr. Yokiyama introduced a carbon racquet in the late 1980s — the "Carbonex 8" — first used by the great Channerong. For today's skilled and experienced players, Yokiyama's "Yonex" is the racquet of choice. Contemporary graphite models, weighing from 75 to 84 grams and with synthetic strings, can be strung up to 30 lb. Overall costs range

147

itself well. Vancouver's Helen Kelesi beat Germany's Claudia Kohde Kilsch in an early round. Germany took the Cup, defeating the Americans. Steffi Graf beat Chris Evert, Kohde Kilsch took Pam Shriver, and the two Germans won the doubles. Several other big name players represented their countries, including the gorgeous Gabriela Sabatini from Argentina, Jana Novotna from Czechoslovakia (who had every stroke in the book), and Carling Bassett from Canada. Big-time tennis was being played in B.C.

1970s

from $100–$350, and size standards are regulated by the International Badminton Federation (IBF).

Today the bird is lighter. With the heavier models, players really had to "cream it," as Jeannie Bardsley said. The lighter bird, combined with the lighter and tighter-strung racquets, has resulted in much quicker and stronger shots. The rallies are longer, and good players can now smash and clear with their backhand. No question badminton has benefited.

Goose feathers attached to cork make the best birds. Plastic shuttles cost less and are suitable for beginners, but for the best feel and true flight, plastic cannot compare to mother or father goose. The feathers used to come from geese in Southeast Europe — three feathers plucked from the left wing. Now China's geese are the principal source. About 100 brands of birds are on the market, some of the most popular being RSL, Yonex, Black Knight, and Victor. A tube of 12 birds costs $20–$35.

Badminton Coaching and Prize Money

In the early days most of the Club's better players — Art Peel, Bev Rhodes, neat left-handed Nora Maw with her almighty smash, steady Jocelyn Pease, and others — would help our developing players for free, as also did a few schools in the 1970s and 1980s. Club member Ray Stevenson produced a 20-year "badminton dynasty" at St. George's and as a VLTBC member, took many team and provincial titles.

Ram Nyar came to the Club in 1999 from Winnipeg, succeeding Abdul "The Great" Shaikh as Club pro. As a level five coach, Ram, along with his assistants and volunteers, works with about 130 junior members plus 100 adult members who also gather for monthly dinner socials. His program covers promising "Guests of the Pro" such as Chris Lee. The juniors also participate in several International At-Homes in India, Scotland, England, Guatemala, Jamaica, the United States, Hong Kong, Australia, Singapore, New Zealand, Trinidad, Tobago, and Malaysia. They do get around. The attendees pay half their transportation and lodging costs and the Club's Legacy Fund takes care of the rest.

In 2006, Ram led the 10-person Canadian National Badminton Team to the Commonwealth Games in Melbourne. B.C.'s Lyndsay Thomson recently joined Ram as a coach.

The Club has several outstanding young players. Jimmy Van Ostrand won our men's singles in 2001 and 2002 and Tyler Hislop triumphed from 2003 until 2006, while also winning the Jamaica Open in 2003. Kate Woznow in 1997, 1998 and 2000; Davita Fuchs in 1999; Kristy Hislop in 2001 and 2002 — now on the University of Western Ontario team; Tory Hislop in 2003; and Danielle Bensles in 2004 and 2005, who also won the junior Nationals in Montreal. The Club's up-and-coming juniors include Tatjana Wimmer and Jeremy Chao, who captured bronze medals in the under-14 Nationals in Edmonton.

In Canada, badminton has not been nearly as commercial as tennis. In years past, winners of tourneys often used to get a ribbon or a miserable six-inch wooden ruler — the prize that Bert Jones and I won when he carried me through to a B.C. badminton "B"

©John Hill

1970s

Teresa in Calcutta. Jerry Falwell's U.S. Moral Majority. Sony Walkman. Trivial Pursuit. Isle of Man Parliament 1000 years old. Mountbatten blown up by IRA. Granville Island Market opens. CPR's last scheduled passenger train. Vancouver's new Law Courts

doubles. Bert was horrified! In later years a cup, a medal, or perhaps a free racquet were awarded — but until fairly recently no prize money. B.C. has a provincial "Best Out of the West Circuit" that consists of six or seven tournaments. Based on singles and doubles, the prize money ranges from $50 to $500 per person. The B.C. Closed tournament has $2,000 available with about $250 for the winners and $100 for second place. Depending on the budget, some additional national prize money is available, as well as some for international play, but overall, badminton does not attract big bucks as tennis does.

Badminton Serves, Grip, and Etiquette

Until the early 1980s, the standard serve for the singles game was as high as possible and right to the back line — a style that John Samis perfected. Some players tried short hard serves — driving the shuttle above their waist — which is clearly a callable fault. Wily Jimmie Forsythe, an excellent singles player and a huge supporter of badminton, got a great charge out of doing this. (Over the years he hired many Club members to assist him in his business interests — Tony Finnerty, Dick Hibbard, Art Jeffery and Sid Winsby.) However the more easily controlled backhand serve for both singles and doubles became, and still is, the standard serve. When it was first introduced, some even spun the serve — hitting the feathers first — to make the shuttle jump about. This tactic didn't last for long as the IBF affirmed the longstanding unwritten rule that the cork portion of the shuttle had to make primary contact with the racquet. The IBF had already ruled out wood shots — where the

shuttle made contact with the wood frame. The serve had to be clean to count. The player's grip on the racquet has not changed much, except that one's hand is now choked further up the handle for better leverage. And for increased flexibility, the racquet is held more loosely between the fingers.

Court etiquette has varied too. An opponent usually would retrieve a bird and gently return it over the net to the server. Now many players slide it along the floor and in tournaments, players no longer test the shuttles. Delay of play and "tipping" — the spreading or compressing of the shuttle's feathers — are not permitted, and if there is a problem, the umpire is quick to decide and can award penalty points if necessary.

The IBF has proposed some major changes in the game, ostensibly to make it more marketable and television friendly. Overall that game will be faster with a point awarded on every shot, not just on serves. Doubles will not have a second serve and games will go to 21 points. Deuces will require two points until 29, and then the first to reach 30 wins. Matches will be best two out of three. A 60-second break will take place when one side reaches 11 points and between games a two-minute break for a pause that refreshes.

Squash Play

Upon the advent of squash at the Club in 1961, I wrote an "edifying" (oh dear — pride of authorship!) two-page article categorizing squash as a "whirling, exhausting physical and often very rough and tough battle requiring power,

149

1980s

opened by Lord Denning. B.C.R.I.C. shares. Bill Bennett loses four seats but wins second term. **1980** Ronald Reagan elected President. Trudeau re-elected. John Lennon murdered. Ted Turner's 24-hour CNN news. Rhodesia becomes Zimbabwe. Iraq invades

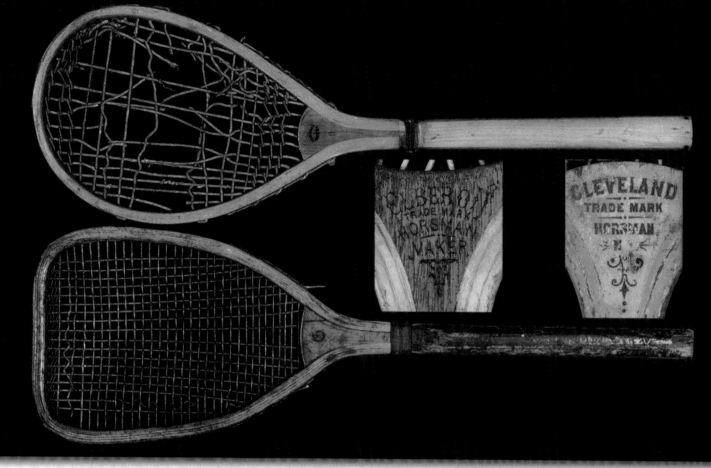

Early squash racquets, dating back to about 1885.

speed, endurance, racquet control, and cunning." The court is about the size of an upper middle class living room — 32 feet long, 18 feet 6 inches wide and 16 feet high. The game can be dangerous, for within this confined space players need to not only dodge the ball, which travels at over 125 mph, but also avoid the follow-through of the opponent's racquet. Fortitude is an enormous factor.

When compared to other racquet sports, the main attraction of squash is that a beginner can have as much fun and exercise and work up a just as good a sweat as an expert. As well, there is little inconvenience. If you book a court at five, you play at five. But book you must.

"Squash tennis" is a variation and uses a green ball similar to a small tennis ball and a racquet that looks like a small tennis racquet. It's played mainly in front of the T and the players are in a constant turn, spinning like a top. If you're not prone to dizziness, you'll have a good time. Squash tennis is much played along the Atlantic seaboard in the United States. Our Ed Kemble starred, and I often had a swell game with him. He well-dizzied me.

1980s

Iran. Roller blades. Canada, U.S., Japan and West Germany boycott Summer Olympics in Moscow. B.C.'s cancer fighter one-legged Terry Fox starts his cross-Canada run. Mount St. Helen erupts. Blackcomb opens. B.C. Penitentiary and Boeing's Sea Island

Squash Racquets and Balls

Squash racquets have not changed much over the years. The length has remained the same — 27 inches. The first models were wood with a 7.5-inch diameter head and strung with gut. Today most are of graphite with a somewhat larger and teardrop-shaped head — and much lighter and synthetically strung. As with tennis racquets, the size of squash racquets is not regulated. A Wilson, Dunlop, or Black Knight racquet costs about $145. The balls developed from the soft or "squashers," the golf-ball-hard, and the in-between compromise, which for singles is the Dunlop's Yellow Dot.

Squash Coaching and Prize Money

As mentioned previously, good friend Abdul was our first squash pro. Up till then one mainly learned on the job, but it is by far the easiest of the racquet sports to get the hang of. Now we're graced by Melanie Jans — a great enthusiast and a great player — Canadian-ranked No. 1 since 1999, world-ranked No. 25, and a Pan Am Games gold and silver medallist. In 2006 she received Premier Campbell's Athletic Award for squash. Good on you, Melanie. She runs our On-line Squash Ladder, Thursday Night League, Calcutta Doubles, plus all sorts of in and out of House Leagues, tournaments and junior sessions. Busy lady.

Apart from international pros, squashers are extremely amateur-oriented. Visitors were often billeted and occasionally transportation expenses were subsidized, but it wasn't until the late 1980s at the World Doubles Professional Squash Association

tournament that some moolah became available. International stars at exhibitions, special tournaments, and teaching clinics now receive something too. In December 2005, at the Saudi International, Jonathan Power of Montreal beat Anthony Ricketts of Australia three sets to one and garnered No. 1 world ranking. Way to go, Jonathan! Prize money totalled US$127,500. Way to go, Canada! And also, "Way to go!" to our Brad Desaulniers, who coached Power — then a 10-year-old — at the Montreal Athletic Club.

The Pro Shop

Initially it was run by Paul Willey and from the mid-1970s for 20 years by the gentlemanly Basil Favelle, and then for the next eight by our extremely accomplished tennis and squash star Reidar Getz. In 2005 the board awarded a contract to *Racquets and Runners*. The Club charges for a manager plus an operational contract, and the operator provides the merchandise and keeps the revenues from the sales.

Table Tennis

Ping pong (as table tennis was best known as) was most popular here. The table was at the north side of the main floor of the McLure clubhouse and it was always busy. And we had tournaments — singles and doubles — but unfortunately not so now. Let's hope they can be re-invigorated.

This game named "gossima, whiff-whaff," and later "ping-pong," which sprouted in the 1880s, enjoys quite a history. In London, F.H. Ayres Sporting Goods — subsequently to be absorbed by Slazengers — sold a "green baize court laid on the floor or on a table, with

151

1980s

plant close. **1981** Solidarity—Poland—Lech Walesa. AIDS rapidly increases. Prince Charles marries Lady Diana Spencer. Rene Levesque's Separatist Parti Québecois elected. News anchor Walter Cronkite leaves the air. President Reagan survives being

a light, but firm, knitted ball to avoid damage to furniture." A sponge rubber one followed. Celluloid balls arrived in 1901 and throughout the world table tennis' popularity took off.

Today the balls are white or orange and a little larger — 40 mm as opposed to the original 38 mm. Racquets are mostly "sandwiched" — wood, sponge, and rubber. In 2000 the scoring changed and now it's played to 11 points, not 21, with each player having two serves, not five. Deuce continues. However, apart from extensive training and the resultant skill of the competitors, little else has changed except the serve. Nowadays, the ball must rest in an open palm, and be elevated about 6.5 inches before it is struck. Squishing or spinning it onto the racquet constitutes a fault.

In 1926 the International Table Tennis Federation (ITTF) was formed. It subsequently standardized the tables, the balls, and the required floor space, which for competition is 40 by 20 feet. In 1929, tennis great Fred Perry won the table tennis World Championships in Budapest and that provided a boost. In 1988 it became an Olympic sport. Over 180 countries belong to the ITTF, and the number of table tennis competitors participating in World Championships ranks above those in the Olympic Games and World Cup Soccer! Amazing!

Our Club's Dr. Chandra Madhosingh is a wonder. He's coached, won the Canadian Team Championships from 1964 to 1966, has been president of the Canadian and B.C. Federation, and is also up-front and centre with the Olympic and Commonwealth Games. Most knowledgeable and a table tennis supporter bar none.

Swimming

The pool is in use year round and has enjoyed enormous popularity with members of all ages and been the venue for many events — the father-and-son and mother-and-daughter relays, the Tony Bardsley Dog Paddle Challenge, and the Timed Mile. The Club held meets with Crescent Beach and Richmond and for a time used the pool to successfully entice prospective members. For five bucks the Club gave them a swim and a drink plus a Patio Special. They liked that.

Swimming continues year round under bubble in winter and is mighty popular. There are lots of meets and no end of children have been taught — freestyle, breaststroke, backstroke, and butterfly. Also instruction is available leading to Red Cross life-saving status, synchronized swimming, and aqua-aerobics. Plus scuba diving and artificial respiration courses for the adults. Needless to say our ladies' swimsuits are eye catchers. Never before has so little meant so much to so many! Throughout we've enjoyed excellent teachers and lifeguards plus hosts of in-house events. It's family participated and has been a winner since day one, and today is led by Erin Wilkins and D.J. Feenstadt.

The Hot Tub, the Sauna, and the Steam Rooms

The Club's swirling hot tub, constructed in 1978, never fails to assuage aching muscles, as do the men's sauna and the two steam rooms. The Club's sauna was the first in Vancouver, thanks to squash-playing J. Ronald Grant, who discovered saunas, along with many other pleasures, while visiting Sweden. The

1980s

shot. Reagan fires 12,000 striking air traffic controllers. Egypt's Sadat shot by Islamic fundamentalists. CUPE strikes—garbage piles up on public tennis courts. Devonshire Hotel imploded. **1982** Canada's constitution repatriated from the U.K. Bank prime

Our Pool.

skipped rope, and some exercised à la Charles Atlas. Mark Lidster continues to take that route, do his own thing, and one fit son of a Kiwi is he!

In the early 1970s, Abdul, also started our first organized fitness program — with its popularity growing like Topsy. Involved running too. Tony Wooster, Dick Lyons, and Ian Turnbull accumulated hordes of miles. I remember Ian puffing into the Club, being teasingly asked if he'd just run to New Westminster and back, replying, "Yes, I did." Wow! Today Mark Mitchell thinks nothing of running from the Club around Stanley Park and return. Fit, fit. Whew.

Kate Le Blanc — our first full time fitness program instructor — followed Abdul and our cheery and very professional Amanda Lee took the helm from 2000 until 2006, when Heather Nivison took over. It's an in-house operation that has and does everything but tanning, and its increase in usage is enormous. It's open from 6.00 a.m. until 8.00 p.m. with classes and one-on-ones utilizing about $32,000 of equipment. Plus there's yoga, aerobics, and pilates (not Pontius). All of which is being even more utilized following the expansion of those facilities into our former TV room. The whole nine yards and quite a change from running, skipping, pushups, some weights, and stretching.

✦
153
✦

ladies got one too, but it was converted to a steam room in 1997. Before the men's steamer was constructed, an athletic male member in search of a little relaxing heat slipped into the ladies' facility late one night. No harm was done, however he was spotted and duly censured.

Fitness Machines and Programs

All of our top-flight racquet folk were fit — they had to be. Apart from playing, they mainly ran. A few

Emergency Response Procedure

In 2004 the Club produced an excellent Response Procedure to be followed in case anyone falls by the wayside for whatever reason, or there's a major calamity. Let's hope none of this will happen, but all of us should be prepared. So, read it!

1980s

lending rate rises to 22.75%. Falklands War—Thatcher vs. Argentina's Galtieri. Acid rain. Jimmy Connors takes McEnroe at Wimbledon. "Cats" opens on Broadway. Prince William born. First artifical heart. Clifford Olsen pleads guilty to murdering 11

Tennis juniors, 1964. Back row (L-R): Mark Tindle, John Kenmuir, Brian Baker, Norah Ashmore. Front row (L-R): Diane Baker, Janice Tindle, Bob Kaplan.

CHAPTER 9

Other Organizations

Funding Assistance For Our Juniors, and Awards For Our Outstanding Volunteers

National, Provincial, and Club Organisations

Tennis Canada, one of Canada's largest and oldest national sports associations, was founded in 1890. It is the parent non-profit organization for tennis, and is responsible for its development across the country. Our Bob Moffatt served as president from 1998 until 2004.

Similar associations soon came into being in Western Canada and the Northwest United States. The Pacific Northwest Association was started by Davis Cupper Bobby Powell in Victoria in 1902. It grew to include our grass courts, those in Victoria and Duncan, the hard courts at Multnomah and Irvington in Portland, the clay courts in Tacoma, and the B.C. Electric courts in Vancouver. In 1921, largely due to the leadership of E.J.H. Cardinall, three clubs in Victoria formed the British Columbia Lawn Tennis Association (BCLTA). In 1967, with Alan Skelton as editor, the BCTLA produced its first publication, *Court Lines*.

In 1986, Tennis BC was formed to promote and assist all levels of tennis in the province with a mandate emphasizing the five "Cs" — courts, clubs, clinics, coaches, and competition. A sixth soon followed — cash. Apart from its sponsors, donors, and contributors, Tennis BC receives funds from Tennis Canada's Athletes Assistance Program. Tennis BC soon became involved with many clubs as well as providing clinics in the elementary schools — currently 20,000 students take part. Tennis BC also maintains provincial rankings, plans more than 100 sanctioned and non-sanctioned annual events, and awards Tennis Canada's Coaching Certificates. During Bob Moffatt's term as executive director of Tennis BC, *Court Lines* was replaced by a new quarterly, *Match Point*, under the enthusiastic leadership of publisher Rick Angus and editor Denise DesLauriers. Today it enjoys a readership of some 20,000.

Funding Assistance for Our and Other B.C. Juniors

Apart from the never-ending generosity of the parents of junior members, the Club's first formalized funding assistance was provided by Walt Stohlberg — an ex- RCAF prisoner of war, and a 1948 and 1949 Davis Cupper — and Brian Bramall. Together they founded the Stohlberg/Bramall Fund for Club juniors in the early 1950s. In 1958 it was melded into the more extensive fund of the then new B.C. Patrons Association, incorporated by yours truly, which financially assisted promising juniors throughout the province, plus $100 bursaries for a few attending UBC.

Brian Cavendish, another of our energetic "down-unders," took the helm of the Patrons and worked many wonders. In 1960, the Patrons instituted the prestigious "Mr. Tennis Award," with its first recipient being our famed E.J.H. Cardinall. A year later, the Patrons formed an "Import Plan," whereby foreign players were brought to our region to compete in local and Pacific Northwest events. Canadian Pacific Airlines donated a trophy and financially assisted the Stanley Park Tournament. In addition the Patrons provided $6,000 to help build the four public courts on

Dr. Donald B. Rix

Granville Park — part of our agreement with the City for closing 15th Avenue beside the Club. They also sponsored a six-week course — $3 for juniors and $5 for seniors! — at seven public courts in Vancouver. In 1983 the Patrons became part of Tennis BC, and in 1997 the B.C. Community Youth Foundation took over.

A more recent funding project is the Rix Rookie Tour for Boys and Girls (ages eight to 14), financed by Club member Dr. Donald B. Rix. It includes 21 events province-wide and has proven to be the starting ground for many of B.C.'s promising tennis juniors.

Our Members' Legacy Fund

The Club continued to explore ways to assist the development of its promising players. In 1995, thanks to the leadership of Peter Jackson and Lois Ker, we established the Members' Legacy Fund to provide some dollars — primarily for travel expenses — for the development of our high-performance junior members in the three racquet sports. Recently, a total of $2,700 was made available to Rebecca Marino and Ian Harvey (tennis), and to Danielle Bensler (badminton). Funds are sourced from donations, which currently are not tax deductible. Half of the annual donations is available for grants while the remaining half is placed in an interest-bearing endowment, with about $48,000 now on hand. Also Rick Angus, assisted by Peter Jackson, "sweetened the deal" by importing and donating some excellent long-distilled "highland dew" from Scotland. Nice guys. Make a donation. Get a bottle! Unrelated to this, in 2005 Tennis Canada honoured Rick for his outstanding support for tennis over the years and awarded him its Distinguished Service Award.

1980s

children. B.C. Place's inflated dome - world's largest. **1983** — Reagan denounces Communism - "Focus of evil in the modern world". Thatcher's second term. Poland's Lech Walesa awarded Nobel Prize. U.S. invades Grenada. Apple computer. Mouse. Michael

In August 2006, we hosted our 8th Annual Legacy Clay Court Challenge with a record number of teams and great players. Bob Wright's squad, which included the Bardsley brothers and Don McCormick, took the honours. The event raised $1,000 for the Lower Mainland Youth Racket Sport Charities and $1,000 for the Legacy Fund.

The Martini Club

Upon the request of the Legacy Committee, the board agreed to formalize the "Martini Club," to which its members would twice a year donate $37.50, to be followed by an annual "On-the-House" Martini Tasting for the donors. The concept was spawned by Ian Adam. He'd buy one, then donate the price of another to the fund and soon it caught on. A dandy initiative with already over 60 contributors.

Rebecca Marino

Olive, onion, and a twist, please.

In 2005 our then 14-year-old Rebecca Marino, our all round athlete from Magee Secondary School, became the youngest ever women's singles champion at the 74th Rogers Open at Stanley Park. She repeated the feat in 2006. Since its inception in 1931, the Rogers Open has become North America's largest community tennis tournament. Rebecca also won — for the third time — our Club's ladies singles, and is now the top-ranked player in B.C.'s Open singles. She was privately tutored by former Washington Huskies Coach Wes Nott and most recently by Henry Choi.

In June 2006 she was recognized by the Martini Club's "Big Olive." Following which, she played an exhibition match against Bob Bardsley and with her almighty serve, bested him 6-4, 6-3. Wouldn't her great-great-grandfather William Farrell, who leased the Vancouver Lawn Tennis Club its land in 1898, be proud!

Honorary Life Members and the Bill Keenan Award

Honorary Life Members, as described in the Club bylaws, are members recommended by the board for outstanding service to the Club and elected by Special Resolution at a General Meeting. Over the years a few have been elected, but since 2005 we've only two — Ken Meredith and me.

The distinguished Bill Keenan Award and trophy was initiated in 1998. The award recognizes a member who has best demonstrated devotion and caring for the Club and who has volunteered his or her advice and assistance above and beyond the call. Bill Keenan was the first recipient. In 2000 it was awarded to Bill Crawford, in 2002 to Doug Shellard, and in 2005 to Herb Evers.

157

1980s

Jackson's "Beat It". $3,000 car telephones. Australia wins America's Cup for the first time in 132 years. Soviets shoot down Korean airliner. Crack. 40,000 Solidarity rally in Vancouver. . Bill Bennett's government re-elected. New Westminster's Royal Columbian

Harold and Mary Haggart, 1945. The Haggart Cup is as much a social event as a tennis competition.

CHAPTER 10

The Haggart Cup

Bowen Island, The South Cowichan, Cribbage, Showers, and so forth

The Haggart Cup

There's always lots of spirited activity and many chuckles at the VLTBC. Of all our events, our parties, and ongoing happenings, one of the most enduring and popular features has been the annual competition for the Haggart Cup — donated in 1945 by Harold and Mary Haggart for tennis mixed doubles handicap for married couples. Mary was an excellent player and reached the finals of the women's doubles in the Canadian championships of 1934.

The handicapping was something. Jim and Jean Bardsley won and won and once even faced having a minus 50. That was a record, especially as some of their opponents were plus 40. Les and Freda Mason were not in the Bardsley's class, but quite a team. Sturdy Freda was punishing at the net and "No Strokes" Les made all the returns and could run like a deer. A few of our male hot shots wanted to win at any cost, so they scooted their wives off the courts, almost played sin-gles, and relentlessly drilled the ball at their hapless female opponents. Not the best of form. Genial Harold and Mary, who were excellent hosts at their impressive Tudor

Haggart Cup winners, 1965. Garde and Helen Gardom (and Kim).

home on Beach Avenue with its enormous fish aquarium, mended all spats.

For divorce lawyers, the Haggart Cup was a bonanza! Well do some members recall a man bellowing at his beloved, "Get out of the way, fatso, I'll get it!" She didn't and nor did he! But in trying, he ran into the stone wall at the south end of our grass courts and knocked himself senseless. They made up — but it took a while.

Apart from matrimonial hazards, the Haggart Cup was as much a social as a tennis occasion. However, in reality there were few rows and most participants behaved exceptionally well, like Sid and Shirley Kaplan — the latter who at one time had sung with the famous Glenn Miller.

Partying – Sometimes Too Much – and Rental Revenues

As in any social club, the directors faced problems with our members. Some of the miscreants were amusing, however a few were anything but. Most often the villain was an oversupply of the demon rum or demon whatever. At one stag party a long-time member and politician invited as his guest a provincial court judge, only to have an overly lubricated member hurl insults at His Worship. An observer wrote a furious letter to the president who, after apologizing on behalf of the Club, hauled the offending member on the carpet.

Some year later the directors had to deal with five male members who had invited two "ladies" (who weren't members, and certainly not "ladies") into the men's locker room. The board took a serious view and

160

Deryk and Grace Leader, winners of the Haggart Cup in 1952 and 1962.

newspaper ceases publication. Vancouver Art Gallery moves into refurbished old Courthouse. The Queen and Prince Philip arrive in "Britannia" and invite the World to Expo '86. **1984** Bhopal explosion in India. Indira Gandhi assassinated. Arnold

suspended them for a month, a ruling that was successfully appealed as being unnecessarily hasty and harsh. In review, two of the accused were acquitted and the suspensions for the remaining three were commuted to one week. Art Jeffery and his sister recall a much wilder occasion some 50 years ago, when an amorous tosspot had an *affaire de coeur* on a chesterfield in full view of everyone. Again, the lady was no "lady," nor a member, and the member — who was no "gentleman" — was summarily expelled.

Sometimes, but fortunately very occasionally, a function can get a little out of hand, as did a lavish private affair on New Year's Eve 2004. A member took almost all the responsibility for the organization of the event, assuming the cost of promotion, security, music, décor, and additional insurance, as well as selling the tickets, mainly to outsiders — some 700 — at $75 each. The Club assumed the cost of the post-party clean-up and received 100% of the beverage and other sales revenue. Apart from an accidentally shattered window in the pub, which the host replaced, the evening was successful and the Club netted about $15,000.

The income was attractive, but discussion quickly spread as to whether the Club should be rented for "outsider" events, or should it only be used for members' meetings, receptions, meals, weddings, wakes, and the like. Also, whether a director should be present at anything beyond that. While searching for a solution, the directors had to consider the competing priorities. The Club needed the revenue that large functions generated. In 2004 the annual August Pool Party, with about 700 attendees and no damage, net-

ted $24,796, and in 2005, $18,740. However the Club is not a commercial undertaking, and the directors had to keep the interests of members foremost in mind, which called for a compromise.

As a result of their deliberations, in June 2005 the directors promulgated a Functions Policy with several conditions. All events would end at 1.00 a.m. except New Year's Eve, when the curfew was extended to 2.00 a.m. Every function would require a sponsor and the Club would not permit advertisement to the general public for any event where liquor was served. Regular and long-standing functions would require a deposit of $500 and for functions during the Christmas season $1,000. The annual August Pool

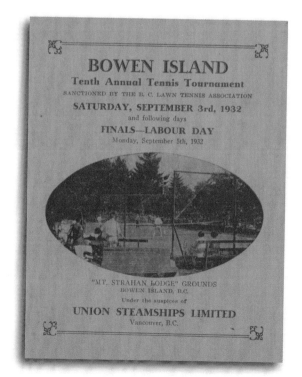

161

Schwarzenegger's "Terminator". Bill Cosby. Tutu receives Nobel Prize. Trudeau resigns. Soviets boycott Summer Olympics in L.A. Britain agrees to return Hong Kong to China in 1997. Granville Island Lager goes on sale. Vancouver Sun and Province strike

Party would be capped at 725 attendees — a member could buy seven admissions and use five of them to invite non-members. To placate a neighbour of the Club, still upset about the Club's noisy New Year's Eve parties, the directors offered him and his wife complimentary hotel accommodation for the following New Year's Eve. He accepted. And finally it was decreed, that member access to the pub and to historic buffet events such as Easter, Thanksgiving and the Wassail would always be available — a formal affirmation of the Club's unwritten policy for many years.

The Bowen Island Bash

In the 1920s, the Bowen Island Clay Court tournament marked the end of the tennis season. It was a big event on the social calendar, with devotees boarding a Union steamship in Vancouver and cruising on what became heralded as the "Booze Cruise" to Bowen Island, where they stayed at the Union's picturesque Mount Strathcona Lodge. The tournament, interspersed by rounds of never-ending parties and excellent meals, went on for three days. In the mid-1950s it came to an end when the lodge burned to the ground and the Union Steam Ship Line went out of business. Too bad — it is missed

The South Cowichan Sectionals

For many Club members, the small laid-back South Cowichan Lawn Tennis Club annual tourney in Duncan, B.C., was an event unto itself. The club hosted the Pacific North West Sectionals and its Open. Lots of big name players participated: Seattle's Jack Lowe, the Clegg brothers — Big Bear and Little

Bear — Jim Brink, Mel Dranga and his white poodle, Bob Caldwell, and Portland's Big Emery Neale. Also participating were our "Doggy" and Cy Craig — martinets disguised as starters — as well several other Club luminaries, with the most expert players receiving small honorariums. Most of them found time to hook a salmon! Mel Scott attended the event for years, combining it with his expense-paid business trip to visit his Yorkshire clients on Vancouver Island.

Cowichan had its six grass courts, some surrounded by enormous western broad-leaf Canada maples. Above one of the courts nearest the friendly but dilapidated clubhouse a huge tree limb about nine feet high stretched across half of a court. The ground rules stipulated that if a player hit the ball into the branch or leaves, he or she lost the point. On one occasion a player, Hackaway Daly, hit the ball into the tree on match point. He almost convulsed, but the tree prevailed and he forfeited the point. And then there is the unsubstantiated tale of Jim Bardsley playing a ball that had become lodged in a branch. It didn't come down so Jimmy climbed up — claiming that the rule didn't apply — and, as only Jimmy could, played it whilst aloft! Merton Lechtzier in the first round always faced the top seed. Poor Mert.

The club and the tournament it hosted was delightfully unique. It was not uncommon to see members white-washing the lines, or an ancient horse, clothed with a hat and four felt slippers, pulling a roller over the dew-drenched lawn. The club served up cucumber and watercress sandwiches, sponge and gooey-iced cakes, salmon titbits, as well as cider at 25¢ a shot. The outdoor privy was always busy! And wasps! Wasp City.

1980s

for 7 weeks. Woodwards opens on Sundays. Michael Jackson entertains 60,000 in Vancouver. Pope John Paul II and Billy Graham visit. **1985** Gorbachev's Peristroika and Glasnost. Whitney Houston's "Saving All My Love for You". Aretha Franklin's "Who's

We had a wonderful time at the sectionals, playing tennis all day, partying all night, fishing at dawn (or "Sparrow Phart," as Colin Walker used to say), and then making to the Anchor Café for breakfast, with "Goodnight Irene, Irene Goodnight" playing continuously. Ed Kemble, not noted as a swinger, must have heard it 20 times, yet asked, "That's a catchy tune. What is it called?" Little sleep, sore muscles, and fatigue were part and parcel of the Cowichan experience.

"Baby" and the "Black Job" bunked at the nicknamed "No Tell Motel." Jack Margach coined "Enid, a Beautiful Morning?" — Enid being Hugh Campbell's cute Australian wife. Jimmie Longborn manned the gate. Bob Caldwell's car trunk was chock full of ice, mixer, and everything that went with it, as was the car of Duncan's Edwin Jackson. One rainy night, Artie accidentally flipped a tennis friend's car. With its wheels still spinning in the air, Artie confidently said, "No problem, I can drive it out!" He didn't, but later relieved himself in Colin Walker's pocket. In those days, "road rage" didn't exist.

One year Colin broke his ankle while playing mixed doubles with Jeannie Bardsley. His next match was the men's doubles with Art Jeffery. Refusing to default, he froze his ankle and they won their match. Those Aussies are tough blokes! There was Jack Churchill threatening, "Take the hands off the threads, man." And Stan Hayden asking a member who was toting a freshly caught 35 lb. Spring, "Any luck?" Plus a well-lubricated Ed Kemble hosting a cocktail party and calling Colin Walker "Wally." The name stuck!

In July 1977 the South Cowichan celebrated its 110th birthday, hosting a rousing dinner at Duncan's Inn at the Water. Much flowed, but it wasn't water! All of Cowichan Lawns's notables were there — including Kay Staples and Jeff Hunter — and visitors and well-wishers came from farther abroad, including the VLTBC and the United States. Kay Scott and I spoke. Many reminiscences: The gawd-awful outhouse, which Mel Scott nearly fell in; the "Breakfast of Champions" — one-third brandy, two-thirds port — which was guaranteed insulation for fishing at sunrise; and the yummy teas — wasps notwithstanding! For our First Nations people, "Cowichan" means "land warmed by the sun." And, we'd say, by South Cowichan's hospitality too.

The Club's 29th Indoor Masters

This "Open" tourney started in 1977 and continues to ace, attracting all sorts of durable seniors, both male and female. In April 2006, under tournament director Lois Ker and official referee David Oulet, 285 players took part, playing 384 matches, best two out of three. Eighty-three Club members competed, of whom 19 were either winners or finalists. Club Pro Russ Hartley won the men's under-45 singles, and Ronnie Ng the men's under-75 doubles. The women's under-40 singles, and their 60-70 doubles were taken respectively by Phyllis Money and Annie Oakey. The participants were a lively lot, required lots of liniment, and told tall tales throughout! An excellent stand-up reception followed the matches, with table upon table of delicious edibles. Tournament Chairman John Fraser, together with the representatives from the donors, HSBC and Wilsons, said a few words.

163

1980s

Zooming Who". TV's "Golden Girls". Paraplegic Rick Hansen starts his around the world wheelchair tour. Federal Government issues apologies to Japanese Canadians. Skytrain opens. B.C. Lions win Grey Cup. Greenpeace's Rainbow Warrior – David McTaggert

Ever-Popular Crib

Cribbage, first called "Noddy", was invented by Sir John Suckling in the early 17th century. And, according to some buffs, it's about as close to a way of life as religion, a spirited woman, fine wine, or newly-baked bread. Bridge was always popular at the Club, with duplicate lessons provided by the many-mastered "Flip" Wood. Bingo, backgammon, darts, and whist also had their supporters, as did blackjack, roulette, and poker at the stags. But eventually crib took over — especially low-stake games with soup and

LUCKY DOUG
"THE PERFECT HAND"
October 16, 1987   V.L.T.B.C.

a sandwich at noon. Regular participants included George Carter, Dick Hibbard, Mert Lechtzier, Tom Osler, Rex Jackson, Les Mason, Sid Winsby, Sandy Robertson, Bob Wade, Tim Hugman, Brian Bramall, Richard Raibmon, Ron Weber, Wild Bill Keenan, and Doug Shellard—who got a perfect 29 hand. His plaque hangs in the Snake Room.

Apart from the noon scene and evening games for dinner, our first annual cribbage tournament was held in 1981 — "Doubles and Singles." There was no seeding, and the cards, the board, arm bands, and the visors were supplied for an entry fee of $2. In the

singles, the Old Master George (the "Duke") Carter took on Sandy "Rack" Robertson. Esther Carter and Rosemary Winsby whipped Robertson and Bob Wade in the doubles. Carl Rennix donated a trophy in 1988 and since then, its big-time winners are Dick Hibbard and Merton Lechtzier, who've partnered for over 20 years. However the overall champ clearly is "Tricky Dickie" Hibbard, who has enjoyed more victories in more tourneys with more partners than any other player. Congratulations, "Admiral!"

Darts

At the VLTBC idle we ain't, for we're always doing something on the courts or in the pool, the exercise parlours, the bar, and the many eateries. Cards and backgammon are popular, and we have darts in the pub — for a pub is not a pub without darts. Play for a drink or whatever. Sometimes tourneys. And with darts, once more with their hand-eye coordination, usually our best athletes prevail. Sid Winsby and Sandy Robertson could run up an almighty score. Doesn't seem to be played much now.

loses an eye. Boris Becker at 17 becomes youngest man to win Wimbledon. **1986** Reagan, Ollie North - Nicaragua Contras funding. Reagan meets Gorbachev at Reykjavic and refuses to stop SDI. Chernobyl disaster. "Phantom of the Opera". Prince Andrew

Man's Best Friends

Erwin Elliott would say that was anyone who ponied up a bottle of Hudson's Bay Rye, but here we're referring to dogs on the Club's premises. Against all regulations, a member who insisted on bringing his "mutt" into our grounds and fouling them was suspended for a month. Then a year later for two months for a second offence. But it was not always thus — for there are dogs, and dogs. Colonel Leader had two English bulldogs that he would bring to the Club and which, apart from their incessant drooling,

David Strachan, aka "Doggy!"

behaved themselves. Also it was the feisty Colonel who, capriciously observing the resemblance and honouring his beasts, looked at David Strachan and said "You dog face, you!" — That term of affection stuck and David became "Doggy" forever.

Locker Room Showers, Towels, and Accessories

Over the decades, probably there were more justifiable beefs about our showers than anything else. E.g., in 1953, "They're shocking." But for two good showers in the men's locker room. This appears to continue. Déjà vu all over again. All too plastic. Too small. Too slippery. A lack of hand rails. Some wimpy shower heads. Criticisms also ranged from temperature control, pressure, and for too often being out of service. About these, the Building Committee's Bill Keenan was unmercifully and constantly hectored, although in a kindly manner.

In 2001, we spent $10,525 for 18,000 disposable razors. Big beards. And changing the men's aftershave lotion resulted in complaints. Worse was when the men got hairdryers. Some beefed about the noise, others were horrified that a man would even think of using a hair dryer, albeit noisy or quiet. Also, and as now, the directors were more than infrequently concerned about the members' misuse of the locker rooms, the most common being leaving valuables on the benches or in unlocked lockers — an open sesame to thievery.

When we provided large new towels, once 177 were "lost" (taken?) in the first five weeks. And some members used them excessively, but it's better than slipping on a wet floor. Also no end of members, when they're finished, never put them into the bins. One doubts if any of us would get away with that at home. But their disappearance continues, notwithstanding various *Hi-Lights* admonitions:

> Semi-annual reminder to the effect that TOWELS still seem to find their way out of the Club, and do not appear able to find their way back. Should you find any sneaky towels nesting in your residence, please return them — if they need a thorough scolding and lecture, we'll do that.

165

marries Sarah Ferguson. Lions Gate Bridge illuminated. City of Vancouver becomes 100 years old. Expo '86 is opened by Prince Charles and Princess Diana. P.M. Margaret Thatcher, V.P. George Bush and all sorts of Heads of State, and Princess Margaret

And more:

> Please return to the Club any towel that may have inadvertently found its way to your home. In two months some 300 were involved in a mass exodus; their counterparts in the Club are lonely.

In 2001 over 3600 towels disappeared at a cost of $11,000.

To end on a lighter note, a player was once asked why he didn't take a shower after his match. He replied, "I've just been hosed by Bob Bardsley!"

Grits, Grub, and Bills of Fare

Since the days of our McLure clubhouse we've always enjoyed good food, and some better than others. From our teas, and high teas — and it was always an honour to be asked to pour — from our players' and junior lounges, and snack bars. From our pool, patio, and special functions, and from our more formal dining room. And, it's always been imaginative, providing good value for the dollar and most often well utilized, however, never enough to create a needed profit. We couldn't do without our food chain but profitable it isn't, so one way or other, it's always been subsidized, plus a minimum charge which reared its head in the 1980s. Bob Thorpe novelly suggested in 1986 that one's bar bills should be offset. Didn't happen.

Cigarettes and Whisky

Smoking and drinking in the Club have always been topics of discussion. In the early years, cigarette smoking was widely accepted, so the Club's regulations made no reference to it. Pipes and cigars, however, generated some controversy, especially in our dining areas. For a time they were tolerated, with the directors even considering providing "ecologizer" ashtrays, designed to keep them out of sight and eliminate the odours of cigar stubs and pipe dottle. As in society at large, now all forms of smoking inside our premises is prohibited and today that is graciously accepted.

Liquor licenses, rules, and regulations shaped much of B.C.'s lifestyle from the wide-open times of the Gold Rush and Gassy Jack's Globe Saloon in present-day Gastown. And liquor's always been a moneymaker. At the turn of the last century, a man could go to the bar at the old Hotel Vancouver and buy a beer for a nickel, a schooner for a dime, or two shots of whisky for a quarter plus all the food he could eat. Wouldn't that be nice today?

The United States introduced prohibition in 1920 and a well known but equally disregarded Vancouver family brewed during the day but ran rum and whisky across the border at night. "Speakeasies" flourished in the United States, well stocked by enterprising Canadians. In B.C., liquor was not available, apart from at a few golf and other private clubs that the Liquor Control Board (LCB) licensed. Here it was strictly BYOB — bring your own bottle — until 1954, when a Dining Lounge License let us buy a drink provided it was accompanied by a meal. With the advent of our new clubhouse in 1957, members could drink in the bar, which is now the Boardroom. Its windows were deliberately set high, as the LCB folk didn't want our well-used bar to upset the neighbourhood! It didn't.

1980s attend. The anticipated attendance of 14M tops 22M. Vander Zalm becomes Premier. Alex Fraser Bridge opens. Bank of B.C. sold to Hong Kong Bank. Jamaica Joe Fortes - who died in 1922 – named Vancouver's Citizen of the Century. Sun Yat Sen Gardens

"Beer then cost 55¢ and now $4.50 for a bottle and $5.50 for draft. A coke cost 25¢ and now $2. A cup of coffee was 15¢ and today it's $1.75."

The most purchased brands then were Johnny Walker and Dewars Scotch, Gordon's Gin (vodka was then not "in"), and imported wine — then B.C.'s wines were barely a step above paint remover and not excellent as they are today. It wasn't until the mid-1970s that members could enjoy a drink poolside, but male members could always belt one in our senior men's locker room! In those days the drinking age was 21 and in public establishments to get a drink you had to buy food. B.C.'s beer parlours were even more austere, with a ban on music and food and no fraternisation with the opposite sex. And available to "men only," unless there was a "ladies and escorts" section.

In 1957 the Club's corkage fee for a bottle was 75¢. A comparison of prices between the 1970s and the present provide yet another reminder of how times have changed. Beer then cost 55¢ and now $4.50 for a bottle and $5.50 for draft. A coke cost 25¢ and now $2. A cup of coffee was 15¢ and today it's $1.75. Cocktails or mixed drinks ran from 85¢ to $1 and are now $4.25 and up — and this is for a 1 oz. mixed drink or a 2 oz. martini. However the famous "Mallory" (Smith) Martini was larger, cost more, and did more! Corkage fees are now LCB prices plus $10–$12 a bottle. Add to all of this the Club's minimum food charge and it becomes clear that both the Club and the government do well, but our members pay, pay and pay.

Mercifully, apart from a few members sometimes being over-served, liquor in the Club has never caused significant problems. And apart from dues and entrance fees, the sale of alcoholic beverages is our only consistent money-maker. So wine bibbers, beer drinkers and liquor imbibers of the world unite and a toast to it! But drink responsibly, remember CounterAttack, and do not drink and drive.

✦
167
✦

open. **1987** Black Monday - $22.6B of stocks tumble, doubling the 1929 loss. Supreme Court of U.S. orders Rotary to admit women. AIDS becomes epidemic worldwide. Condom commercials on TV. Rick Hansen completes his 26 month tour around the

Left to Right:
A. W. Jeffery,
Jack Pedlar,
Jandi Fraser,
Chuck Underhill.

Left to Right:
Ronnie Ng,
Scott Pothast,
Ed Kendall,
Brenda Cameron.

Left to Right:
Sally Cates,
Sandy Sutherland,
Tony Bardsley,
Bob Bardsley

CHAPTER 11

1972-1993 • Accomplishments

More Tennis, Badminton and Squash Stars, Gifts to the Club, and the Snake Room

During this period and from 1993 on, our racquet sports thrived. However, in a sense the golden years of play had passed and its level never returned to that of the earlier years. Only a few members achieved significant success in open competitions, although several excelled in seniors' and masters' events.

Tennis in the Olympics

Tennis was first admitted to the Olympics in 1896 and play continued until 1924. From then until 1988, tennis was not included apart from two demonstration events, one in 1968 and another in 1984, which eventually led to its reinstatement on the Olympic Calendar. In 1988, Canadians Carling Bassett and Jill Hetherington won the longest doubles match in Olympic history, defeating the Argentine twosome of Mercedes Paz and Gabriela Sabatini 7-6, 5-7, and 20-18. In 2000, Canada's Daniel Nestor and Sébastian Lareau captured the gold medal in men's doubles. To date, Steffi Graf enjoys the best overall record in singles play — 10 wins, one loss — an impressive feat which included winning the gold medal in 1988 and the silver in 1992. She also won the demonstration event in 1984.

More VLTBC Tennis Greats

The year 1974 saw saw the demise of the Western Canadian, but carry on we did. In Club singles, Mike Bolton with three victories, and the Bardsley brothers — Tony with four and Bob with three — were the best. Although not a member when he was winning major tournaments, Don McCormick earned renown in 1991 by taking the over-45 World championship in Australia. He, Tony, and Larry Barclay also played

> ❝Skiing also became big time, and in other clubs, skating and hockey too. For in Vancouver now there was much more to do.❞

Davis Cup when Jim Skelton and Fred Bolton were the non-playing captains. At Mont Tremblant in the Senior Nationals, Bob Bardsley took the over-60 singles and with Don McCormick the doubles. Among our younger competitors in the '70s, John Nicolls was top drawer. Besides his badminton prowess, he played, and still plays, excellent tennis. In 1980 and 1998 he won our Club's tennis singles — another example of a talented racquets player who crossed over.

Amongst our female tennis players, Janice Tindle was a standout. Coached by Abdul Shaikh, she won the Canadian Closed singles in 1972 and 1973 and became the top-ranked Canadian after having edged her way up since 1967, when she held ninth place. Janice shares with Susan Butt the distinction of having played doubles on the centre court at Wimbledon in 1969. More recently our Club singles has been dominated by Mrs. Tutu Mahal, who won it six times since 1980, and Miss Marina Levin, who took the title five times from 1999 until 2003.

The Starr–Reynolds and Denny–Cardinall Matches

The first international tennis event in which the Club competed was the Starr–Reynolds Matches, wherein member clubs of the Pacific Northwest Lawn Tennis Association played annually in a Davis Cup format — four singles and one doubles. Initiated in 1910, it was discontinued several years ago, replaced by the regional Denny-Cardinall tournament, named after Victor Denny of Seattle, past president of the United States Lawn Tennis Association, and our E.J.H. "Cardy" Cardinall. Once every three years, B.C., Washington, and Oregon select players over the age of 45 to play in each region. Club members who have competed include Art Jeffery, Jim Skelton, Jack Pedlar, and Chuck Underhill — son of the eminent badminton player Jack Underhill.

Badminton — Level of Play

During this period, it was down from former years and particularly noticeable, Jean Bardsley said, among those in their late teens and early twenties. Abdul Shaikh agreed, saying that there was considerable interest among the juniors, but at the age of 19 or 20, they went on to university and other endeavours. Jean thought that their involvement was lessened not only because of college but also by virtue of our indoor tennis and its year-round play. Skiing also became big time and in other clubs, skating and hockey too. Yes, in Vancouver now there was much more to do. Fortunately many returned as they reached their 30s and 40s.

Our junior development, with many promising youngsters presided over by Shaikh and assisted by the dedicated Doug Shellard, was most encouraging. They started with five- and six-year olds, teaching

1980s

world. Queen Elizabeth II attends Commonwealth Leaders' Conference in Vancouver and grants B.C. its revised Coat of Arms. Expo '86 flagpole - the world's highest - sold to Guilford. Trade and Convention Centre opens. Meech Lake Constitutional proposals.

them the feel of a racquet, how to judge the flight of a bird, plus eye-to-racquet coordination. In six weeks a 10-year-old novice could progress to the point of enjoying rallying. Deserving youngsters were moved to play in a higher age group and also given a chance to play with seniors. Those who showed real promise got additional court time and as much play with competent seniors as could be managed, plus advanced coaching — the principles of our program being those established by Badminton Canada.

Also, badminton attracted more and more tennis players, particularly those not akin to squash. Saturdays and Sundays drew huge numbers — you got a quick sweat and had many a laugh and in the mixed, the girls were cute beyond description. One of our habitués was Dudley Meakin — a truly grand fellow. He was on the Building Committee for about forever, plus he owned, along with Jim Spilsbury, his *Blythe Spirit,* in which Captain Dud took his tennis pals on many a fishing expedition and was the inspiration for a great 25-paragraph poem by Tom and Laurel Osler. We love this excerpt:

> Behold the fisherman!
> He riseth early in the Dawn
> And disturbeth the whole household.
> Mighty are his preparations.
> He goes forth full of hope
> And when the day is well spent
> He returneth,
> Smelling of strong drink
> And, the truth is not in him.

"Uncle" Dud's fun philosophy was, "Spend your money or your heirs will," of which his pretty wife "Gladi" more than occasionally cheerfully reminded him. Dudley was good at badminton, but loved to crosscourt drop — a real "no-no" in doubles. So we'd always ask him not to. And he always agreed. But, he always did, cheerfully singing — which was not his long suit — "Oh, it's hard to be humble."

Optimism about the future of badminton in B.C. and in Canada grew and grew, aided and abetted by it becoming a British Empire and Commonwealth Games (now Commonwealth Games) sport in 1966 at Jamaica, plus an Olympic sport in 1992 at Barcelona. In the 1994 Commonwealth Games in Victoria, the three most-attended events were track and field, swimming, and badminton.

Also giving it a shot in the arm has been the immigration of Asians. In Indonesia and Malaysia, badminton is now a part of their culture, almost a religion, and their governments build facilities and handsomely reward top players, e.g., two Indonesian champions were given US $500,000 each! Malaysia, described by Badminton BC as "the greatest badminton nation in the world," builds courts on a grand scale. Brent Olynyk travelled there for training sessions in 1993. Asians have become the world's best players — they're wiry, extremely fast, have amazing stamina, and hit powerful shots. And many are short — and as Dick Birch put it, "small compact people move quicker." Also, as Ken Meredith pointed out, "It's natural for them to play in hot, humid climates which would enervate European or North American competitors — the great Erland Kops excepted." There are now many Canadians of Asian descent playing here and at the Racquets Club, where they make up about 90% of its players.

171

1980s

1988 Canada's winning Olympic sprinter Ben Johnson disqualified for doping. A million fax machines sold in U.S. Pakistan's Bhutto first female Muslim leader. Prozac. Pan Am 103 blown up at Lockerbie. George Bush becomes President. Salman Rushdie's

Left to Right:
Judith Rollick,
Samantha Reynolds,
Dougall Molson,
Jimmy Van Ostrand.

Left to Right:
Brent Olynyk,
Andrea Neil,
Ross Mitchel,
Lois Reid Johnson.

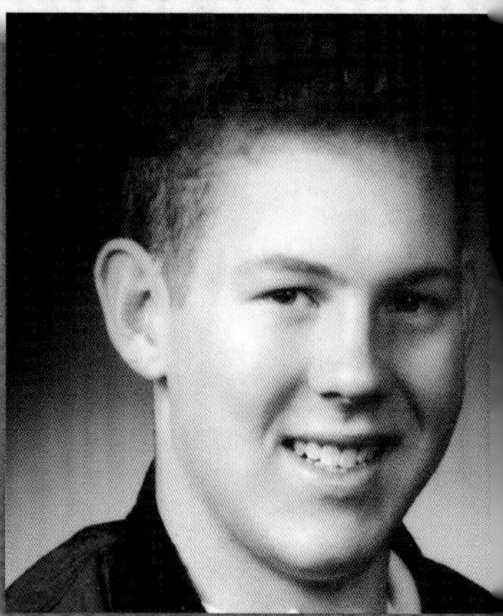

✦
172
✦

Left to Right:
Rex Moore,
Bruce Rollick,
Sharon Bleuler,
Daryl Thomson.

Satanic Verses. Expo '86 site sold to Li Kay Shing of Hong Kong. Bennetts and Doman charged with insider trading. **1989** Berlin Wall tumbles. Tiananmen Square. Panamanian drug dealer President Noriega surrenders. Exxon tanker oil spill in Valdez,

VLTBC Badminton Greats

Claire Lovett and Jean Bardsley, who by the early 1970s were playing as seniors, continued to be at the forefront. Jean won the last of her seven Club singles in 1975. In the same year, she and Claire won their fourth consecutive Canadian senior doubles. No female Club member has equalled their accomplishments nor those of Eleanor Young, Anna Kier-Patrick, and Eileen Underhill before them. However, we have several other excellent players such as Shaheen Shaikh, the daughter of Abdul and Val Shaikh; Mimi Nilsson; and Judith Rollick. In 1977, Mimi was a triple-crown winner in the Canadian seniors and in 1979 won its singles and mixed. Judy, who joined the Club after her career peeked, won the Club's women's title in 1984 and later played in seniors' events with great success.

A promising young junior, Andrea Neil, won the provincial under-16 and under-19 singles, and with a partner from Quebec, won the National under-19 doubles. Among the younger male members at this time, several stood out. In the mid-1970s, John Clark won the men's singles three times in succession. John Nicolls (eldest son of the late John) first came to prominence in 1973 when he took three titles at an invitational junior tournament. Between 1979 and 1999, John won the Club singles, a British Columbia singles, and a silver medal when playing for Canada in the Pan American Games.

Eric Nilsson, Mimi's son, won the singles in the provincial championships as well as taking the Club singles on four occasions. Perhaps the most outstanding young male player of this era was Brent Olynyk — best known for his skill in doubles. He and Nilsson were the only Club members to hold national rankings in the Canadian Closed. In 1998, Nilsson was ranked 11th in singles and 15th in mixed doubles while Olynyk was ranked sixth in men's doubles and 20th in mixed. As seniors, the ever-fit Bruce Rollick and Rolf Paterson won the 1955 Canadian men's doubles.

Squash

Unfortunately, because of its confined court and small gallery, only a handful of spectators can watch the game, although a few courts have glass rear walls to provide a better view. However for some years the world's leading pros have used a four-walled portable see-through court that travels with them. It's a glass, plexiglass, or whatever, one-way composite, providing spectators an excellent view

1980s

Alaska. World-wide ban on ivory trading. Stealth bombers. Ford buys Jaguar. "Miss Saigon". Science World and SFU's downtown campus open. Vancouver Port handles more imports and exports than any in North America. False Creek Dragon boat races

Left to Right:
Edward Trevor-Smith,
Laura Ramsay,
Hilda Ward.

Left to Right:
Abdul Shaikh,
John Osburn,
Neil Desaulniers.

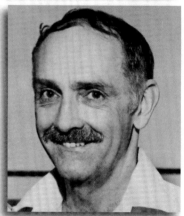

✦
174
✦

Left to Right:
Ruth Castellino,
Michael Desaulniers,
Brad Desaulniers

1990s

commence. **1990** Nelson Mandela freed. Gorbachev resigns and Boris Yeltsin chairs the U.S.S.R. John Major replaces Margaret Thatcher. Smoking banned on all U.S. domestic flights. Spotted Owl becomes an endangered species. GST introduced. East

from all four sides, and for the players it blocks the outside. Excellent technology. It's been in B.C. and in 2006 was handsomely quartered in Egypt at the foot of the Giza pyramids for the World's Open. But, apart from its usually limited spectator appeal, squash, like badminton is neither television nor radio-friendly. TV fails to capture the speed of the players and the ball is hard to see.

Also, our racquet players prefer an audience, e.g., in tennis our ground courts are way more popular than those on the roof. Abdul noted that juniors felt somewhat cloistered on a squash court and more or less out of sight, so their interest diminished. Yet the Racquets Club doesn't seem to have so suffered because, according to Bob Wade, there were lots more "hot shot" juniors playing there than here, plus it had more courts. Bob felt our Club's level of play was governed more by a desire for exercise than competition. However, for a quick workout, even for the duffers, it's a winner. Also, for older folk, doubles not only provides more chuckles but significantly extends their careers. And, for a youngster with any sort of coordination and racquet sense, squash can be easily and quickly learned. However, Abdul, who also coached squash, was leery of putting very young children on its courts because of squash's inherent dangers, and preferred to start them at an older age than badminton.

Classes of Squash Events

In squash the court size, the scoring, and the type of ball differ. For competitive play, there are four classes: A, B, C, and D. In tennis and badminton tournaments, players are dealt with by the seedings and by the draw, although in Club tournaments they're often graded at four levels, as in squash. In squash a D player — the lowest level — can play in a higher category but for an A player to play in a D tournament would be *de trop*. So squash players enter a tournament at whatever level he or she thinks appropriate, thus avoiding the embarrassment of a good one overwhelming a poorer one, as happened in tennis for that unfortunate "rabbit" Jack Bromwich encountered.

VLTBC Squash Greats

The Club has not produced many squash players who have won open tournaments, and in competitive play it lags behind tennis and badminton. However, if the measure of success lies in the boundless enthusiasm and loyalty of its aficionados, then our squash is way up there. Bob Wade was one of the many who came to us from the Racquets Club in the late 1950s — a migration that triggered the construction of our courts in 1961. He had marvellously white-bushy-eyebrows and crafty strokes and also retained his membership in the Racquets Club. He gained renown for the VLTBC by winning successively the over-50, the over-60, and the over-70 titles in the U.S. Nationals.

Bob's victories were in the hardball events played on the narrow American-size court, and when doubles arrived, he often partnered Sandy Robertson. His son Robin took a gold medal in the under-18s in 1972. Also "Spoon" — Hilary Wotherspoon — and Ron Weber were pretty good, winning the Oregon State doubles in 1970. Another British Columbian, who though not a member often played tennis and squash

175

1990s

and West Germany unify. Meech Lake proposals collapse. Mohawks and the Oka crisis. Vancouver's first Molson Indy race. After L.A. and New York, Vancouver becomes North America's third largest film production facility. Blue Box recycling begins.

"Bob Wade... gained renown for the VLTBC by winning successively the over-50, the over-60 and the over-70 titles in the U.S. Nationals."

at the VLTBC, is George Morfitt, who became B.C.'s Auditor General, and in 1993 won the U.S. over-50 championship. Bob Puddicombe's squash career was not far behind. In 1976 he won the B.C. Open "A" doubles and in 1979 the Pacific North West.

And when talk turns to squash, one name that stands out above all the rest is Desaulniers. Neil (Diz), the father of the tribe, was and still is highly competent. However, Neil and Bobby's sons, Mike and Brad, outshone their father. In 1973 Mike won the under-16 Canadian singles, the first B.C. player to do so, and that year, playing with his father, also won the Western Canadian doubles. Two years later he won the under-19 at the United States Junior National championships. Among the many other tournaments that he took part in that year, he was a finalist in, but not the winner, of the Australian juniors. In 1976 he repeated his 1973 victory by winning the Canadian juniors — a hardball tournament. Illustrating his ability to move from the hardball to the softball or vice versa, in 1975, '76, and '79, he won the Canadian Open softball titles as well as the Canadian hardball championships in '76, '78, and '79. Mike turned professional and in 1981 and '82 won the North American Professional championship.

Mike is no longer a member, but his brother, Brad, is. Brad was the Canadian junior champ in 1978 and

1980, when he also won the Canadian men's Open softball event. In '83, '84, and '86 he took the Canadian doubles; in 1985 and '86 the North American doubles, plus the United States Professional doubles and became world-ranked in professional doubles in '86 and '87. He's won our "A" singles four times. Would that his jokes were as swift. Still another Desaulniers, Greg, took seven of our Club titles between 1991 and 2000, and the youngest brother, Blake, is good too. In 1955 Neil Desaulniers along with Harry Kermode was a member of Port Albernie Athletics basketball team which won the Canadian title. He was also Canada's and the U.S. singles and doubles squash champion, and in 2006 "Diz" was still at it with Lorne Main capturing the -70 tennis doubles in our Indoors Masters.

Women at the VLTBC, compared to their male counterparts, have historically dominated badminton and tennis, so one has to wonder why relatively so few take up squash. How come, girls? Hilda Ward is a notable exception, being six times our Club champion, plus our mightily talented Club pro, Melanie Burke.

The Tennis Calcutta and the Triathlon

The "Calcutta," first held in 1968, and the more rigorous "Triathlon," which started in 1991, are two of the Club's more popular tournaments. In the Calcutta — a hard-fought, take-no-prisoners affair — a com-

176

1990s

1991 Rajiv Gandhi assassinated. Operation Desert Storm in Kuwait and Iraq. South Africa repeals apartheid. Ted Turner marries Jane Fonda. International Olympics ends its 21-year boycott of South Africa. B.C.'s Rita Johnson becomes Canada's first female

mittee selects men's teams, usually pairing weaker and stronger players together. In 1999 it was expanded to include women and in early 2005, mixed play. The tournament is handicapped and requires an entry fee of $25. A draw is made, and then there is a barbecue, and then the teams are auctioned — sold to the highest bidder — and a set of play is held over two days. The winners split the pool, which has reached $10,000, and the team "owner" getting 50% with the competitors divvying up the rest. In 2006 the pot contained $2,455, with the successful men's gladiators being Ron Wierstra and Biraj Bora, and for the women, Julie Kucher and Joan Grant.

The Triathlon takes place every two years and requires male and female play in tennis, squash, and badminton in one day in that order. Twenty-four points are needed to win each of the games, which can be won either when serving or receiving. The winner for its first two years was Curtis Brennan — a strong badminton player who had won the Clubs singles in 1981 and '82. So far, the Triathlon has been well-patronized by our men, with limited interest by our women.

Members' Own Tennis Tourneys

We've always complimented those who've arranged and put on their own show, be it for drinks, for dinner, or for what have you. The Big John Clarke Invitational, known as the "Nooners," started in 1985 and Bill Sauder, Bent Ewald, Ron Stanford, David Saba, and Bill Crawford were some of the originals. Winners sometimes got trips to Vegas. Big John died in 1988, but his handicapped event carries on with some 25

entries under the tutelage of Mike Ryan and is capped with much libation, a dinner, and a trophy. In 2005 it was won by Big John's son Peter — who also provides the Club with excellent plaques and trophies. In 1978, Ted Trevor-Smith sponsored his East Langley Open for eight teams of men's doubles. It lasted for 25 years with TTS always producing his very tasty self-chefed dinners. Lotsa calories.

The VLTBC Tournament Champions' Dinner

This was initiated by president Bruce Gandossi in 1997. All Club champions were invited, highlighted by Claire Lovett with 12 championships in tennis and 12 in badminton — the most wins in more than one sport. Jean Bardsley and John Nicolls in badminton and tennis plus Bob Puddicombe in tennis and squash. Art Jeffery, who garnered 13 championships over 24 years from 1942 until 1966, and Bob Bardsley, who held seven from 1967 until 1997, plus our president champions Ken Meredith and Bruce Gandossi in badminton, and Sandy Robertson in squash. Also from 1999 until 2000, an excellent brother-and-sister act — Michael and Marina Levin in tennis. It was a welcomed initiative, went well, and bears repeating.

Gifts to the Club

Over the years many members have donated trophies, prizes, and memorabilia — e.g., the bench at our front door honouring Bill Keenan. One of the earliest recorded was the anonymous gift by a director in 1947 of a flag pole, bunting, pennants, and a mahogany sign outside our gates. But until 1986 no

177

Premier. Oakalla Prison Farm closes. N.D.P. premier Harcourt elected. **1992** Bosnia civil war. U.S. Olympic basketball "Dream Team". Johnny Carson leaves his "Tonight" show, replaced by Jay Leno. Rio's Environment Conference to reduce gas emissions.

one had made a testamentary bequest. The first to do so was Erwin "Scoop" Elliott — so nicknamed during his badminton days when he was noted for being able to scoop up a bird just before it hit the floor. As said, Erwin, a McGill graduate, was a long-time member and one of the anti-Monk camp of 1947. He and his companion, Lorna Ross, always had the welfare of the Club in mind, but teamed in raising almighty Cain with the directors and management — and Lord help you if you weren't on their side.

I, as Scoop's friend, lawyer, and executor, was instructed by him to provide in his will "a bequest to the Club of $5,500 for capital expenditure plus $500 for a wake in the Snake Room." That was a howler. The Club purchased a dignified grandfather clock for $3,500, which graces the entrance to the Tudor Room, and spent the rest upon a Werner Forster-designed drinking fountain — "Fons Erwinorum" — near the pool. Rick Angus speculated that it was deliberately built high to discourage its use by small children, whose presence was one of Erwin's many "could-do-withouts."

178

Scoop was a character. He liked Al Stevenson, but used to outrageously hector "Ya Mutt," as he often called him. During their trip to Montreal, the right front wheel of Erwin's car flew off. Al told him. Scoop responded, "Shut up, Ya Mutt!" before they plunged into a ditch. Years later, recovering at UBC Hospital from a broken hip, he was almightily berating his nurses with his favourite, "The trouble with you is you're basically stupid." I was visiting and said, "Come on Scoop, you can't treat your nurses like your friends," then ducked.

David Jeffery, Don Ellison and our "Fons Erwinorum," a Werner Forster-designed drinking fountain that Erwin "Scoop" Elliot bequeathed to our Club.

Vancouver Airport's former chief meteorologist, David "Doggy" Strachan died in 2001. He requested me to draw a codicil to his will wherein he left $10,000 to the Club for "capital improvements and refurbishments" for his [and our] beloved Snake Room, "where I have enjoyed many happy times, much camaraderie and lots of spirited discussion." He loved puns. In those days (before CounterAttack against drinking and driving), people used to say, "Have one for the road," which Doggy converted into "Unus pro via" and with his Druid interest, also quipped, "Have one for

1990s

Grunge rock. Nicoderm patches cut smoking. Clinton elected President. Charlottetown Constitutional Accord rejected. P.M. Mulroney resigns. Block Quebecois become Her Majesty's "Loyal" Opposition. **1993** Palestine's Yasser Arafat and Israel's Yiztak

Ian Adam stands beside the grandfather clock that was purchased from Erwin Elliott's bequest to the Club.

me — during our major 1960 additions and was followed up by successor President Jack Allan. It's open to all our men plus by invitation to ladies for hallmark occasions. Lorna Ross, Jean Bardsley, Jeanie Clarke, Helen Gardom, and the daughters of John and Nan Nicolls have been aboard. It's small, cozy, and a great place to have a chat about one's game, one's victories, one's losses, one's ills, politics, the news of the day, all while having a snort or two. There are few rules — none prescribed — except to be of good humour and BYOB. Pictures of many of our greats adorn the room and the names, nicknames, and dates of death of habitués when they joined the "Snake Room in the Sky" are distinguished by plaques on the wall. Thankfully so far there are only 15, with lots of "Sons of Snakers" still snaking about. Many memories. And all of them spirited.

It's great for the after-game and after-exercise pursuits of many and has received lots of non-Club financed tender loving care from the likes of David Jeffery, Tony Hugman, and Don Ellison. In 2006 David and Tony set up a dandy Christmas tree decorated with lights and miniature bottles. Nice gesture. Grinches they weren't. But the administration felt they could be a fire hazard — which they weren't — and removed them! The "Snaker" continues to be daily used plus for wakes for departed Snakers, for gatherings of "Sons of Snakers," for a few birthday dos, and for highland malt tastings — initiated by "Big Sip" Bob Sung and ably joined by Willie Laurie, Matthew Cheng, and Jonn Wu, also for some vodka and gin snifting too. Conviviality at its best.

✦
179
✦

my baby and one for the woad." A small committee led by Bob Sung, Iain Perkins, and David Jeffery attended to his bequest with some handsomely framed pictures, new chairs, and lamps as well as repainting the joint. Plus a few habitués made donations. Nice job. Doggy would be pleased.

The Snake Room

The member-led Snake Room, in the men's locker room, came into being under Eric Beardmore's leadership — with strong support from John P.R. Nicolls and

© Denise Grant

1990s

The Snake Room, 2007

CHAPTER 12

1974–1993 • Decisions & Renovations

The Pool. Our Lawn Courts Come to an End in 1984. Our Suggestion Box, and Staff.

1974 — Gallery of Champions

The institution of our Gallery of Champions — photographs of members who have achieved prominence in the racquet sports — caused a few skirmishes. In 1974, President Bill Whittall unveiled 25 framed photographs of "members who had become Canadian champions in badminton, squash and tennis." The idea was spawned by Dr. Bruce Cates, and Al Stevenson collected the photos. A year later Sharon Bleuler, a badminton star who joined the Club in 1970, asked whether those who like herself had earned a Canadian racquets title before becoming a member could be included. The directors ruled that the Gallery would be restricted to those who had won their "major title" while a Club member. But then the question arose: What exactly is a "major title?" Is it limited to a title in singles, or should it include doubles, and what about seniors' events? In any case, the board soon reversed its decision, and Mrs. Bleuler's pho-

tograph is in the Gallery as is that of Bruce Rollick — another outstanding badminton player who won his major titles while a member of the Racquets Club. At one time Susan Butt wasn't in the array, which also has been taken care of.

1975 — We Eliminate Four Grass Courts and Build and Bubble Four New Tennis Quick *Hard Ones*

During this period the long-existing lobby to remove the grass courts sadly gained momentum. Our clay courts had long disappeared and much as their loss was lamented by a few, their reaction was mild compared to the tumult that arose when the directors decided to do away with the last of our grass courts. The events leading to this began when the City earlier refused to let us install a protective bubble over our four roof courts. This prompted the directors to consider laying *Tennis Quick*, a porous concrete, over the

The player's lounge, c. 1990.

four westernmost grass courts — one being the pro court — as well as covering them with a bubble.

As he strongly disagreed with these decisions, Doug Shellard — a director, chairman of the Club's Building and Planning Committee, and a gentleman of firm conviction — followed parliamentary tradition and resigned. Ironically, about five years earlier he had led the charge for not three but four indoor courts. Shellard was replaced by Bill Keenan who took on his fourth expansion program in 20 years — a remarkable record by a remarkable member! A similar disagreement took place in early 2004 when Director Jandi Fraser, also of firm conviction, resigned from the board because of her opposition to the board's reconstruction proposal, which included the elimination of one tennis court. In November of 2004, she was re-elected as a director.

So in 1975 it was decided to proceed in stages — remove the four grass courts and replace them with *Tennis Quick*. Then a year later, bubble them for the winter. The City granted the permit on condition that neighbouring landowners be consulted, and that the permit would be renewed annually. The Club invited our 17 neighbours to discuss the project, but only two showed up. The board then called a special meeting of our members to consider this proposal. Only 60 attended, but their approval was overwhelming, demonstrating no qualms about losing half of our eight grass courts — an attitude which must have influenced the directors' decision many years later to do away with our remaining four. Sadder still.

Soon the board received the unpalatable, but not unsurprising news that the original estimate of

182

$200,000 for this work had risen to $263,000. This was scaled back to $240,000 but, in the exercise of caution, the directors postponed the bubble for a year, and under the presidency of David Black installed our new *Tennis Quick* hard courts for about $150,000. That decision was ratified at the AGM a month later, when the members also gave the directors authority, if needed, to borrow money to complete the project. Subsequently, the costs rose by 5%, mainly because of more City of Vancouver bylaw requirements. However, those extra costs were handled by arranging $20,000 short-term financing with the rest to be paid from from accumulated surplus. The bubble was in place by September 1975. So now we had four rooftop courts, four inside courts, four courts bubbled for the winter — all *Tennis Quick*-surfaced — and still four lovely grass courts.

1984 — Farewell All our Remaining Lawn, Hello Omni

As mentioned previously, until the mid-1970s we enjoyed nine lawn courts, the most westerly of which was surfaced with asphalt and reserved for the exclusive use of our pro, Paul Willey. In their prime they were marvellous — pristine and aesthetic. The grass

Canada's first female Prime Minister. Ballard's fuel cell bus. U.B.C.'S Michael Smith awarded the Nobel Prize for Chemistry. Largest Fraser River salmon run in 80 years. **1994** Blacks gain vote in South Africa. Chechen war. Rwanda's civil war - Hutu extremists

was of excellent quality, meticulously manicured, and possessed a sweet smell of its own — especially when freshly mown. Regular maintenance kept the courts top-dressed, levelled, mowed, reseeded, watered, re-turfed when necessary, fertilized, and rolled hard. They never wore as much as did Wimbledon's and without question, play on the lawn was the best of any. A joy and a luxury too. Also, they were great on the legs — bad knee-ers and bad hip-pers take note!

However in 1982, following the Tennis Committee's recommendation, the directors approved in principle a decision to convert the remaining four to some kind of all-weather surface. Unfortunately, continuance of the lawn had become increasingly impractical. Also the makeup of our membership had dramatically altered. In earlier days play on the grass would commence in the afternoon after work. But with the VLTBC becoming a family club, members played on the grass throughout the day (obviously they liked it), and without costly intensive maintenance it couldn't withstand that amount of wear and tear.

So, in 1983, the directors reiterated their 1982 stand, but decided to reconsult the membership before doing all of this. The board, conscious of arriving at a decision which would irrevocably alter the ambience of the Club, insisted that the Tennis Committee prepare a report detailing what was in mind. Although an alternative surface had not then been settled upon, the general consensus was that it should be *Omni-turf.* Then, armed with information from the Tennis Committee, in May 1984 the directors put the issue to the membership by referendum. Of those responding, 374 approved the removal of the grass and only 53 said "Nay."

However, many of our traditionalists battled on. At that time our property was still owned by our holding company, which was not wound up until two years later. The Company Act provided dissident shareholders with the right to requisition a special meeting provided they could muster the required percentage of the total membership. This the dissidents were able to do, and they formally notified the Club's holding company to convene on July 5 an Extraordinary General Meeting to consider a motion to amend its articles to prevent the directors eliminating the lawn courts without the approval of the members by special resolution — i.e. one passed by a 75% majority. In the interim they compelled the board to maintain the grass.

It was a spirited meeting, with members passionately speaking pro and con. Former president Bill Whittall led the charge for those opposed to its removal — supported amongst others by Doug Shellard, Rosemary Cunningham, and Jack Brawn's son Doug. Among those speaking in favour of taking them out were President Gavin Connell and Ron Weber, a director. By a vote of 189 to 26 the "retentionists," as they were also sometimes referred to, were defeated. Events then moved swiftly. *Omni-turf* arrived and by the end of August, our lawn courts were no more! The grass went to UBC where, by virtue of inadequate TLC, it lasted only a year. Gone but certainly not forgotten in the hearts of many members. Today there is only one grass court in Vancouver — at the home of Pat McGeer. Little wonder his knees are better than Ron Weber's!

Once it was decided to abandon grass, the choice of *Omni* seemed appropriate. Hence the 1984 installation

✦
183
✦

1990s

vs. Tutsi – 2 million flee the country. O. J. Simpson charged with murder but aquitted. Tom Hanks' "Forrest Gump". Walt Disney's "Lion King". Channel tunnel opens—England to France. Canada, U.S., Mexico Free Trade Agreement. Vancouver Grizzlies

was somewhat of a compromise between those who favoured retaining the grass and those who preferred firmer underpinnings. Also *Omni*, barring snowfall, is an all-weather surface and playable within half an hour of a heavy rainfall. Some members played it year round. But it did tend to be slippery, and sand accumulated in little mounds, causing some bad bounces — but perhaps the same could be said about bouncers on the grass.

However, one question remains: How long can we continue to be named the "Vancouver *Lawn* Tennis and Badminton Club"? Most hope forever. We've been loath to alter our name. Although in 1983 the board gave thought to requesting Royal Warrant to become "The Royal Vancouver Lawn Tennis and Badminton Club," but decided against it.

More Proposals, More Referendums, and More Renovations.

In 1988, the directors once more began to plan large-scale renovations — a combination of refurbishing and adding new facilities — especially for the juniors, plus improvements to our clubhouse. Architect Vladimir Plavsic produced a concept that was to include an elevator from the middle of the players' lounge, various amenities, and some underground parking. Its cost was estimated at $2,850,000, which was well beyond our available cash. So, late that year, the membership was polled. Although a majority of those responding favoured the proposal, which included taking out a mortgage for roughly $2 million, it fell far short of the 75% special resolution requirement. Hence, back to the drawing board, with

all but the most pressing maintenance expenses being deferred in order to conserve cash.

At the 1990 AGM the issue of the directors' spending powers emerged again, prompting them once more to reflect on our members' opposition to the exercise of powers which the directors believed they had. Their consensus was that an organized minority who attended the meeting diverted full attention from the board's initiatives. However it was agreed that a method should be found to reverse the impression of the board's powers to spend all of the Club's cash reserves without recourse to the membership.

1990-1993: Phase I Improvements

To conserve cash, the directors decided to divide the project into two phases and to proceed with the first one which, costing about $1.5 million, could be paid for by monies on hand. So the board instructed its consultants and our newly-appointed architect, Werner Forster (formerly Plavsic's partner), to proceed. Werner's forte was also designing Mediterranean restaurants, kitchens, and some homes. Apart from general upgrading (carpets, chairs, bay windows, and the removal of the outside walkway to the south of the dining room), the main floor was handsomely renovated, including additional office space, much desired exercise rooms, plus a corridor to allow juniors access to their lounges without having to traverse the senior lounge, together with a pro shop further to the west. These improvements were all very well received, especially the exercise/fitness rooms which were an instant hit both for our racquets

184

Dinner in the dining room, c. 1990.

ize borrowing $250,000 to cover them. Fortunately they were able to whittle down the contract price by eliminating some of the items, so with a line of credit for operating expenses from the Bank of Montreal, the Club was in a position to proceed. The contract was awarded to Homar Construction in September 1992, and a year later on 9 September, 1993, the official opening took place.

The Pool and Its Use

Suggestions to provide other facilities caused far less controversy. In 1981, the board briefly considered whether to build a racquetball court, but decided against it. I suggested enclosing the pool with removable plexiglass sides and a highly pitched, removable plastic roof. However the final decision was to bubble it, which was acceptable to all.

Our pool has been the subject of some amusing episodes. Dr. Joe Badre recalled one afternoon when his wife was swimming and a bird pooped on her. She didn't mind — "It's my good luck," she said. In July 1979, a female member wrote to the board complaining about the rule that her diapered youngsters were not permitted to use the pool. Probably this was prompted by an episode witnessed by Director Jone Brodie-Fraser, when a toddler's nappies failed to contain his big job. The pool was cleared and our maintenance staff unsuccessfully attempted to recover his droppings. Soon afterward a man did his customary 20 laps, later to ask, "Why, on such a lovely day, is no one else swimming?" Hmm. Nowadays kids can use the pool provided, thanks to modern technology, they are properly diapered with pool pants.

185

devotees and also for those whose sole object was better health. However, because of all of this, the Club was forced to comply with the City's regulations for earthquake proofing, fire protection, and bringing our wiring up to code — all of which significantly added to the cost.

This was placed before our members in October 1991 at an informational meeting presided over by President Rick Angus and his successor Peter Jackson. Opposition was expressed, however the board decided to proceed without putting the matter to a formal vote—with which Angus and Jackson disagreed—believing that they had the support of a substantial majority of the membership, and that if the members were unhappy they could throw them out at the AGM to be held a month later.

The revolt simmered out, the dissidents didn't put up any candidates, and in March 1992, Phase I went to tender. The lowest bid almost matched our total cash on hand plus our estimated cash flow to completion, but it didn't take into account contingencies — which the directors fixed at 15% of the contract price and contemplated calling a special meeting to author-

1990s

Her Majesty Queen Elizabeth II and Bert Fergus (left) at the 1994 Commonwealth Games in Victoria, B.C.

CHAPTER 13

Members, Directors, and Administrators

The hroughout our history, we've sought to balance the compatibility of applicants for membership with our need to maintain enough members to ensure financial stability. Also we had to make sure our facilities didn't become overloaded. Perennial problems faced by most clubs.

Number and Classifications of Members — Current Entrance Fees

The Club has always had a cap on our Playing membership. It used to be 960, however in the fall of 2000, this was changed to include spouses in the count, hence the present cap rose to 1,500. In addition to Playing Members there are 998 Social, Non-Resident, Life, Interim, Honorary, Courtesy, and Complimentary members, reaching a complement of close to 2,500 apart from their children.

A member includes his or her "partner" i.e., the husband or wife, or if not married, significant others who have lived together for two years. All of this went well unless there was a family break-up. The member belongs, but what about the partner? If the de-maritalization was harmonious, fine. But if not, and when the member didn't want his or her former beloved about, all sorts of cantankerisms arose. So the board established a middle ground — and if the non-member partner elected to join upon complying with the usual processes, she or he could. 'Tis easier to remain hitched.

We also instituted a corporate membership — where a company joins and nominates one of its principals or employees to represent it, who could change from time to time. And the Club always took into account the compatibility of the company's nominee. In 1976, this was discontinued. However in 1993, "corporates" were restored and they work well. Much the same arrangement is in place for interested members of the B.C.

187

Consular Corps, who are also a welcome addition.

In August 2006, the president announced that we had a waiting list of 12–14 months. Also that effective 1 October, 2006, our entrance fees would be increased to $25,000 for a Playing Couple, $15,000 for a Single, Social Couples $15,000, and $9,000 for a Social Single.

Life Members

In the past a member who reached the age of 65 years and had been a playing member for 30 years automatically became a life member and did not have to pay dues, but of course had to pay for bar bills and meals. As life expectancy in society at large increased, so did the number of our life members, resulting in some erosion of our financial base. At the 1985 AGM, a motion to "grandfather the situation" proposed that life members between the ages of 65 and 70 had to pay 50% of regular dues but after 70 they would become exempt. The motion failed, and the meeting voted to continue with the existing policy.

Thirteen years later the board tackled this again and on 1 June, 1998, our bylaws were amended to include those who weren't life members before to receive that designation up to 2009, but with the qualifying age being increased to 70. Also our "lifers" lost their right to vote, to qualify as a director, and additionally were called upon to pay dues — except those who reached 80 prior to October 2000 — which were set effective 2000 at 10% of playing members' dues; effective 2001, 20%; and effective 2002, 30%; but no assessments. Apart from the non-assessment aspect, the same applied to our social members.

Needless to say this did not sit well with our life members, who for many years had supported the Club through thick and thin and paid for that which we now enjoy. And their opposition was compounded as they were being denied any right to vote, notwithstanding they had to pay dues, reduced though they were. Not fair

Lawsuits

There have not been many lawsuits of members vs. the Club, except for damages for alleged negligence, and less of Club vs. members, unless it was failure to pay dues or improperly perform a contract. However, as a result of our life members losing the right to vote but having to pay dues, this came before the courts. A major revision of our bylaws in 1974 stipulated that upon our life members surrendering their voting shares for $100, they would no longer have to pay dues. But in October 2000, the voting members reversed this and called upon our life members to pay reduced dues, but continued to deny them their vote.

Only a few life members were concerned about the imposed cost, because initially it wasn't too much and those who used the Club received all of its usual benefits. However, the reversal in policy much troubled them. Also the formula is not frozen, for it increases the dues of lifers when the dues of voting members are increased. Our dues never go down.

The life members expected to continue to be dues-free, as they had become when they surrendered their shares, but since they were now compelled to pay dues, they felt it was most unright that they should also become disenfranchised. The board didn't go along with their requests to change this and, on a mat-

1990s

control U.S. Congress. Body piercing becomes popular. Princess Diana's confession on TV. Queen Elizabeth urges Charles and Diana to divorce. Air France's Concorde rounds the world in 31 hours 27 minutes. John Major re-elected. CBC's Front Page Challenge

Bill Crawford, Sandy Sutherland and Jim Skelton, late 1960s.

ter of principle, former president Bill Whittall — who joined the Club in 1954 — with support from many life members, commenced an action in April 2003 seeking rectification of the issue. He, and they, lost. This was appealed and on 7 September, 2005 the B.C. Court of Appeal also found in favour of the Club.

Most members agree that a social club, like a legislature or parliament, is not fettered from altering policy — unless a contract was involved, wherein damages could be claimed for its breach. But the court found this wasn't a contract. Times and circumstances do change, but the loss of any right a dues-paying member may have for some kind of franchise — restricted or whatever — essentially constitutes

taxation without representation, something which George III ran into resulting in the "Boston Tea Party" in 1773 and eventually the loss of his American colonies in 1776. So, notwithstanding the lawsuit's outcome, perhaps it would be appropriate for the Club to take a second look. Maintain the reduced dues, but see if the voting issue could be dealt with, as have other clubs. Harmony is not an unrealistic goal.

Women on the Board

As referred to earlier, few women have been elected to the board. However, Director Nicki Perkins became our first vice-president and also our first president. A record-breaker. But none have been treasurer. Our

1990s

first female director, Doris Belchley, was elected in 1953 and served four years and was, she said, regarded as "somewhat of an oddity." Doris was appointed secretary, a post designed, she felt, to keep her quiet as she took the Minutes. Jone Brodie-Fraser, à la Doris, following her election in 1978, spoke to a female lawyer member, who on learning she was on the board and was also secretary, expressed surprise and remarked, "Jone, I didn't know you could type."

Directors and Events

Following election as a director, the president is elected by the board, and he/she selects the directors' portfolios. At one time our directors had their own tennis and badminton doubles tournaments. Former president Leonard Read presented a trophy for the tennis tournament, which was last played for in 1941. Later it became reinstated as a handicap event. The first winners were Angela Doyle and Bill Keenan. It was such a good idea that a year later Director Mike O'Brian presented a trophy for directors' badminton doubles. It was first played in 1976, to be won by him and Angela Doyle, who that same year repeated her victory in the Read Trophy with J. Ross Southam. Those tourneys seem to be no longer.

Another well-attended function — initiated in 1966 by me — is the annual Past Presidents' Dinner which, apart from an evening of good food and drink, is a great get-together and stimulates lots of discussion about the activities of the Club, its financial shape, and where it's going. During Ken Meredith's presidency, the past presidents were established as a standing committee. Now re major matters, sometimes

they are consulted by the incumbent president. They have the interests of the Club at heart and in one way or another continue to assist.

Suggestion Box

Throughout our history our directors have kept our members well-informed of their endeavours, appreciating the fact that their's is no rose garden and they can't please everyone. So if you've a suggestion, put it in writing. Much better than management or the board having to rely on osmosis or receiving it verbally. Way back in 1927 we initiated a "Suggestion Box" — still useful, still good. But those suggestions should be made known — circulated or placed on our notice board. All the board's work is gratis and regretfully often without much thanks. Sometimes they receive dinner at an evening meeting. The president has a reserved parking space. And, for the past 10 years, prior to the AGM, they've held a well-received cocktail and canapé reception for our committee members. It also helps to ensure a quorum. Hardly fat perks. We owe them a lot.

Staff

Over the years a very loyal and competent Club staff has attended to the needs of our members — the only exception being in in 1928, when the directors fired everyone save the secretary manager! We now have 87. "Cardy," Harry Monk, and Tom Myring would be spellbound! The 10 in administration include Club CEO Janis Ostling, a Comptroller, a Membership and Marketing Manager, an Operations Manager, a Programs Manager, a Front Desk Supervisor, a Players'

190

bill. **1996** VIA's new $260 million terminal. B.C. Securities Commission finds Bill and Russell Bennett and Herb Doman guilty of insider trading. Pacific Press moves to Granville Square. Three Tenors at B.C. Place. Premier Harcourt resigns. Glen Clark MLA

Lounge Manager plus our ever-assistive, competent, and conscientious Clubhouse Manager George Walker — who has been with us since 1993. Chef James Schaffer has presided in the kitchen since 1993 and our cordial Chief Bartender Kevin Luther, has slaked our thirst since 1989. The professionals for our racquet sports are all independent contractors. And who can forget Gerry and Rita in the players' lounge, Alice in the dining room, and Mary Clarkson and Lam Ngo at the front desk.

The Club operates an in-house laundry to clean the uniforms, towels, and table linens. The maintenance and food services staff — including bartenders — belong to Local 40 of the Hotel, Bartenders and Culinary Workers Union. Although there have been threats of work stoppage over the years — and strike votes have occasionally been taken — mercifully none have occurred. The staff members are good people and the Club treats them well. A Harassment Policy is in place — at the VLTBC? Heavens! — which we are glad to say is rarely called upon.

Employees hired prior to 1996 have an annual bonus provision. And for the past 20 years the Club has held a much-enjoyed and well-attended staff Christmas party — which for the last while has been held at the Royal Vancouver Yacht Club. Our longest-serving employee is now retired Gino Danesin, who spent 35 years with us maintaining our property and courts. Bartender Tony To is not far behind — in 2006 he celebrated 32 years of employment. Tommy Wong has been with the Club for 19, Henry Sui in Maintenance for 26, and Norman Wu was at our watering hole for 20 years before leaving in 2004.

Secretary Managers

From our beginnings, the duties of our managers were very much those of greeting and mixing: arranging games and organizing tournaments; religiously attending functions; plus ensuring that our operation was up, running, and kept up to scratch. This kind of modus operandi, like others, does change and over time their mingling with members became increasingly secondary. From 1965 to 1999 three managers stand out. England's Tom Myring, whom we earlier highlighted; Graham Laxton; plus Australia's Jim Robson. Robson had worked in the Laurentians, knew his food, and insisted on excellent and changing bills of fare. He brought true professionalism to the position but was lured away by the Seattle Tennis Club and later to a club in La Jolla. He was succeeded by Reg Tobin, who after serving four years was dismissed with subsequent litigation, which eventually became settled. In 1977 we hired Graham Laxton — first as an administrative assistant, then assistant manager and following Tobin's departure, as Club manager in 1978. Graham held the position for a record 22 years — by far the longest of any manager in our history. Great staying powers had our ever-courteous Graham! The life of a Club manager is not easy. On the one hand he, and now she — our most capable and cheery Mrs. Janis Ostling designated as our chief executive officer — is answerable to the directors for administration of policy and is also on the front line for information-seeking, concerned, and complaining members. It's not only a tough role, but an art too. We have been, and continue to be, very well served.

191

FROM HERE TO THE *F*UTURE

VANCOUVER LAWN TENNIS & BADMINTON CLUB
BUILDING IMPROVEMENT PLAN

Cover of the 2003-2004 Vancouver Lawn Tennis & Badminton Club Building Improvement Plan.

CHAPTER 14

1996-2006 • Our Centennial

More Plans and More Improvements

1997 — We Celebrate Our 100th Birthday

In 1897, when the idea of a club was but a gleam in the eye of a few tennis enthusiasts, the *Vancouver Province*, with its banner "Free Trade and Direct Taxation," was our only newspaper, selling for 2¢ a copy, which was also Canada's price for first-class mail to anywhere in the British Empire. Sir Wilfred Laurier was prime minister and Queen Victoria was celebrating her Diamond Jubilee. Five thousand gold-rushers climbed — and several perished while doing so — the Yukon's Chilcoot Pass on their way to the Klondike. Canada's first gasoline-driven car was built in Quebec. Everyone in Vancouver lived less than a mile from the new CPR station at the foot of Granville Street. The Burlington Railway advertised "No dust in the car seats. No litter on the floor. No foul air. Nothing to remind you of former occupants." (Men's locker room, please take note!)

Jamaica Joe Fortes taught swimming at English Bay — men to the east of a large boulder and ladies to the west, clad top-to-toe and wearing hats. Childcare cost 10¢ a day, department store employees received about $4 a week and beef cost 12½¢ a pound. Well water was replaced by that from the Capilano River, piped under the First Narrows. Fines paid the salaries of the police. Once a chain gang went on strike. However, "after three days of bread and water, they came to terms." No union bosses then.

Everywhere enormous firs, cedars, spruce, and hemlock. Lots of logging. Teams of 14 oxen plied the skid roads. Kerrisdale, Point Grey, and Kitsilano didn't exist. Nor did Shaughnessy. One could easily catch the best of fish. And, notwithstanding an abundance of bear, deer, cougars, coyotes, raccoons, and skunks, an early Vancouver by-law stipulated: "Within City limits, no more than 25 cows shall be kept by any one person, family, partnership, or corporation." The Club didn't have any.

Our century of progress was a many-

The March/April 1997 edition of *Match Point* celebrated the 100th anniversary of VLTBC.

splendoured thing and in 1997 under President Bruce Gandossi, ours was a time for great rejoicing. And rejoice we did. It took a lot of planning and lead-up peaking in August when the world-famous Australians Ken Rosewall and Roy Emerson played in our "Legends of Tennis." Hosts of activities were carefully organized and well carried out. Our *Racquet Hi-Lights* printed a heads-up. There were colourful articles in the *B.C Historical News* and in Rick Angus' *Match Point*. A handsome eight-page letter-size brochure was produced plus an anniversary calendar, each with a wide range of photographs.

The official celebration took place on Sunday, September 28, at 2 p.m. Every member received a special invitation accompanied by a six-page program, and many attended — 450, the largest crowd in years. It was tremendous fun. The directors encouraged members to wear period attire, and many did, and Pipe Major John Mager, my piper, led the official procession. In my capacity as Lieutenant Governor of British Columbia I gave the official address, after which a number of distinguished people spoke. Messages of congratulations from other distinguished individuals who weren't present were also read. Next came exhibition matches in the three racquet sports

plus table tennis. We unveiled the Centennial plaque and Gordon Maxwell sang a Centennial song composed for the occasion. Light refreshments followed, with my wife Helen and our then four-year-old granddaughter Cara cutting the cake. Also we're sure that following the cake, coffee, and cookies, the bar did very well! It was the best event the Club organized in many years, and it's unfortunate that not many of us will be around for our 200th. As kids our four daughters: Kim, Karen, Brione, and Brita — "Baby" — were members, enjoyed what the Club had to offer, learned to play tennis and badminton and together with Helen, tolerated my coming home late after a game with all sorts of interesting strays in tow. Baby once ran into trouble — got a finger caught in the chain of an exercise bike. That smarted!

2006 — Revision of Our Rules and Regulations

On March 1, these were again revised. Read 'em. "'Smart Casual' in … Centre Court … all cell phones strictly prohibited … smoking … restricted to the south side of the pool deck." Good stuff.

More Proposals, More Improvements, and More Renovations

In 1993 under the presidency of Peter Jackson, our $2.1 million Phase I development got under way. The main floor and the players lounge were handsomely renovated, the corridor was installed, and the fitness rooms were established. They were an instant hit — both for our racquets devotees and also for those whose sole object was a workout. "No pain, no gain."

194

© Service photo de Matignon
1990s

12 stroke win at U.S. Masters. **1998** President Clinton faces impeachment. U.S. bombs Iraq. Viagra developed. India and Pakistan nuclear test. El Niño. Jean Charest leaves Federal Tories to lead Quebec's Provincial Liberals. **1999** Aging population increases.

The omni was removed to make way for the underground parking garage.

In 1996, during President Bruce Gandossi's leadership, the larger expenditure of $4.2 million was proposed for the Phase II — when our four most easterly courts were changed to clay, the men's locker rooms were refurbished, and a steam room and new showers were installed — of which two are great apart from some now rectified dry rot. "The Saga of the Showers." As anticipated, good old Keenan again affably weathered a lot of heat. A members' elevator was installed, which was a godsend for our oldies, plus very costly underground parking — parking being the Club's continuous nemesis. Henry Ford contributed much to the success of the world but also to the ruin of some of it. Now we have 161 parking spaces — 73 underground, 18 in the covered lot, 22 on its roof plus 48 in the front — hopefully more than enough.

Our architect for both of these undertakings was Werner Forster, and Homar Construction served as the contractor. Unfortunately the costs rose to $4,985,000, mainly because the underground parking cost $1 mil-

lion more than anticipated. Also it took a little longer than expected (as always) but it got done and done well. This was to be paid by cash in hand of about $1.5 million, by borrowing $2.5 million at 6% (paid off in April 2005), plus a Long Range Plan (LRP) Assessment of $15 a month from our dues-paying members.

Eight years later, on 30 March 2004, at a well-attended Extraordinary General Meeting in the badminton hall, Club members were asked to approve a proposal for another major renovation. Led by President Ewen Cameron and past president Herb Evers, who served as chairman of the Building and Planning Committee. This had taken months of thought and extremely ably chronicled work, rafts of detailed information, and no end of presentations to our members. Surprises there weren't — but nonetheless, it failed to make the grade.

This 2004 proposal, entitled "From Here to the Future," was exceptionally well-presented and outlined the suggested "key facility upgrades." These included

1990s

DVDs. First around the world balloon flight. Julie Payette—Canada's first female Astronaut. Russia's Yeltsin and Premier Clark resign. NDP Caucus selects Dan Miller for Premier. Euro dollar introduced. **2000** Billions welcome the new millennium. Quebec

improvement to the facilities for tennis, social, squash, badminton, fitness, administration, family services, life safety plus other proposals for the future. To pay for this the directors sought authority to mortgage the Club's property for $8.5 million, amortized over 15 years. At no time in the 128 years in the Club's history had directors ever presented such a detailed submission. The timing for this project also seemed fortuitous — mortgage rates were at an all-time low and there was a good pool of available labour.

The members voted. Valid ballots, in person or by proxy, totalled 892, about 67% of the Club's 1,328 eligible voters — a healthy turnout. Of the members who voted, 541, or 61%, were in general agreement, but 351, or 39%, were not. The principal objection appeared to be the loss of the most easterly rooftop tennis court. Since the proposal required a 75% majority under the Societies Act, it failed to pass, notwithstanding the directors' promise to fine-tune it following a survey of the members and once more seeking their input.

Following this rejection, the directors soldiered on and submitted a rezoning application to the City to erect a bubble over the clay courts. This appeared to have been approved in principle in the spring of 2005, however, due to Vancouver's construction boom the development permit didn't materialize until mid-January 2006, which deferred the installation of the bubble until October. To our dismay its projected cost increased by $360,000 due to more work and materials than earlier forecast.

The board continued with its other endeavours, kept the membership posted, solicited their views, conducted a survey, and following a response rate

In October 2001 Jack Pedlar and Rod Laver were inducted into the USTA/PNW Hall of Fame.

of 35%, posted its results in July, which were 62% favourable, with 23% opting for total redesign and 15% for only modest upgrades. Consequently, in August 2004, the directors established a 20-member Building Improvement Plan (BIP) Committee, again chaired by ex-president Herb Evers, which in October presented four remodelled Development Options:

- Plan A – $5,500,600
- Plan B – $12,425,000
- Plan C – more long range – $14,650,000
- Plan D – another longer range – $20,940,000

Member response — 15% — was underwhelming, but most voiced a desire to get on with something. With this in mind, the board held more information meetings in November.

Newly elected President Andrew Bibby, following the advice of the BIP Committee in May 2005, requested that the Club's new architects — Proscenium Architecture and Interiors Inc. — present a new three-phase BIP. Projected costs for Phase One were $8,257,000; Phase Two, $4,300,000; and Phase Three, $10,500,000; for a total of $23,057,000.

Phase Three, which suggested major excavation for underground tennis courts to the west of the underground parking garage, would have been a huge, costly undertaking and was considered much too far down the line for a present decision and was eliminated.

So the remaining two revamped proposals were put to the members at an Extraordinary General Meeting on 19 September 2005, in the form of four Resolutions:

(1) An ordinary (50%) resolution to "Approve the Building Improvement Plan including the Clay Court Bubble."

It passed with 516 members (65%) approving it and 276 members (35%) voting against it.

(2) A special resolution (requiring 75% approval) to "Approve financing our $8,500,000 project."

This dealt with renovating the dining room, kitchen, pub, and Tudor Room; building new administration offices and storage as well as a new TV room; and improving the squash facilities and expanding the fitness facility as well as ensuring that the Club conformed with all the necessary seismic and Life Safety Code requirements. It also proposed a new entrance for the badminton hall, upgrading and relocating the family lounge, plus upgrades for the ladies' and men's locker rooms. This resolution failed to pass, with 507 members (63%) approving it, while 287 members (37%) voted against it.

(3) A special resolution to "approve $725,000 financing for the Clay Court Bubble."

This passed with 636 members (80%) voting in favour and 152 members (20%) disapproving.

(4) An ordinary resolution to approve the clay court bubble.

It passed with 709 members (91%) approving it and 77 (9%) voting against it. Yearly operational and maintenance costs will be approximately $50,000. The principal bone of contention this time came from the squash fraternity concerning the deletion of that which had been proposed for them in 2004. Others were troubled about the cost. Could we afford it?

In November 2005 the directors, within the ambit of their authority, decided upon a much more modest initiative involving a $1 million line of credit and about $2.5 million of improvements. This project, chaired by ex-president Ewen Cameron, got under way in 2006 and involved expanding the fitness centre, expanding and renovating the family lounge and its dining area, sprucing up the men's and boys' and girls' locker rooms, providing seismic upgrading for the tennis hall, installing sprinklers and upgrading the floor in the badminton hall, renovating the main floor hallway and Champions' Gallery, and (unfortunately!) relocating the TV into the family lounge. This pleased the juniors but according to many senior members, was too far removed from its well used prior location.

Members welcomed the striking blue and green indoor tennis courts, as well as the spacious and spectacular main floor quarters for the juniors, which are probably the best of their kind in Canada.

And one thing for sure, there's been an awful lot of work by an awful lot of people, and we owe each of them our gratitude.

✦
197
✦

Vancouver Lawn Tennis and Badminton Club

**2005
Men's
& Ladies
Calcutta**

Thursday, July 7th to
Saturday, July 9th, 2005

*ENTRY DEADLINE
Monday, July 4th, 2005*

Team lists will be available by
12 noon, Thursday July 7th

Tournament Director: Erin Wilkins
Referee & Auctioneer: Russ Hartley

****In the event of poor weather, (rain) the event will
move indoors and the scoring system modified.****

Please return completed entry form to the Front Desk!

New York World Trade Center twin towers. Garde Gardom retires as B.C.'s 26th Lieutenant Governor. Canada's Firearms Act. B.C. Liberals elected—Gordon Campbell Premier. Ladysmith's bosomy Pamela Anderson bouncing in *Bay Watch*. **2002** 11 EEC

The west end of the courts at the Vancouver Lawn Tennis & Badminton Club.

CHAPTER 15

2007

A lot went on in 2007 but unfortunately we were unable to publish *Love Game* then, so this is a brief recap of that year.

Our tennis events and programs continued to flourish and a few members rose to new heights, à la Rebecca Marino, who became No. 1-ranked Canadian Junior and is slated for a scholarship at Georgia Tech. Many of our seniors attained Canadian national rankings. In the men's, Stephen Kimoff was rated No. 1 in the 45 singles, Ken Dahl in the 60 singles and doubles, and Chuck Underhill in the 70 doubles. Among the women, Leslie Van Santen and Tessa Breukels were rated No. 1 in the 40 doubles, Janice Holloway in the 55 singles and doubles, and Pamela Rosenbaum in the 55 doubles. In Club play, Ian Hartley was our Men's singles champ, Julie Reynolds took the Women's title, and our top Male junior was 18-year-old Vasek Pospisil.

On a more recreational level, Art Jeffery

199

became the "King of the Dogs," playing doubles with Arnie Booth, Murray Chambers, Tom McCusker, and Victor MacLean. Artie doesn't move all that well, but can still whip many an irretrievable ball at his lesser lights.

In big-time professional tennis, impeccably mannered Roger Federer continued to shine, losing only one Grand Slam — the French Clay — to Rafael Nadal. Pete Sampras and John McEnroe think Roger's the best ever. In the Women's, the now divorced and much calmer Justine Henin, with her amazing one-handed backhand, rose to new heights, and gorgeous Maria Sharapova became more gorgeous by the moment — notwithstanding her outrageous grunts. And for the top players, their winnings, in addition to their handsome endorsements, grew and grew.

Badminton continued to be gung-ho at the Club, with a record number of promising juniors learning the game. And our senior aficionados experienced more games, more fun, and still more laughs. The 15th World Championships were held in Madrid, with China's shuttlers winning everything — except the Mixed, which went to an English team. Talk about dominance!

As always, our squash enthusiasts were busy. Doug MacDougall took our Men's singles, and Lara Ramsay the Women's. She also won the 55 + division in the Canadian Nationals in Calgary. Ruth Castellino took the 45 + division doubles in the Nationals in Toronto, and John Osburn captured the 65 + division in doubles. All this while our regulars continued to pound away.

The International Squash Doubles Association (ISDM), formed in 2000, grew like Topsy. It is played by professionals on a North American doubles-sized court — which we have —with a hard ball which makes for snappier points. The Aussie pros, Ben Gould and Paul Price, lead the pack in tournaments in major American cities and one at Hollyburn in West Vancouver.

The Club's social scene was as active as ever. Art Jeffery's son David put on his second annual "Sons of Snakers Christmas Party," with Ian Beardmore, like his father before him, serving some fluted and almost lethal "Brown Velvets" — which, needless to say, in short order made everyone most merry. As do our Thursday night malt tastings for "Scots wha hae" and for those who don't, but drams for all, high-spiritedly led by Rollie Haebler and the irrepressible Bob Sung — "Joy gin" Bob. Also there's our nightly "Sun's over the Yardarm" ginners and vodkers — who've also gone up-market — quaffing Plymouths, Brokers, Quintessential, Grey Goose, and Ted Trevor-Smith's Effems. Plus the occasional sherry for Richard Raibmon and Irish whiskey for Micky Sehmer. The array of empties is a collector's dream.

Our Martini Club (MC) flourished with John Fraser as its current "Big Olive," having been appointed in absentia when he missed a meeting. That'll teach him. Who knows who "Swizzle Stick" will be, but we do know that the Martini Club installed "Pater Olive" Ian Adam as its first honorary member. The MC boasts 87 members and a kitty of $113,075, of which $82,000 is earmarked as an endowment for our promising juniors. An outstanding member-initiated and member-supported success. Do join.

200

2000s

countries adopt the Eurodollar. Lionel Hampton dies. **2003** Canada's first space telescope launched in Northern Russia. Weapons of Mass Destruction. U.S. invades Iraq. Kelowna forest fires. **2004** 17-year old Maria Sharapova wins Wimbledon. Roger

We continue to have fun events — breakfast with Mr. and Mrs. Claus, Dickens' Lunch, Gung Hai Fat Choi evenings, specialty food smorgasbords, and shows at the Stanley Theatre. The only "downer" is that the Club cancelled our Crib Tournament and Bingo, which for years have been most appreciated and well attended, plus our New Year's Eve Party. But apart from that, there's no keeping us down — notwithstanding increases in our dues, together with hefty ones in our city taxes. Up. Up. And, up!

Sadly, the Club suffered a number of deaths among our members — Jeannie Southam, Bill Sauder, Bill Lane, Les Mason, Dick Fairleigh, Bud Spiers, Ralph Carle, John Chikites, June Wark, Larry Barclay, Claire Lovett, Werner Forster, Bill Thorpe, and 93-year-old Harry Wilkinson. A few others had to be hospitalized, including Steve Bramall who had a foot lopped off. But he's back exercising and playing tennis too. Way to go, Steve!

On the brighter side, Tony Bardsley was admitted to the BC Sports Hall of Fame and Museum, and Matthew Cheng was elected president of Badminton BC.

There's been more renovating to the pub, the dining room, the players' bistro, and the squash-viewing areas, plus on-going maintenance. However, we hope — but please don't tell our insurance company — that those dangerously slippery floors beside the men's showers will be attended to — at least provided with more mats. And security continues to be security, yet the filching continues. Oh, to catch them!

Yes, 2007 was a good one also.

Maria Sharapova

Photo by Boss Tweed via Flickr

Roger Federer

Photo by Laurent Sauvage

✦
201
✦

2000s

Federer wins U.S. Open and Wimbledon. World Junior Badminton tournament in Richmond, BC. Oil/gas prices soar. Tony Blair re-elected. Avian 'flu. Paul Martin becomes Prime Minister. San Francisco permits same-sex weddings. South Asia's

Above: Our signage on the southeast corner of 16th Avenue and Fir Street.

Left: Our outdoor parking lot along the north side of the Club, on closed 15th Avenue.

CHAPTER 16

Quo Vadis, the Dear Old VLTBC?

Amateurs, Dress Code, Follies, How Blessed We All Are, Plus Some Lasting Thoughts

How does the Club stand? What are the future prospects for our racquet sports? And what are the prospects for the Club itself, and will it remain where it is?

Amateurs — or Pay for Play?

The days are long past when a talented amateur could reach the top rung in Open competition. Nowadays it would be next to impossible for the skilled amateur badminton players from Duncan in the late 1920s and early 1930s to dominate badminton competition in Canada as they did in their time. Nor will we again witness the remarkable achievements of amateur tennis stars such as Eleanor Young, Jean Milne, and Susan Butt. (However, as they freely admit, even in their day modest "expense money" would be passed to them under the table. Susan recalled that Wimbledon gave her £75 — a princely sum she thought — to assist with her "out of pockets.") The move by racquet sports to the imprinted professionalism which we now know came about in 1968 when tennis pros were first granted access to Open tournaments.

Today tennis is big money. The umpires, referees, lines people and legions of players are all paid. And the current crop of up-and-comers are all mighty young and from everywhere. Russian-born Maria Sharapova is a prime example of how money dominates the current tennis industry. As a child, Maria immigrated to the United States with her father to become relentlessly schooled in a Florida tennis factory. In 2002 at the age of 15, she made her professional debut in Vancouver where she captured the Jericho Junior's Open and the $10,000 prize money. In 2004, when only 17 years old, she won the ladies singles at Wimbledon and enjoyed a No. 2 world ranking. She continues to win all sorts of major titles. Apart from being vivacious, breathtakingly attractive, bright, and

Melanie Jans and Rafik Bhaloo were the female and male recipients of the Premier's Athletic Awards for Squash. The awards were presented by Premier Gordon Campbell on March 20, 2006.

extraordinarily photogenic, she's pictured in no end of magazines and receives enormous endorsements — about $21 million in 2005 and even more in 2006. A nice girl but we wish she didn't grunt so much — an unfortunate legacy predominantly initiated by Monica Seles. Lots of male players do it too. Decorous it isn't. A new buzzword was conjured at the 2006 U.S. Open — but not often used — replacing "love" with "bagel." Love is more fun.

There's some money available for top-level badminton competition — certainly for the representatives from countries such as Malaysia — but nothing compared to the tournament money, TV revenues, and endorsements found in tennis. In squash, a few pros do well, but on the whole their revenues are limited.

Few would dispute that the top level of the racquet sports now belongs to the professionals. And Club members, however gifted they may be, will not be able to break that barrier unless they're prepared to make it "racquets and racquets only," and forego all other interests. Hence the competitions remaining open for talented amateurs are primarily in local or

regional tournaments plus some junior and senior events. A classic example of the latter is 94-year-old Club member Ed Kendall. As a youth, "fast Ed" played football at King Edward High School and also practiced coming out of the blocks with the then Olympic sprinter Percy Williams, where Ed always led for the first 10 yards. During World War II, he served six years overseas with the RCAF's "Demon Squadron," flying Hudsons over the North Sea to hinder the Nazi's shipments of iron ore. For his service he received the Distinguished Flying Cross. Later, Ed became Chief Navigator for Canadian Pacific Airlines, somehow finding time to win 16 U.S. Nationals. Talk about elixir! Wow!

Appreciating that the instruction, training, and equipment has greatly changed over the past century, it's difficult to say who would be the best player of the twentieth century, but here's a go: Tilden, Borg, McEnroe, Sampras, Laver, Roger Federer, upcomer Rafael Nadal in tennis? I'd pick Rod Laver. For the women I'd consider Alice Marble, Billy Jean King, Chris Evert, Steffi Graf, and Martina Navritalova. Martina's my choice. Badminton is tough — Erland Kops and Channerong. And for squash — the Khans.

Susan Butt graduated in psychology from the University of Chicago. Her Ph.D. thesis, *The Psychology of Sport: The Motivation, Behaviour, Personality and Performance of Athletes,* was an indictment of the competitive ethics and commercialism of modern athletes. Her premise was that someone who engaged in sports should do so from intrinsic motivation rather than from external considerations such as overly pushy parents, win-or-else coaches, and playing for money

2000s

earthquake—started tsunami. **2005** George W. Bush's second term. Pope Benedict XVI. Prince Charles marries Camilla Parker Bowles. Hurricane Katrina devastates New Orleans. Trial of Iraq's Saddam Hussein. Iran working on its nuclear capacity. Victoria's

and endorsements. She also felt that lesser athletes could achieve personal fulfillment in whatever sport they chose. How true. And that applies to by far the most of us, for by just playing ("because not in the prize the glory lies") — or by winning (which is mighty agreeable too) — so be it. We get our exercise. We have our challenge. We have our fun. The game *is* the thing. And, that is our fulfillment.

Dress Code

In the early days, gentlemen players wore long neatly pressed cream flannel trousers, or cotton ducks along with cable-knit sweaters and crested blazers. For the ladies it was white ankle-length, corseted or tucked-at-the-waistline cotton and silk dresses or skirts (perhaps a crinoline now and then), with high-necked blouses, white stockings, garter belts (we suppose), and straw hats. Some even sported fans and parasols while waiting. *Très chic*! Both men and women wore white Oxford-shaped runners — Converse, Tretorn, and Purcell were the favourites. In the 1960s at the VLTBC the Watts twins, Maureen and Lindsay, caused a stir with their tennis haute couture — neat and cute beyond description. They were a joy!

The question as to what constitutes suitable attire, both on and off the courts, has recurred over the years. The long-standing "white only" rule was once relaxed for a short time by allowing 10% colour, but now the Club has returned to white. In 2005 there was talk of the Canadian International Badminton staging a tournament at the Club. Anticipating the television coverage that such an event might attract,

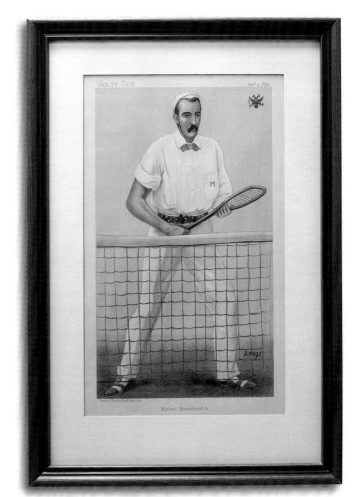

the directors granted permission to the participants — providing four countries took part — to wear team colours and uniforms. However that tournament didn't materialize and so the directors passed their dispensation along to our Pan-Am Games fixture.

In the 1930s, Club directors somewhat grudgingly approved of shorts for men, "provided they reached the knee, with knee length stockings." Shorts and ankle socks for both sexes didn't appear until about 1940. Many members recall Jack Churchill and his meshed see-through tops, and English Dudley Carter

2000s

Steve Nash becomes NBA's MVP and Sam Sullivan Canada's first quadriplegic Mayor. Conservative PM Harper forms Federal minority government. Terrorism and suicide bombers plague the Middle East. Canadian troops in Afghanistan. Jeannie Southam

referring to his undergarments as his "smalls." Never mind Dudley, we'll never tell. One wife once gave her other half a fur-lined jockstrap, which was the talk of the men's locker room. Guess who? And, when a member continued to fail to soap and water his gear, his locker mates recommended Airwick.

And, apart from sweat (remembering that horses sweat, men perspire, and ladies merely glow), there's the usual locker room aromas — wintergreen, eucalyptus, shaving lotions, and a host of deodorants. The men's locker room is a great place to get some heat or ice, work out cramps and dehydration, have a salt pill, drink some tea with lots of sugar, or have a ginger ale, a beer, a glass of wine or a shot of some sterner stuff.

But most of all, from all the men, our everlasting gratitude to our racquet wives for their constant painstaking and unpaid laundering of their beloveds' strip. We're fortunate they didn't cotton on to becoming unionized!

In the clubhouse, the dress policy has been less consistent — as is always the case with style and fashion. However the Club continues to favour propriety. At one time the men had to wear jackets and ties after 5 p.m. In the dining room, board room, and Tudor Lounge, appropriate attire is still called for and fortunately, most of the time members comply. Jeans are prohibited — most certainly those with rips in the backside or holes at the knees! Plus, thank the Lord, no caps on the men or cell phones for anyone. As at Wimbledon, togs on our courts continue to be white and white only — a nice and continuing tradition, although in some tourneys and Grand Slams one sees just about everything.

Follies

Hindsight, always a piece of cake compared to foresight, does serve to identify mistakes — which most often were the result of haste and abandoning planning. In 1957 we tore down our stately McLure clubhouse and where it stood constructed a dull, aesthetically sterile, concrete parking garage that obfuscated our premium view. Then we built our incorrectly sized pool. Also, we didn't purchase our neighbour on 15th Avenue, the Terminal City Bowling Club. In 1984 we sacrificed all of our grass courts. In addition we did away with our Saturday-night dances, de-emphasized the charm of the Tudor Room, scaled down the Friday Happy Hour, and did away with the ever-popular Christmas Bingo and the Crib tournament. From 1990 to 1992 we took out Tennis Quick — our best ever hard surface — and substituted LayKold, also known as PlexiPave. Many are overjoyed with our new bubbled clay courts, notwithstanding having to change shoes when entering the clubhouse. It's tough not to track in some dust. Ah well, who can win 'em all? And, notwithstanding our karma, the adage, "Profit from the past, but don't become shackled by it," stands on both counts.

How Blessed We All Are

Periodically we have our gripes — that's human nature — but we who live in beautiful bountiful British Columbia, compared to the rest of the world, have precious little to complain about. We have fresh air, clean water, pure soil, and an abundance of natural resources. B.C. is aesthetically exquisite, peaceful,

2000s

with a relatively small population plus a standard of living enjoyed by about only 4% of the world's population, with opportunities that are almost unlimited. Blessed? I'll say.

The Good Old Club

Over the years the directors have engaged in a lot of soul searching in attempting to precisely define what sort of club the VLTBC is, or should be. Soon after the Arbutus Club opened in 1964 with its courts, ice rinks, and huge swimming pool, competition for members caused concern and there was talk of acquiring additional land. A month or so later sober second thoughts prevailed, with the directors policying that "We are first and foremost a racquets club, the oldest one in the city, and as such are unique, and that the best course for us is to improve and expand our existing facilities."

In 1981, once more there was considerable agitation about court times for our juniors, baby-sitting facilities, nannies, and the use of the pool by infants — whereupon the board proclaimed, "The Vancouver Lawn Tennis and Badminton Club is an adult club in which children of members have certain privileges." That somewhat terse edict led to the resignation of one of our tennis luminaries. However, a month later he changed his mind, was reinstated but subsequently re-resigned and joined the Hollyburn Country Club where, he said, "They not only have ice, but juniors were treated as equals with adults." Methinks the ice was the persuader.

In March 1993, the board restated the Club's ethos that it is a leading racquets club, and that emphasis is justified. It is the niche that the Club has occupied for more than 100 years, and which, with luck and good management, will occupy for another hundred. To quote our rehoned Mission Statement:

> The Vancouver Lawn Tennis and Badminton Club is a leading racquets club, providing outstanding tennis, badminton and squash facilities. The Club offers a range of competitive and recreational playing opportunities for members and their families in a congenial environment. The Club provides ancillary fitness, recreational and social programs and facilities include casual and formal food and beverage services of the highest quality.

Critics have often accused the Club of being snobbish and elitist — accusations that are quite unfounded. To maintain a stance held by the members for over a century may be viewed by some as somewhat inflexible, but it cannot fairly be categorized as exclusive in the pejorative sense. Without being guilty of *lèse majesté,* the All England operates on the same principles as do we. It would be unthinkable for Wimbledon to build skating arenas, enjoyable though they may be, and would not emphasize there, as here, that it's racquets that are *numero uno,* which has engendered the loyalty of two and three generations of many families. In fact, the Club is graced with one four-generation family: Victor and Joan MacLean, their daughter Dewey Parker, their grandson Andrew Parker, great-grandson Aidan, as well as their granddaughter Elizabeth Dobell, great grandson Alexander and great grand-daughter Sophia. That's a record! Joan joined the Club before Victor and was a junior badminton champ. Another record is held by long-

207

2000s

of California. Roger Federer wins Australian and U.S. Open and Rafael Nadal and Henin-Hardenne the French on Clay. Federer and Amelie Mauresmo capture Wimbledon. For second time in history China wins two Grand Slams—Women's Doubles in

time member Harry Eng who, with his wife Fudge, were the first family of Asian descent to join the Club.

Move? No Way!

What then lies ahead? In the short term, Phase II of the 1993 renovations was completed in 1995, consisting of improvements to the lobby, installation of fire protective sprinkling systems, and expansion of the pub by taking in portions of the Tudor Room which regretfully, but not unexpectedly, had become been somewhat under-used. But what of the long term? Every member we spoke to was unanimous in agreeing that the Club should stay where it is. In 2006, the land was assessed by the City at $4,509,000, that is to say 20 town lots on the edge of Shaughnessy with an assessed value of about $225,450 each. Add to this the value of the buildings and improvements, which were assessed at $3,944,000, for a total of $8,453,000. A fair market value could be much more, depending on the use. As well, with nothing being more certain than death and taxes, property taxes for 2006 came to $263,481, to which the new GVRD Parking Site tax of $1.02 per square meter, or $4,832 must be added.

In 1957 some members flirted with the idea of selling the Club property and moving to a less developed area, such as Richmond or Port Moody (which had one of the first lawn courts in B.C.). That idea was quickly rejected. Nowadays there is not much affordable land for the Club outside of Vancouver. And of course, it is the "<u>Vancouver</u>" Lawn Tennis and Badminton Club. So any question of a "move" will hopefully remain academic.

The Club should stay exactly where it has been since 1914. It has survived all sorts of financial crises — sometimes more through good luck than anything else — but it has survived and the members enjoy and are indeed blessed with excellent premises as well as historic, enviable, and unique traditions. Apart from the squash courts, the improved facilities, bar and pool, the Club is not much different than it was in 1936. When Secretary Manager Harry Monk left, many predicted the Club's demise 10 years later. But it didn't kick the bucket — it survived, eventually prospered, and continues to do so. Hosanna!

Mighty Members, Mighty Competitors, and Mighty Deeds

Giants, such as Erland Kops and the Choongs in badminton, and Hashim Kahn and Geoff Hunt in squash have played here. Tennis greats such as Norman Brookes, Gerald Patterson, Vines, Budge, Bromwich, Emerson, Rosewall, Kramer, Alice Marble, and Mo Connolly have graced our courts. These and many other superb players, and most especially thousands of well-served and well-satisfied members, have granted the Club a cachet we still enjoy. Yes, the VLTBC has been the source of tremendous camaraderie and many mighty deeds. And, no question, more will come.

Traditions

Every club has its traditions. Every club must balance past values against current expectations. The nostalgic demands of older members sometimes conflict with the expectations of younger members, which is probably healthy, as stagnation is far more degenerative than change. And over the years the Club has been

2000s

Australia and at Wimbledon—Yan Zi and Zheng Jie. U.S. twins Bob and Mike Bryan win Wimbledon Men's Doubles. Martha Piper retires as President of U.B.C. B.C. Lions win Grey Cup. Helen Mirren stars in "The Queen". Vancouver real estate prices continue

amenable to change. It discarded croquet and lawn bowling. It discarded the clay courts, but they have been restored. Members discarded the lawn courts, with their ambiance and friendly surface, when their upkeep became impractical — just as the U.S. Open did, when it moved from its Forest Hills' grass to the hard surface at Flushing Meadows. And if past events are any indicator, no doubt our tennis surface will be revisited in the years to come.

Some say that the members make the Club, others that the Club makes the members. But I'd say that it's the ever evolving melding of the two. However the drawing card is clearly the Club, for its hand holds all the aces, and its spirit and ambiance overshadows all. The brilliant eighteenth century essayist Edmund Burke described society as "a partnership between the dead, the living and the unborn." How aptly that describes the Club. And there is every reason to believe that the dear old VLTBC will be able to accommodate itself to the future and any changes that may occur. In short, the Club can meet challenges. It always has. It always will. And, well.

Victor and Joan MacLean and their family represent four generations of membership in the Club. Back row, left to right, Victor MacLean, Joan MacLean, grandson Andrew Parker, daughter Dewey Parker. Front row: great-grandsons Alex Dobell and Aidan Parker.

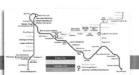

2000s

to take off. Property taxes continue to soar. Start of RAV line construction on Cambie Street. Including endorsements, 31 year old Tiger Woods earned $101.1M U.S. and Maria Sharapova $21.1M US. Iraq convicts and hangs former dictator Saddam Hussein.

APPENDICES

Interviews

Ian Adam
Peter Allen
Rick Angus
Bob Annable
Jean Bardsley
Jim Bardsley
Tony Bardsley
Ann Barling
Ian Beardmore
Peter Bentley
Andrew Bibby
Dick Birch
Sharon Bleuler
Arnold Booth
Brian Bramall
Jone Brodie-Fraser
Susan Butt
Leslie Cliff
Gordon Cooper
Bill Crawford
Richénda Crawford
Rosemary Cunningham
Brad Desaulniers
Neil Desaulniers
Bert Fergus
Bruce Gandossi
Garde Gardom
Helen Gardom
Patricia Graham
Louis Hanic
Russ Hartley
Dick Hibbard

Ted Horsey
Maria Horvath
John Hungerford
Tony Hugman
Peter Jackson
Melanie Jans
Art Jeffery
David Jeffery
Mildred Jeffery
Lawrence Jones
Bill Keenan
Lois Ker
Ross Ker
Anna Kier (Patrick)
Amanda Lau
Graham Laxton
Deryk Leader
Merton Lechtzier
John Long
Claire Lovett
Wayne MacDonnell
Victor MacLean
Alan MacNeil
John Madden
Chandra Madosingh
Lorne Main
Pat McGeer
Edwin McLaughlin
Joan McMaster
Doris Magee
Kenneth Meredith
Joan Milne

Ram Nayar
John Nicolls
Rod Nicolls
Laurel Osler
Janis Ostling
Dewey Parker
Malcolm Perry
Bob Puddicombe
Richard Raibmon
Sandy Robertson
Bruce Rollick
Judith Rollick
John Samis
David Savage
Kay Scott
Mel Scott
Abdul Shaikh
Doug Shellard
Jim Skelton
Ted Trevor-Smith
Al Stevenson
Eleanor Stonehouse (Young)
David Strachan
Jean Thompson
Chuck Underhill
Dick Vogel
Bob Wade
Charlotte Warren
Bill Whittall
Laura Williams
Kay Wilson
Sid Winsby

  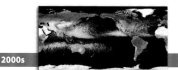 

2000s

4 and 5 bladed Schick and Gillette razors. For much of the world, warmest year on record. And thanks to the Pineapple Express, B.C.'s wettest weather plus violent windstorms – 3000 trees downed in Stanley Park. 250 anniversary of Mozart's birth.

Take the QUIZ

NICK-NAMES AND SAYINGS

Who were they?
Written answers SVP.
First prize: Take the author to lunch.
Second prize: Take him twice.

Arf-Arf
Scoop
The Count
The Duke
Planter
Wild Bill
Pheasant Head
Beebs
Slim
Big Noise
The Hungarian Cavalry
Willy White Shoes
The Gov
Little Bear
Me Hearty
The Rooster
Big Lil
The Great Danes
The Bryde
Stomper
The Black Job
The Mighty Arts Players
Ni Hao

The Colonel
One Side
The Penguin
C.B.C.
Doggie
R. Kives
The Hornet
Camel Driver
Big Bear
Crazy Otto
Up Charles
Bones
Up-Up
Murd the Turd
Stick
J. P.J.
Big John
Vials
Jezzilin
Genghis
Placebo
The Sergeant
The Captain

Bugs
Wally
Trixie La Rue
Stud
The Wife
B.B.S.
Machine Gun
Old Fellow
Moose
Rollie
Jungle Jim
Shadow
The Ballerina
J.P.R.
The Doc
Woody
Big Mac
R.G.C.
Diz
Fault
Rupert
Beady Eyes
Man

211

2000s

Nanaimo's songstress Diana Krall, Vancouver's Sarah McLaughlin and Murrayville born tenor Ben Heppner knock 'em dead. Emily Carr painting auctioned for $431,250. Population in Canada 32,750.000. B.C. 4.1 million. Greater Vancouver (one of the

Sayings Heard Around The Club

"I guv him the thumb"

"Trouble with you is you're basically stupid"

"Erland was nervous"

"I'll have a dresser"

"Don't Matter None"

"Yah Mutt"

"You mustn't treat your nurses like your friends"

"I don't like your face"

"My best friend"

"Golly Wally, wall to wall carpet"

"Please hurry up—my pressure cooker is on the boil"

"Any Mrs. Edwards stuff?"

"The problem with your game is that it is basically unsound"

"First in a long line of weak Presidents"

"The girls from Courtenay are mean and dirty, but I'm from Comox"

"Like a Homer?"

"It's not a flamer"

"I didn't see it, it must have been out"

"You got bott'l?"

"If I want to call the pigs I'll rattle the buckets"

"Any Schmucks?"

"Have one on me, Chaps"

212

© KitAy / flickr

2000s

Club Presidents

R. Marpole	1897 - 1904		E. Beardmore	1959 - 1962
E. Lewis	1905 - 1906		J. C. Allen	1962 - 1964
C. M. Beecher	1906 - 1907		G. B. Gardom	1964 - 1966
A. McCreary	1907 - 1908		E. A. Robertson	1966 - 1967
E. Cave-Browne-Cave	1908 - 1918		W. Y. Crawford	1967 - 1970
J. H. Griffith	1918 - 1925		E. Trevor-Smith	1970 - 1972
W. G. Murrin	1925 - 1926		E. W. Whittall	1972 - 1974
A. P. Horne	1926 - 1927		W. D. Black	1974 - 1976
T. H. Boggs	1927 - 1928		B. M. Brydon	1976 - 1978
P. L. Lyford	1928 - 1929		R. A. W. Elliott	1978 - 1980
W. H. Malkin	1929 - 1931		W. M. Ferrie	1980 - 1982
P. L. Lyford	1931 - 1934		W. F. Keenan	1982 - 1984
L. Read	1934 - 1936		J. G. Connell	1984 - 1986
N. L. Ker	1936 - 1937		J. H. Fraser	1986 - 1988
G. E. McCrossan	1937 - 1939		W. D. Welsford	1988 - 1990
R. D. Pears	1939 - 1945		R. Angus	1990 - 1992
J. B. Storey	1945 - 1946		P. Jackson	1992 - 1994
S. V. T. Jeffery	1946 - 1947		H. M. Evers	1994 - 1996
E. D. Bolton	1947 - 1948		B. Gandossi	1996 - 1998
H. Sutherland	1948 - 1949		P. Trapp	1998 - 2000
L. Boulter	1949 - 1950		Nicki Perkins	2000 - 2002
S. Winsby	1950 - 1951		E. Cameron	2002 - 2004
C. B. Walker	1951 - 1954		A. Bibby	2004 - 2006
K. Meredith	1954 - 1957		D. Anderson	2006 - present
C. E. Morris	1957 - 1959			

Club Managers

YEAR	TITLE	NAME
1897 - 1900	Honorary Secretary	A. P. Horne
1897 - ?	Secretary	W. Hayes
1905 - 1909	Secretary	E. Cave-Browne-Cave
1909 - 1910	Secretary	C. E. Merritt
1910 - 1915	Secretary Treasurer	H. Lockwood
1915 - 1920	Secretary Treasurer	E. N. Maltby
1920 - 1921	Secretary Treasurer	J. G. Stark
1921 - 1930	Secretary Treasurer	E. J. H. Cardinall
1930 - 1932	Secretary Treasurer	H. L. Haines
1932 - 1935	Secretary Treasurer	R. D. Kinmond
1935 - 1947	Secretary Manager	H. N. Monk
1947 - 1948	Secretary Manager	M. G. Dexter
1948 - 1949	Secretary Manager	A. Laithwaite
1949 - 1950	Secretary Manager	G. T. Turley
1950 - 1952	Secretary Manager	H. Wilkinson
1953 - 1954	Secretary Manager	A. E. Cox
1954 - 1956	Secretary Manager	Mrs. Moo Furney
1956 - 1965	Secretary Manager	T. Vossen
1965 - 1970	Secretary Manager	T. J. Myring
1970 - 1972	General Manager	J. A. Robson
1972 - 1974	General Manager	T. J. Myring
1974 - 1976	General Manager	L. E. Dubay
1976 - 1978	General Manager	R. C. Tobin
1978 - 2000	General Manager	G. Laxton
2000 - 2003	General Manager	J. Stokes-Rees
2003 - Present	Chief Executive Officer	Mrs. Janis Ostling

Early records are not complete but it appears that from the outset, A.P. Horne was Honorary Secretary and the first Secretary was W. Hayes. Compensation for their services, at $300 a year, didn't start until 1908. During Mr. Maltby's tenure, hard times reduced the salary to $200. With the arrival of E.J.H. Cardinall, it was increased to $450. Most Secretaries were also Treasurer, and each was a Club member until the days of Harry Monk, when the position became a full time but modestly paid job. Monk's starting salary was $75 a month, which was increased to $90 in 1937.

Bibliography

For additional reading

Cherry, Jean. *Tennis Antiques & Collectibles.* Santa Monica, CA: Amaryllis Press, 1995

Partington, H. R. & A. J. F. Peel. *The History of Badminton in British Columbia.* Vancouver, BC: British Columbia Badminton Associations, 1949

Stevenson, Alan. *First Service: One Hundred Years of Tennis in British Columbia.* Vancouver, BC: Tennis B.C., 1987

Horne, A. P. *Lawn Tennis in Vancouver from 1890 to 1938.* Vancouver, BC: The Vancouver Lawn Tennis and Badminton Club Ltd., 1938

Corporate Design Consultants. *Vancouver Lawn Tennis & Badminton Club.* Vancouver, BC: 1972

The Officers and Executive for the Year 1927. *The Vancouver Lawn Tennis Club Constitution.* Vancouver, BC: The Vancouver Lawn Tennis Club, 1927

Davis, Chuck & Roy Carlson. *Greater Vancouver Book: An Urban Encyclopaedia.* Surrey, BC: Linkman Press, 1997

Francis, Daniel, editor. *The Encyclopedia of British Columbia.* Madeira Park, BC: Harbour Publishing Co. Ltd., 2000

◆
215
◆

Additional resources that were accessed in preparing this book include:

Numerous back issues of *Match Point.* Vancouver, BC: The official quarterly magazine of Tennis BC.

Numerous back issues of *Racquet Hi-Lights.* Vancouver, BC: Published by the Vancouver Lawn Tennis & Badminton Club.

All available Vancouver Lawn Tennis & Badminton Club Board and Committee Minutes, Notices and Reports, Vancouver, BC

All available Press clippings.

Index

Suzanne Lenglen, a French tennis player who achieved much success in the French and British women's game from 1919 to 1926, winning 25 Grand Slam titles.

Caroline Wozniacki at the 2006 Wimbledon final.

© 2006 Ricky Diver

John Pius Boland, represented Britain at the 1896 Summer Olympics.

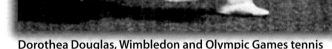

Dorothea Douglas, Wimbledon and Olympic Games tennis champion. Picture taken in 1903.

◆
219
◆

Li Na 2007 Sydney Medibank International.

© 2007 Glenn Thomas

Cours centrale de Roland Garros.

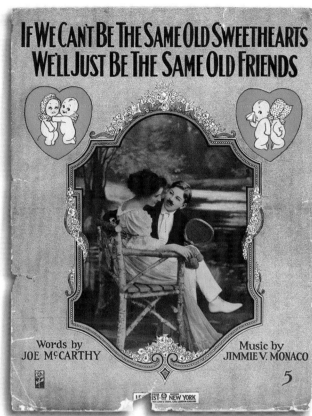